The Canadian Guide to
HOME ENTERTAINING

The Canadian Guide to
HOME ENTERTAINING

Una Abrahamson

Macmillan of Canada / Toronto

ISBN 0-7705-1314-X

Printed in Canada for
The Macmillan Company of Canada Limited
70 Bond Street, Toronto M5B 1X3

Contents

FOR MY MOTHER

whose parties are among
the memories of my childhood

Acknowledgments

The splendid photographs were taken by Fred Bird. To Anna Carr, who prepared the setting for the photographs, and to Carol Ferguson, home economist, who prepared the food, particular thanks.

A special word of appreciation goes to the following people who graciously permitted their homes and grounds to be used for the taking of the photographs:

Mr. and Mrs. Tommy Ambrose
Toronto
Mrs. Dorothy Bird
Toronto
Mr. and Mrs. Jeff Brown
Toronto
Mr. and Mrs. Ross DeGeer
Toronto
Mr. and Mrs. David Eisen
Toronto

Mr. and Mrs. James Findlay
Milton, Ontario
Mr. and Mrs. R. Keating
Toronto
Mr. and Mrs. Frank Kinzinger
Caledon, Ontario
Mr. and Mrs. John O'Connell
Toronto

And to the following firms that provided special items for the photographs:

The Bronze Dolphin
1365 Yonge Street
Toronto, Ontario

Worcester Royal Porcelain Co.
(Canada) Limited,
Toronto, Ontario

Preface

This is a personal book, not only because it grew out of my own experience in entertaining—I have cooked all the foods mentioned and have tried the gamut of parties from dinner for two to cocktails for fifty—but also because it reflects my interests and tastes. It is filled with my own experiences, and hopefully with what I have learned over the years; for I, too, have had disasters. I hope that the book will help keep you free of these, that it will encourage you if you have ever hesitated about inviting the "nice people who moved into the corner house", and that it will generate ideas to give new twists to parties given by those who are old hands at entertaining.

I have lived this book. My education in homemaking and entertaining was, in my youth, somewhat sketchy. I never really thought that I would actually have to get into the kitchen and whip up a small storm. Like my knowledge of books and music, my knowledge of entertaining has been acquired by experience. Most of it was acquired happily, and in the main by watching and remembering how admired friends managed to have delightful parties that are part of memory. As soon as I realized that the most successful party-givers really enjoyed their own parties, I knew entertaining was to be one of my pleasures. For years, I have not been able to resist a new entertaining idea, I can't let a month go by without planning an entertainment, and whenever I buy an article for my home, I do so with its end use in mind, to hold food, fruit, flowers, or as a backdrop to my home and enhancement for entertaining.

Behind all the suggestions, ideas, tips, and recipes, there is the underlying philosophy of sensitivity to others which is so important to successful entertaining. When you radiate confidence and show warmth toward your guests, then the party can't help but succeed—no matter whether it is large or small, formal or informal. Your home comes alive—and so do you. There is nothing quite as exhilarating as planning, organizing, anticipating and enjoying a successful entertainment. In this book I hope to share with you some of the pleasures I have found.

This is a book to generate ideas, a helper from one who has tried everything in it. If you have an easier way, or a method that suits your way of life better, then by all means keep to what is successful for you; you can use this book for menu ideas, or to check up on tips and pointers. This not a textbook—no two homes could be alike; neither can hosts or circumstances be identical. Nor is it a book on etiquette or cookery (although it has plenty of both); there are many specialized books in libraries and book shops on those particular subjects. I hope that this labour of love will help those who wish to entertain smoothly, within budget, and without fuss, and who often hesitate to invite friends because of inexperience. With each successful party experience grows. I know; I could barely make coffee, came from a different country with a different set of traditions, and had no idea how to get all the food for even one course on the table at once, and at the correct temperature.

Keep it simple, is a cliché that I hesitate to use.

But it is the truth and the basis of success. No one wants twenty different types of canapé, or a choice of ten hot dishes at an informal buffet supper—or a formal one for that matter. Plan ahead is another cliché, but equally valid. After years of party-giving I confess to keeping a diary of what has to be done from the moment the guests are invited. This not only helps planning but gives me a certain confidence so that I never have a last minute panic, rushing out of the kitchen and into party clothes as the guests come up to the front door. I am against hosts pottering in the kitchen while guests are relaxing, I am also against hosts disappearing back into the kitchen for long periods while the party is in progress. Above all, I am very much against hosts who don't dish up food until several hours have passed. Hosts who have to work while guests are trying to relax create a glum left-out feeling that eventually hangs overhead like a little black cloud and soon communicates itself to the guests.

Some of the ideas and pointers may make the reader say: "Surely, everyone knows that!" Not everyone! That's the point and the reason for noting seemingly elementary rules. Similarly, some situations are not discussed at all because they depend too much on special circumstances and would mean generalizing for the few, and the subject would not be dealt with justly. So while you will get tips on giving a wedding in the home, you won't learn how to decorate the wedding cake, however simple it may be.

One of the guiding principles has been to cover the most usual situations as well as esthetics—the exercise of taste. The book attempts to set up awareness of that elusive quality—suitability—that governs all entertainment decisions. In the book I have kept a respect for accepted traditions and while we all have our own inherited or acquired traditions of observing the great holidays and feasts, there are other traditional occasions where custom dictates forms and procedures. With the traditions related to Thanksgiving, and the many religious festivals celebrated by different Canadians at different times in different regions, I have let those inherited traditions be the silent guide and must be forgiven for ignoring them in the main.

And finally, throughout this book, I have used the word, "hosts". Occasionally the word "hostess" seems to have crept in. Frankly the word host applies to both men and women. Hostess is a word that sounds archaic to me, but it is used when the occasion is traditionally a feminine entertainment.

UNA ABRAHAMSON

The Canadian Guide to
HOME
ENTERTAINING

1
Hospitality: the Whys and Wherefores

There's a reason behind every party: to celebrate a friend's birthday, to get to know a casual acquaintance better, to repay hospitality, or simply a need to be with people. There are family occasions, ranging from a christening to a marriage, as well as the holidays of Thanksgiving and Christmas. Beneath all the reasons is the sheer pleasure of giving and receiving hospitality.

Let's give a party!

It is fun to entertain friends in a relaxed atmosphere with good food, drink and company. It brings about that intangible warmth and fellowship we hope for. And, of course, if you want to go to parties, you have to give parties yourself! If you've never done it before, or have tried and didn't have a roaring success, try again. Whether you prefer a non-organized impromptu party or an entertainment that is somewhat more formal, the basic rules of planning and preparation are pretty much the same. Once you've learned the formula, stick with it. And practice makes perfect.

Gone are the days of lengthy menus, matched dishes, silverware by the ton, everything done according to etiquette-book rules (based on having a palace for a home and a retinue of servants); gone, too, is the tense and frazzled party-giver. Today hosts follow simple rules aimed at convenience to themselves, simplicity, and the happiness and comfort of the guests. Parties are geared to the interests, capabilities and budget of the host. These principles hold whether the party is formal, informal, indoors, outdoors, dinner, after-theatre coffee, or a TV election night get-together.

Don't let the shortage of possessions, the lack of fine china, or the smallness of an apartment keep you from entertaining. Guests do not look forward to invitations because of your Chippendale chairs; their smiles will be brighter if the food is excellent and the planning unobtrusive. An invitation should mean that something nice will happen. Let it.

Parties are remembered for different reasons, but a true liking of people is a must for both party-giver and guests. And planning is part of this.

Give—and Take

Social life is built upon give and take: When you invite guests, it's like throwing a pebble into a pond; the waves and ripples get bigger and broader. Guests will return your invitations and, in turn, you will meet new people. Of course, you will find some people are tardy in returning invitations, and some never seem to get around to it. What do you do? Well, if you give parties because you enjoy this particular person's company, nothing. If you feel someone offers little and is, in effect, "free-loading," then drop the name from your list. But never gossip about it.

Some guests hesitate to return invitations because they feel their home is too small, they can't cook, they don't own this, that, or the other. Fortunately, you can repay one kind of invitation with another. If you can't cook or haven't much time, you can repay with a supper supplied by the local delicatessen. Or you can have a Sunday brunch based on a dozen different types of bread, buns, cakes and cheese plus fruit you bought on

Saturday. If you are asked to an elegant dinner party, you can still repay by asking the party-giver to a Sunday afternoon tea, or get theatre tickets and then serve coffee, liqueurs and pastry after the show. It isn't how much, or repeating in kind, but *how* that matters. Today there's no excuse for not returning hospitality. No matter how demanding your work, or that you live in a small apartment, that you are alone, that there are children, there's always a way to return friendship in keeping with your pocketbook and life style.

□ A person living alone can invite the minimum of two to four people. Food can be served from a card table and eaten with a plate on the lap or, serve from the kitchen counter and seat the guests around the card table.

□ With slightly more space you can become an expert in buffet meals and all your guests can eat comfortably if you acquire a set of folding tray tables.

□ If you can't afford to give cocktail parties or serve liquor, don't. Guests come to be with you, not for the money you spend.

□ If you want to serve wine and know little about it, then learn by trying varieties for your own pleasure, by reading books and by asking the experts who staff the liquor or wine store. Never be put off by wine-upmanship—that red meat requires red wine, that wine should not be sweet. These are reasonably correct rules, but today rules are forgotten and you serve what pleases you (see Chapter 6).

□ If you are new to entertaining, that's still no excuse. You must start someplace, somewhere, sometime. Start by inviting a few friends in for an after-dinner get-together. Serve a drink if you wish. End the evening at a reasonable hour by serving tea or coffee and a few small sandwiches and pastries which you purchased. Get this organized, and you'll move on to a buffet dinner, although the after-dinner group is always a pleasant, inexpensive and happy way to entertain, especially on a Sunday night.

□ No matter the type of party, sincerity is one of the keynotes to success. Hospitality is given from

Fall Family Dinner

The combination of the natural wood with the red and yellow tones of the food and accessories gives an immediate feeling of warmth and hospitality. The food is the centrepiece on the informal table setting which has earthenware plates, flatware placed family-style, and candles and colourful fall leaves on up-ended saucers.

The food is hearty traditional fare, delicious to come home to after a drive to see the golden trees or after a fall fair. The main platter has orange-glazed pork chops and baked squash, served with creamed onions, red cabbage pickle, home baked bread and whipped butter, apple pie and cheese with cold milk.

the heart, and foremost is the desire to be generous, thoughtful, kind and interested. The French call it *ambience,* a sympathetic and pleasant atmosphere that can't be bought with money, but which is the root of gracious and graceful entertaining.

Stop! Plan Before You Make a Move

Before plunging in and inviting the block, the office, and then some, stop and think. Take a look at your home and decide how many you can entertain comfortably. How many can you entertain if they all stand around talking, how many if you borrow or rent some chairs? How many if you decide you want to sit down to a meal, whether it is at the dining-room table, on tray tables, or at a fun table on the patio that's a heavy plank on sawhorses? How many people can you entertain and still cope with food, conversation, introductions and budget? Not only are personal preferences and numbers important in party giving, but so are costs.

Today most people find that eight is a big enough dinner party unless the home is very large and there is help in preparation and serving. Twenty-five at a cocktail party allows for conversation, but fifty is a crowd and will require outside assistance of barman and maids. Room for hanging guests' coats and storing plates, trays and glasses, let alone the space required for serving food and drink, often take more space than is realized.

If space is a major consideration, money is another. A cocktail party increases the amount of liquor required, and a practised host knows that plenty of food is necessary. Generally, preparing cocktail-party food takes more time and requires more expensive ingredients than a buffet or a dinner party. And all parties have incidentals that up the cost: invitations, decorations if you've chosen a theme party, flowers, fruit, nuts, and niceties from guest towels to soaps, cigarettes, after-dinner liqueurs and mints, and so on. Not really essential, but nice to have.

Dessert and Coffee

In the living room for coffee, dessert, and liqueurs or alternatively, ask guests to join you after dinner and serve a scrumptious rich dessert, liqueurs, and coffee. The picture shows a tempting Brandy Alexander pie with a selection of liqueurs that will enhance its flavour.

Party Patterns

Every successful host has a favourite way of entertaining based on personal preference, budget, and the help and space available. But within the seven main types of parties there are many variations, and it is these variations that make the entertainment personal.

THE COCKTAIL PARTY: Very versatile, it is generally semi-formal to formal and guests can vary in number from six to as many as the home will hold comfortably. With a small number of guests the name is somewhat pretentious, and generally the invitation is "come for a drink and talk after dinner," or "how about dropping by for sherry" —although the drink need not be sherry.

THE BUFFET: It can be given at any time of the day, for any number of guests. Make it informal, after church, after tennis, or for a birthday, or very formal with all the family silver, candles, flowers, and possibly black tie before a special event or to honour a special person.

THE SEATED DINNER: The party most conducive to the enjoyment of guests, conversation, food and wine, it usually consists of six or eight guests— small enough so all can get acquainted, large enough for varied points of view. A dinner party can be as small as four persons, but when the number rises above eight, consider two tables and a buffet service.

LUNCHEON: Even today when many women hold two jobs, the luncheon is still a popular and pleasant way to get a few old friends together, or to introduce a new neighbour or an out-of-town guest. Luncheon parties, on particular occasions, include both sexes.

BRUNCH: Essentially it's luncheon at the weekend, but the hour is earlier and the company will likely be mixed. The food is based on breakfast dishes: juices, fruit, eggs, ham, and a variety of bread, cheeses, and preserves.

THE KAFFEE KLATSCH: This can be any hour of the day, informal to formal, with or without food. Evening coffee parties start after dinner, or after a show and this party at its most glamorous includes a rich and elegant dessert and liqueurs.

THE TEA PARTY: The one truly feminine gathering, the traditional tea party brings together women and may be used to introduce a graduating daughter, a new daughter-in-law, or a visiting friend. It runs the gamut from a casual tea with neighbourly guests to the formality of candles if the day is short, and festive food and flowers for golden weddings, christenings, pre-wedding entertaining, and for club members to meet a new executive.

Today there is a new type of tea party: the Sunday afternoon invitation, where a glass of sherry or Madeira may be served, followed by tea with small sandwiches and a pound or fruit cake. It is a pleasant way to spend a few hours in conversation, listening to new records, or as a preliminary to going out for supper, to a movie or a meeting. And, of course, both men and women are invited to this entertainment.

What's Your Kind of Party?

No two hosts are alike, no set of friends are exactly the same and neither are homes and equipment. A number of factors determine the way you like to entertain. Do you enjoy small or large groups? Can you handle the menu? Will you need a caterer or house help? Regardless of size or style, what can you buy to save energy? What can you afford to purchase in the way of food, help, equipment? It is no longer necessary for the party-giver to personally make all the food from bread to the dessert. Most towns have excellent bakeries and European-style delicatessens to supply an added touch to the party, or even provide most of the food ready-to-serve. The Yellow Pages list not only caterers, but often those who specialize in making a particular dish that is delivered to the house ready for serving and/or heating. You may discover talented people who are not caterers on a large scale, but who will prepare, either in their home or yours, unusual party foods. Some will also provide table service. And, of course, local newspaper food editors often hear of such services.

The lack of china, chairs, glasses, coat-hangers is no excuse for not having a party. There are party services that rent everything from the finest imported dinner services to cheap bar glasses, and some supermarkets rent or lend coffee urns. With a rental service you usually have no dishes or glasses to wash; all the remains are swept into the garbage and the utensils go back in their box to be picked up the next day.

What is formal and what is informal? It is hard to tell today. Great formality is now rare in homes even when the finest of linen, china and silver are used. Everybody uses candles—though maybe not in silver candelabra—even at quite informal gatherings. It is rare for an at-home menu to consist of more than three courses including a salad. The starchiness of old-fashioned formality has vanished, so that formal generally refers to semi-public occasions, or ceremonial and traditional occasions, such as weddings and christenings.

How informal the party is depends on you. Do you have your best times entertaining informally outdoors, or do you prefer evenings of conversation after an excellent dinner? The answers to these and similar questions help determine what is your kind of party. The success of a party does not depend on formality or the lack of it. While there are many kinds of parties (see Chapter 4) which are divided into formal and informal, truthfully there are only two kinds: the small and the large!

The first decision is to have a party! And the reason is basic: you want to be with friends. Then, you check off the people you know, the people you owe, the people you want to meet, and come up with a list of from thirty to fifty. Should you break this number down into compatible groups? Yes, indeed. Then you may have two large groups. Now, do you want to have several small parties: a few quiet dinners, an outdoor patio or pool party, a few evenings of bridge or other games, dinner and the theatre? Or do you want one big splash for thirty? It is a personal choice, depending not only on the physical properties of your home, but, more important, on your personal preferences. Are you happiest with a small group? Some like the big bash. Other successful party-givers change and change around.

The Small Party

There isn't much more work in giving four or five small parties, especially if you simplify the menu, buy whatever you can to avoid lingering over a hot stove, and plan to prevent frazzle. While there are many kinds of parties (see p. 53), the small dinner or buffet is easiest if you are a neophyte. Dinner for six or eight can easily be a pleasant relaxed evening. The first care is to select guests who like or will like each other, and who like this kind of entertainment. Small parties let the host pay more attention to the guests and encourage conversation. Party preparations are simple, you don't need a theme, games or exotic decorations. Remember, too, it is easier to hang coats and house overshoes for six than for fifty.

Keep the menu simple and build around a dish you have success with and which is popular. How elaborate a meal you prepare, is again personal. Today, many people simplify the first course by serving wine or drinks and a tray of small nibbles in the recreation or living room. The main course is served in the dining room or from a buffet and portions are small, since most people confess to dieting. The dessert can be spectacular if the main course was simple, or it can be fruit, cheese and an appropriate wine. Friends come for fellowship and, while they enjoy good food, you are no longer expected to turn cartwheels to prove you can cook.

If you work out one party plan and a menu for one small group, try a second group with an alternate menu. If each party has a meal of three courses, and all are successful, then the permutations for future parties are large. However, it really doesn't matter if you keep serving one of the same dishes. If you make a superb chocolate mousse or cheesecake, your friends will be disappointed if you don't give them the opportunity to taste and taste again. So, if the small party is for you, and you have thirty possible guests, divide them into groups of six. That's only five parties in a year. But then you'll probably enjoy it all so much you'll increase the number of parties.

The key to the small party is compatability, attention to detail and good food. In these days of hurry there isn't enough time to spend with friends, so there is something very flattering about being included in a small group of six to eight. There is, however, a big difference if you stretch the numbers to ten and have a seated meal. Strange but true. Conversation that includes everyone is possible with six or eight people, but with ten the group splits into two. At that point it is time to consider buffet style with guests seated around the room. When you expand the numbers, you lose the intimacy.

The Big Party

For the grand occasion, a wedding or a special anniversary, you will need assistance from hired specialists, and in some cases it is sensible to have a caterer take over. But the big, informal party is still manageable. You won't have close conversation but you will have a lot of fun if you can draw all the guests together, and the best way is atmosphere. This is why big parties are better with a theme, although it is not mandatory. Even those that don't have an actual theme may be based on seasonal festivities or activities: the Grey Cup party, the Tree Trimming evening. Neither does a cocktail party need a theme, but an invitation to an Hawaiian evening sounds exotic and need only add up to lanterns, fruit punch, and paper leis as well as a supply of records. If you like fantasy, you can suggest that your guests dress the part, but find out first if they like this kind of thing. You have to select appropriate food and certainly a theme party requires imagination. The host has to keep the action going, so that planning is particularly important.

Selecting the Guests

One of the most important decisions a host has to make is the selection of the guest list. Numbers are dictated by the size of the rooms and by the type of occasion. Guest lists are the beginning, so begin with a notepad and a pen. Start with the people you want to see. Next come people who, in addition to being friends, have entertained you. Then there are people for whom you want to give a party—new neighbours or people you have met casually and want to know better. Then comes the analysing. Do the guests have some interests in common? A good rule of thumb when drawing people into your circle is to make sure that each guest either knows some other guest or has an interest in common—other than business. A party, unless it is a crowded cocktail party, made up of guests to whom you owe invitations is bound to be a bit stiff, partly because the assortment may not be ideal, and partly because you may look on the entertainment as a duty rather than a pleasure.

We all have friends we love to entertain—they are fun, enter into the spirit of the occasion, and are uninhibited in showing their enjoyment. At the same time we all have close and dear friends whom others find difficult or dull, too talkative, too wallflowerish, too opinionated. In spite of the fact that you are fond of them, there is a tendency to leave them out. Usually, these people blend into the big party. And, while it is a chance, the most unlikely guest combination can make a successful party. This is usually a result of good luck and a knowing host who has the time and talent to devote to melding. But don't plan to invite an odd mixture of people and expect all will have a happy time. There is both subtlety and know-how in planning a guest list.

Have the courage to change the faces around. Even the closest friends, the most brilliant conversationalists, the most entertaining people, get bored with each other if they keep going to the same parties together. This is where a record book is useful. The liveliest parties mix sexes and interests. Invite new people to whom you are drawn as soon as you can. It is a mistake to wait for them to make the overtures. However, if you met them in the home of a mutual friend, it is kind and correct to ask the mutual friend at least for the first time around. Don't hesitate to take the chance and invite. Remember that no one is too important, too young, too old or too busy not to be flattered by an invitation.

Tips for a Successful Mix

□ If too many of your guests have too little in common, you will wear yourself to a frazzle trying to get them to circulate and the party will be leaden.

□ Choose people who will enjoy each other's company. The smaller the gathering the more important this is.

□ Depending on the type of party, age should be considered in planning a guest list. As a rule, it is best to keep the group within a ten-year range. Even so, there are people who are ageless and fit comfortably into any age group and most party situations. And one of the exciting things about parties and people is that you never can tell—the eighteen-year-old will likely find the well-travelled octogenerian fascinating.

□ Parties with mixed age groups are successful for special occasions, and many entertainments gain a great deal from the blending of age groups. Holiday parties are wonderful when planned to include the family's friends and relatives, children of the house and their friends, friends of the relatives and children too. They may have very little in common, and the idea runs counter to most party rules, but the holiday spirit generates a warm and happy family feeling that envelops all ages.

□ The talented guest is one to be enjoyed for his own qualities. He should never be exploited. If the guest is musical, don't hint that playing the piano will be expected and appreciated. Never ask guests with an ulterior motive, nor make the faux pas of trying to pressure the guest into performing. A refusal can be embarrassing with the assembly watching and listening. If a talented guest wants to play the guitar, start a singsong, or perform feats of magic, be sure the other guests will enjoy the performance.

□ Similarly, don't invite guests to a party in order to show movies of your recent trip or the cute antics of your children. If you want to show your movies, or want to rent movies, then ask the guests explicitly for this and tell them what you plan.

□ If you want to expand your social life and are single, try inviting only single people. Arrange a party for guests who are all interested in the same sport or hobby. Avoid asking the non-enthusiast.

□ Be careful about including an over-opinionated guest unless you can find a counterpart and seat them together.

□ When you mix people who know each other well, there is a danger your guest lists will become ingrown. Invite a combination of old and new friends. This has the best potential for a lively party.

□ Don't invite too many in the same profession to a purely social party or you'll find most of them in a huddle talking shop. If the guests are in related professions, then don't invite guests who are not.

□ If you are planning party games (see p. 63) make sure you are inviting those who enjoy playing games. Some people don't; ask them another time.

□ If you are giving a party with a guest of honour, it is sensible and mannerly to discuss the guest list with this person. But don't be dictated to. There may be a celebrity coming to your home, but it is your party and you set the limit on the size of the guest list and decide on the type of party.

□ Experienced hosts can break all the rules and mix all ages and personalities without worry. The secret? The party-giver is relaxed and able to generate warmth and exude friendship.

Invitations

With today's informality the telephone makes it

easy to get a few people together for impromptu entertaining. Coffee and liqueurs after the theatre, good talk and a simple hearty meal after snowmobiling or skiing, chatter and refreshments after a ratepayers' meeting. But there is a great deal in favour of the written invitation for other occasions. A written card shows that you care, and gives the guest a nice wanted feeling. It also has other advantages. It saves time in trying to phone busy people. It is a diplomatic way that allows a guest to have an out if he wishes to decline the invitation; it is difficult to say no in conversation. Even more important, the written invitation is a reminder of the date, time, place and the reason and allows people to space their social engagements. It can include how to get there and will say if special dress is required, such as skating, swimsuit, costume.

Formal occasions, such as a wedding, require an engraved or printed invitation which is ordered from stationery, department, gift or jewelry stores. The sample books show a variety of styles and give the correct wording which is generally given in the third person. While styles vary with fashion, the plain, simply engraved card devoid of lovebirds, hearts and flowers, is still fairly standard and in excellent taste.

For less formal entertainments you can make or buy cards. For dinners, cocktails, receptions, the small fold-over "informals" with the sender's name engraved on the flap of the white card is a simple yet elegant way to ask guests to a party. The engraved name in the case of a woman may have her married name, Mrs. John Brown; but there is a trend for the hostess to use her own name, Mary Brown. For large cocktail parties you can buy attractive invitations that require only the filling in of date, time and address. For children's parties, costume or theme parties, it is fun, if there's time and inspiration, to make invitations from coloured construction paper using felt pens and a variety of stick-on decorations available from stationery and dime stores. While informal invitations can sometimes be used for formal entertaining, the reverse is not true, a

formal printed card is not sent for a picnic or a patio swim-party.

Informal card
> Please come to dinner with us on Saturday, November 9, at 7:00 p.m.
>
> Mary Brown
>
> 345 Holland Avenue
> Apt. 20
> 123-4567
> Regrets only

If the entertainment is given by a couple, then the invitation is given by the hostess. A husband may issue a tentative invitation in the course of conversation, but it should be confirmed by his wife. The old rule was that you should always write the card and envelope. But if your handwriting is not attractive, type. Many typewriters have attractive italic and discursive typefaces. Formal invitations use no abbreviations. They are never issued to Mr. and Mrs. A.B. Guest and Family. Members of the family old enough to be invited receive their own invitations.

Invitations should be sent in advance of the party or reception. Invitations to formal affairs should be mailed a minimum of one month in advance. For dinners, suppers and other in-home parties, invitations are sent at least two weeks ahead, and during the winter, three weeks is safer.

Are They Coming?

It was once understood that a guest was required to accept or decline an invitation. Today some hostesses put RSVP on the card with the phone number. However, there's a new twist, making life much simpler: you ask people to let you know only if they are not coming. And the note says "Regrets only," followed by the telephone number.

How Many Will Show?

In spite of all these precautions, you can't assume that everybody will respond. Sometimes three days before the party you haven't heard and of course you worry, especially if the party is somewhat formal and you may have caterers, maids and a barman in the offing. It could be that the guest is away, or the mail didn't arrive, or the address has changed; there are any number of reasons for the delay. What you do depends on the numbers involved and the type of party. The simplest and easiest way to put your mind at rest is to phone and say, "We really hope you can come on Saturday night." Or you can assume that everybody who didn't reply will come. Then relax, especially if this is a buffet meal or a cocktail party with drinks and nibbles. At the worst you'll have leftovers.

The Extra Guest

If you are blessed with considerate friends they will phone and tell you they have guests staying with them. They will not ask if they can bring the extra people, but will leave the decision to you. If you have a crowd coming, and it is a buffet or other stand-up entertainment, then one or two extra people won't make much difference to the supplies and the general arrangements. However, if the occasion is a sit-down meal, you have a problem. You may sometimes be able to solve it by rearranging the table. But if it is inconvenient in any way, it is best to give a tactful no.

Cancelled

What to do? First, don't panic. If time is short, get your guest list out, line up the phone directory and call. If there is more time and if the invitation was formal, write a brief note. If the occasion has been postponed, give the new date if possible. You don't have to give reasons unless you want to and even then the explanation should be brief. When the party is held at a future date, you are obliged to re-invite all the original guests.

Being a Guest

Guests are people! They come in all sizes, shapes and temperaments. Some are shy and quiet, others spill over with excitement, vivacity and conversation. In accepting an invitation, guests take on a role as well as an obligation. They must identify with the other guests. At today's gatherings guests should introduce themselves if the host is occupied. In return for hospitality, guests are required to play an active role. If they have nothing to contribute, it is best to stay at home. Guests are obligated to keep up conversation and to ensure that the shy are brought into the picture; at the same time they should acquire the asset of being a good listener. Guests, like hosts, can pick and choose their entertainments. If the high decibel level and the small talk of a cocktail party don't appeal, or if the party is devoted to games or cards and you don't care for either, then turn the invitation down. There will be other occasions to see the hosts.

Guest Etiquette

Always answer invitations promptly and arrive on time. However, depending on the community and the occasion, some leeway is given for time (see below). On arrival guests should make themselves both comfortable and at home. Not, of course, to the extent of taking the best chair, but it is nerve racking to have a guest who sits on the edge of the hardest and smallest chair, who nibbles at the food and shows no real pleasure in the occasion. Equally obnoxious is the guest who fingers ornaments, checks the make and marks on china and silver, or who marches through the house on a tour of inspection without an invitation to do so. Guests shouldn't feed the family pets or reprimand the children. Permission should be asked before using the telephone and conversation should be brief. Of course, no long-distance calls are placed unless charged to the home account.

Problems and Emergencies

Should a guest have to leave a party early, this fact should be told the host as soon as possible before the party particularly if he is expected to make a fourth at bridge. If this is impossible, the early departure should be mentioned quietly on arrival to the host, so that leaving will not appear to be a criticism of the party. And the departure should be as unobtrusive as possible.

Should a guest feel ill, the host should be told quietly and the leaving should be unobtrusive.

Guests should apologize for lateness, but only with a brief explanation. However, if lateness is known ahead of the party—a non-operating car, a tardy baby-sitter—then the guest should phone and give an estimate of arrival time.

If a guest breaks or damages anything, the host should be told immediately. And the object should be replaced as quickly as possible. If it is irreplaceable, a gift of greater value and of interest to the receiver should be sent as quickly as possible. In all events, in addition to an immediate verbal apology, a note should be sent the next day, and it is gracious to send some flowers with it.

Punctuality

Promptness is more than a virtue; it makes or breaks a social occasion. No host wants the food spoiled, and many become nervous and impatient when guests don't appear at the appointed hour. There are occasions when punctuality is mandatory, but like all rules, some of the requirements can be bent. Regardless of the occasion, hosts should be ready to receive guests at least fifteen minutes ahead of the invitation time.

Mandatory

□ For specific and traditional ceremonies such as weddings, funerals, graduations, arrange to arrive at least fifteen minutes before the specified time.

□ Guests should be prompt and on time when meeting a host at the theatre or any place where there is a time factor—for example, a restaurant table reservation.

□ Be prompt for all appointments. Don't keep anyone waiting.

Bending the Rule

The amount of laxness permitted depends on the host, the group, the community and the occasion. A rule of thumb allows a guest more latitude when drinks are served before dinner. However, this permissiveness should never be taken for granted, and ten minutes is about the limit for a small at-home dinner or restaurant dining. Large receptions in hotels or homes, crowd buffet meals permit a twenty-minute leeway. For large receptions, teas, cocktail parties that will be held for a specified length of time, fifteen minutes after the beginning to a half hour before the stated end.

When to Go Home

To some, this is as taxing as knowing when to arrive! If there is a guest of honour, other guests leave only after that person's departure. Otherwise it is a matter for personal decision. Cocktail parties require a minimum attendance of forty minutes—enough time to circulate. Getting guests to leave after a successful cocktail party or an at-home is one of the problems of giving a party. However, a guest, unless specifically invited to stay on, should not force the host to offer a dinner invitation. Luncheons are so informal that most guests automatically make preparation to leave after an hour and half to two hours. With a dinner, it is still customary to stay three hours or so. However, leave-taking should be swift, and pleasant and prolonged goodbyes on the doorstep should be avoided.

Guest of Honour

This was once a complicated etiquette scene. Today, like all entertaining, it has become more relaxed. But there is still enjoyment and fun in giving a party in honour of a visiting friend or relation, to welcome a new colleague, bride or neighbour.

Such a party should be planned with the guest of honour in mind. This is the only rule, but it is simple and basic. However, it is one that is occasionally forgotten. Too often the host invites personal friends and ignores the interests of a young girl or an elderly relative coming to a new community. Aunt Jane's friends will probably be quite different from those normally invited to your home and their interests are likely to be different. But remember the party is for Aunt Jane, the guest of honour. However, the list need not be limited to the guest of honour's friends. As a matter of course invite friends you think the visitor would like to meet, but always include people of the guest of honour's age group and who share similar interests.

Guests of honour have obligations too. Actually, etiquette is merely a pleasant game played to make everybody happy and comfortable. Even in today's atmosphere of informality, the person in whose honour the party is being given must arrive a few minutes earlier than the specified hour. Most hosts feel more at ease if the special guest is fifteen minutes ahead of time. It is still fairly generally observed that no one should leave a reception or a dinner until the guest of honour leaves, but this is more observed in the breach. For informal occasions such as teas and brunches the time to leave is very flexible, but sufficient time should be given to speak to all the guests. When the guest of honour wants to leave the moment should be timed to a lull in activities or conversation.

Dropping In on Friends

Unless it is a local and neighbourhood custom, or a well-established one between friends who are on such intimate terms that an unexpected call is welcome, dropping in without first telephoning is a poor idea. It goes without saying that, should the friendship be so close as to allow for the casual drop-in, no friend should call on another with an acquaintance without first asking. Everyone has the right to decide when, where, and what strangers will be welcome.

Thoughtfulness

The day following the party the guest should write a thank-you note to the host or telephone expressing pleasure. For busy people, the note is preferred and is a lasting reminder. Guests of honour or guests who have been especially welcomed or who feel particularly generous, send flowers or a small gift.

Some community and personal customs include guests arriving at the entertainment, particularly a dinner party, with a gift. While no gift should be spurned or treated lightly, it is possible that the host may be too occupied to say more than thank you. In contemporary homes where entertaining is done without help, it is not possible to greet guests, make them welcome, and arrange flowers or open a candy box. Gifts of wine are always appreciated, but in most cases the host has no doubt arranged compatible food and drink, and this welcome gift may also be put on one side. No guest should feel hurt, and a host will, of course, give thanks at the time of receipt and make a quiet mention of future pleasure when good-byes are said.

2
Planning and Organizing

The Painless Party Organizer

While the game-plan for organizing a party is, in the main, based on the old standby, the dinner, the basic organization and planning is the same for cocktail, barbecue, buffet, and all parties where a quantity of food is served.

□ A positive and constructive approach to entertaining is half-way to success and fun for all, host and guests. If you look on entertaining as work and drudgery failure is practically guaranteed. Every aspect of entertaining—home, decorations, food, wanted guests—should be viewed as pleasure and the creation of a pleasing atmosphere.

□ Never entertain those you don't like, or don't want to know better. It is a colossal mistake to invite someone for the sake of having a name in the paper.

□ When asking guests for the first time there may be doubts about food preferences, allergies, or religious tenets. So take the plunge and ask them—once you know they are coming.

□ Save money by planning ahead, then you can buy at leisure, get the best buys and look for the unusual. If you are arranging a particular purchased dessert or other specialty, order well ahead. If you shop in a rush, items such as toothpicks (nice for smoked oysters and marinated artichoke hearts) will be forgotten. And then a chain reaction of confusion begins.

□ You will enjoy your party more by planning and spreading shopping and preparation over a period of time. In this way, when the first guests arrive you will be ready to enjoy yourself.

□ Guests are sensitive creatures and they like an organized yet relaxed atmosphere. If they find it they will unwind, participate, and help to make the event a success. Guests tend to tense when the host is rushing around looking for corkscrews or trying to find the salad servers.

□ Keep an eye on the timing. Be sure that you plan the entertainment step-by-step so that guests receive food and drink at appropriate times. Nothing spoils a party quicker than one host pouring drinks into guests while the other host fumbles the food and finally dishes it up three hours later.

□ Keep a loose-leaf file or a hostess book. It will be a help even when you are thoroughly practised. List your guests, their preferences, and after the party is over you can be candid in your remarks: "Joan and Bill almost came to a fight over politics", "Ralph hogged the conversation." (You'll know to keep them apart next time, and find another extrovert for Ralph.) Note the menu served; it will help you remember that John doesn't eat shellfish, and that Mary gets hives with strawberries even if they are Strawberries Romanoff. A note will help you remember that Ann is left-handed—seat her at the end of the table—or that Tom is mad about the trifle, so next time he comes you'll make a repeat!

□ Keep an up-to-date address book or a file-card box of names, addresses, phone numbers, and include apartment numbers and postal codes. It saves hours of checking before invitations are given.

□ Use a sheet of plain paper headed "Party Worksheet" to help with your initial planning (see sketch). If you write out the menu, you will be able to work out your shopping list. And if you arrange the table plan you will prevent confusion at the doorway.

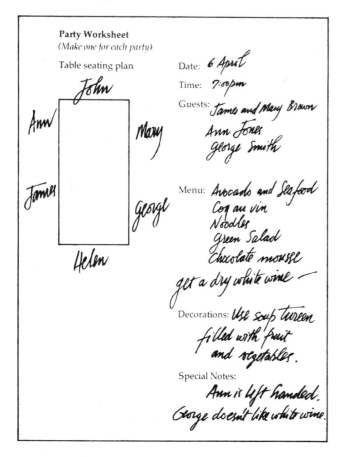

Party Worksheet
(Make one for each party)

Table seating plan

John
Ann
Mary
James
George
Helen

Date: 6 April
Time: 7:00pm
Guests: James and Mary Brown
Ann Jones
George Smith

Menu: Avocado and Seafood
Coq au vin
Noodles
Green Salad
Chocolate mousse
get a dry white wine

Decorations: Use soup tureen filled with fruit and vegetables.

Special Notes: Ann is left handed.
George doesn't like white wine.

Preparing a Timetable

It's easier to plan if you use a written countdown timetable. Don't be hesitant! Such stratagems are used by the most practiced party-givers, although they rarely confess to having these panic savers. On the surface it may seem like an extra chore and a needless waste of time to write everything down, but a little paperwork goes a long way toward making you feel at ease. By organizing you save time, money and above all energy.

And with the countdown, a few things can be organized or purchased each day.

The timetable is a two-part thing. The first part is merely a rundown for the overall planning. The second part deals with the actual cooking and preparation.

Three Weeks Before
(For Christmas, Thanksgiving, or other busy times of the year, invitations should go four weeks before the party.)
decide on the type of party
make up guest list
if you plan on hiring help to serve, using catered food, or renting coffee urns or clothes racks, now is the time to make arrangements
send invitations
plan menu
plan the extras such as flowers, candles and decorations if it is to be a theme party
check table linen
check cookware and tableware

One Week Before
polish silver
make grocery list
make liquor and mix list
wash glasses and china if not recently used
check on guests who haven't answered (see p. 22)
work out seating arrangements and commit to memory or write place cards
check on supply of coat hangers
In winter, get a supply of clothes pins to keep overshoes together
check on guest towels at leisure
iron napkins

One Day Before
shop
set table
put out coasters, ashtrays, matches
do some preliminary preparation of food (check timetable on p. 138 for defrosting poultry)
arrange flowers, candles, etc.

tidy hall closet for the male guests' clothes (use a bedroom for womens' wraps)

The Day

prepare food

set up the bar (a table in the kitchen is sufficient if you are short of space)

get ice delivered if you have no storage facilities

give the washrooms a once-over and put out fresh soap, etc.

Menu Planning

Balance the taste and the colours of both the individual courses and the complete meal. And don't forget texture; the contrast between crisp celery and water chestnuts is delicious with a creamed chicken mixture served in a puff pastry shell, which has still another contrasting texture. All foods are delicious separately but how will they combine? For example, fruit is delicious with many meats—duck with orange or cherries, pork with apples, chicken with pineapple—but fruit doesn't offer the interesting taste contrast when served with beef, veal or shellfish. But shellfish is superb in an avocado container—which proves there's an exception to every rule.

A rich or creamy dish such as Beef Stroganoff or lasagna should be preceded and followed by less rich foods and ones that offer contrasts in colour and texture.

For example:
Consommé with Sherry
Beef Stroganoff
Noodles   Tossed Green Salad
Strawberries and Lemon Sherbet

Melon with Prosciutto
Lasagna
Lettuce and Spinach Salad
Grapes   Cheese

Apart from letting your taste buds guide you, pick up ideas from favourite restaurants. If you've seasoned peas with mint, or served roast lamb with mint jelly, don't follow with a dessert based on Crème de Menthe; try chocolate mousse or a parfait.

Colour is important. A plate with boiled and buttered new potatoes, sole in white wine sauce, and cauliflower may taste superb, but it will look blah. And the guests will be hard pressed to eat and enjoy such a dinner. Change the vegetable to green beans, sprinkle the potatoes with paprika or parsley and chives, add sautéed mushrooms to the sauce. The eye will be pleased and the appetite will increase.

Contrast hot and cold. If the main course is cold, such as cold ham or poached salmon, begin with a hot soup or end with a warm dessert, such as Zabaglione and tart berries or a deep-dish fruit pie.

Every season brings its own traditional foods; enjoy the anticipation of plum pudding, pumpkin pie, strawberry tarts. As well, the seasons bring different foods. In winter there are the root vegetables, including the red and green cabbages; spring brings asparagus; and fall, squash. Not only are seasonal foods plentiful, they are at their peak flavour and, generally, at their cheapest.

A Guide to Contemporary Party Courses

APPETIZERS: Hors d'oeuvres (much easier to serve than canapés which take time to make, become soggy quickly and are, at best, fiddle-some things) can be served with pre-dinner drinks while waiting for all the guests to arrive. Allow twenty minutes to one half hour. If you are without help, pour the first drink (always using a measure). Suggest the guests take another themselves but be sure the dinner is ready before the third drink is wanted.

SOUP: A nice welcoming beginning to a meal. It can be homemade, or purchased and jazzed up with croutons, sherry, and chopped fresh parsley and/or chives. Ladle from the tureen when the guests are seated. Pass the plates or bowls around. Never fill too full to avoid slopping.

When serving soup, put a "service" plate (a bread and butter plate or a dinner-size one) in front of each guest so that any dribbles don't hit the table. (Service plates may be of a different pattern.)

MEAT AND VEGETABLES: Consider the main course from the point of view of easy serving. If you can't carve neatly and quickly, or if the host declines to carve, then avoid roasts. For poultry, from Cornish hens to duckling, use poultry shears to carve into serving portions in minutes, or cook them jointed. When you serve sticky or greasy foods, use the old-fashioned finger bowl. No need to inherit them or go broke to buy them. Fill a small fruit nappy with warm water, float a lemon slice on top and place them on the table before the guests are seated if you have no help.

To save time and work, serve the main course with noodles, rice or jacket potatoes, and pass vegetables, gravy and/or salad bowl. Or you can position individual salad bowls before the guests arrive. Letting the guests help themselves to vegetables, etcetera, speeds the dinner.

SALAD: Served as a first course, or along with the main course, or, if you are serving a fine wine, after the main course has been finished (because vinegar and herbs will spoil the wine's delicate taste). And, gastronomes say, salad dressing alters the taste on the palate.

RELISHES: Bowls or trays of pickles and jellies are put on the table with the main course, and any sauce or gravy for a special dish can be passed with that dish. If the sauce is an integral part of the dish, for example beef in wine sauce, then both meat and sauce are served by the host.

BREAD AND CRACKERS: These are not generally served at a sit-down dinner. However, in some areas it is customary to have bread and rolls on the table. In that case you will need additional plates and knives! The choice is personal, but you can be guided by the fact that people are more calorie-conscious than ever.

DESSERT: This may be served at the table and the servings handed from guest to guest; individual servings may be brought from the kitchen; or guests may help themselves. Usually dessert is served at the dinner table, but for a change of pace a dessert such as a rich chocolate cake or a Brandy Alexander pie can be served in the living room along with coffee and liqueurs.

COFFEE: Serve it in the living room; this prolongs the party atmosphere and continues the conversation. After dessert has been finished in the dining area, at a suitable break in conversation the host rises and leads the guests to the living room. The guests seat themselves. If there is a fireplace, the host may light the fire. Then the coffee is served and liqueurs and brandy are offered. (It is customary to serve coffee only. Guests who don't drink coffee should decline and not accede to the host's suggestion that another beverage be made and offered.) If the living room wasn't used for pre-dinner drinks, the tray, complete except for the coffee pot can be set up earlier in the day. If the room was used for pre-dinner drinks, the host quietly brings a small tray and removes glasses and ashtrays, replacing the latter with clean ones.

SMOKING: Today, since many people do not smoke, there is a return to the old-fashioned courtesy of asking permission before smoking. Smoking is never permissible at the dinner table during the serving of courses. If there are no ashtrays on the dinner table, then it is understood that smoking is not being encouraged in that room. Indeed, the absence of ashtrays in any room is a signal that smoking is not wanted. Cigars should never be lit, regardless of ashtrays, without first asking permission. And cigar stubs should not be left in the ashtrays. Ask leave to use the garbage can.

Planning Is...

Planning can't be over-stressed. It is planning that makes family meals go smoothly even though we are never conscious of it. With experience, the same smoothness happens at parties.

No one feels comfortable if the host keeps sprinting to the kitchen for a forgotten item, or remembers aloud while serving coffee that the salad is still in the kitchen. If this does happen, don't make an announcement. But do make a mental note to toss it out later. If the host keeps disappearing into the kitchen for long periods, the conversations is lost and guests feel they are causing trouble. The general effect is a wet blanket.

There will be fewer problems if you set the table or tables early in the day—or even the day before. Place all the flatware, centrepiece, napkins, salts, relish dishes in position. Then sit at a place setting and in your mind rehearse the meal. Have you spoons for the relish? Are the pepper shakers filled? Is the flatware in the correct order (from the outside towards the plate). It is a good idea to have on the serving table some extra flatware and napkins that can be passed should a guest drop an item. If you've worked out the table setting and the movements for serving, then you should be confident.

After planning, simplicity. There's no need to produce more than three courses, and two are acceptable, plus coffee. What will it be: appetizer, main course, and dessert? or, salad, main course, and dessert? The latter is the most popular basic formula providing both simplicity and variety. Within the formula you can suit yourself and work out a preference. Much depends on your choice, the usual customs of the community, your guests' tastes, the time of the year, and the cooking pots and tableware you own.

You may want to substitute canapés passed in the living room for the first course, or a soup, especially if you own a lovely soup tureen. Hot or cold soups can be served at the table, and a tureen can also be used to serve chili, spaghetti sauce, fish or meat stews. You may want to serve cooked vegetables as well as a salad. Or instead of a tossed salad you may want a moulded one. (In substituting, don't add to your work.)

Appetizers can be served in the recreation room, living room, library, or in fine weather in the garden or sun porch. This method of serving drinks and appetizers has the merit of leaving the living room tidy for after-dinner coffee, liqueurs,

and conversation. The appetizer is never a meal. It can be a tray of cheese, some olives and nuts, or raw vegetables and a tangy sauce which is thick rather than thin and drippy. You can elaborate the appetizer tray with thin slices of spicey sausage or a bowl of pâté. But never serve too many items and be sure that the guests don't make this their meal. How do you stop nibbling? By having the main course ready within twenty minutes of nibbling.

Today people are conscious of calories and wasted food, so keep portions small. If necessary, ask guests individually if you can serve them again when the plates are empty. (Never offer a "second" helping; the host never counts.)

The host who attempts several unfamiliar dishes from new and untried recipes is courting trouble, although many, including myself, find it irresistible. A host who invites guests for seven o'clock, and isn't able to assemble a dinner until ten o'clock has failed, no matter how good the meal finally is. By that time no one really cares. So, if you have to include a new dish, rehearse beforehand. Unless you know that your guests arrive on time, make some allowance in your timetable. In any case, it is best to keep away from rare roasts unless you have an oven that keeps food warm but doesn't cook it further.

If you plan to have assistance, be sure you discuss the hows, whens, and whats before the dinner. Let your helper know exactly what you want done, make her familiar with your reception areas, and work out a series of signals so that she will be present when you require her. Trained help know exactly what to do and how to do it—provided you write out the number of guests expected, the time allowed for hors d'oeuvres and pre-dinner drinks, and the remainder of the menu.

If you are counting on untrained help—the cleaning lady, an elder child, or your babysitter—you may find the assistance will be more valuable if they work behind the scenes dishing up the courses, keeping the kitchen neat and tidy, or putting the children to bed.

The Help-Less Dinner

It isn't difficult to cook, serve, and entertain without help. The meal will go more smoothly if the first course is served where the guests gather on arrival, or if it is placed on the dining room table in advance of the guests' arrival (for example, devilled eggs in a lettuce nest, or pâté accompanied by warm crisp melba toast). While your guests meet each other and have a drink, you leave half way through the allotted time and go to the dining room. Place the appetizers on the table, light the candles. Check the main course and if you are serving hot vegetables, start to cook them. If it is a salad, take the prepared greens and toss with dressing; replace in the refrigerator. Lead the guests to the table and direct seating (p. 52). (If the party is given by a couple, then the servicing chores should be divided. However, it is quite possible to serve a dinner unaided.) After the first course the host pours wine, and the hostess goes to the kitchen. If service is swift she can dispense with warm plates; if she prefers them, she returns with them and places them on the dining, serving table, or sideboard. She then returns to the kitchen for a serving platter on which portions of food are arranged for easy service. The platter in position, the host begins to serve. The hostess returns to the kitchen and brings in vegetable dishes and gravy boat if required and places them on the dining-room table. This saves time, speeds service and ensures that everybody has a hot meal. The host keeps an eye on the wine and as necessary refills glasses.

Simplifying Dinners When the Cook Is Host

The menu can and should be reduced to two courses. Bread plates can be omitted; service plates eliminated from soup bowls; salad plates and forks dispensed with. The salad can be eaten from the dinner plate. (If you do the latter and serve wine, make the dressing with lemon juice instead of vinegar.)

The Formal Buffet Dinner

The afternoon set-up where everything to be used in the way of silver, china, including serving dishes, and flatware, is put into position to check that nothing is forgotten and that the traffic will flow. Guests will begin with the plates and move around the table ending with the napkins and flatware. The wine and coffee service is close by, but in separate locations for the ease of the hosts who will serve.

The chosen theme is red, silver, and gold with the lace tablecloth placed over a red undercloth to pick up the colour of the china. The candles are secured with soft wax to ensure they don't lean or drip. The centrepiece is gold-sprayed artificial fruit arranged on a flat board or platter with a few fresh flowers tucked in. For an exotic touch consult a florist for inexpensive small orchids or other unusual flowers supplied with their stems securely sealed in a tube of water.

Flower Centrepieces

A charming example of using possessions in an unconventional way to decorate a dinner table, a buffet, or a sideboard. The glass-covered cheese board is filled with flowers and greenery arranged on a saucer placed on the board. The glass dome seems to enhance the flower colours and prolongs their freshness for several days. The same idea can be carried out for a Victorian-style table using small dried flowers under the dome.

Christmas Open House

Red, white, and blue is a pleasant Scandinavian change instead of the conventional red and green. The plentiful use of one colour for candles, cloth, plates, and apples gives a feeling of warmth and spaciousness and it shows off the white-painted tree branches and the blue grapes. See illustration opposite p. 112.

Dinner for Two

Elegant simplicity is the message of this table and the use of black, white, and glass actually gives a feeling of warmth and hospitality. The candleholders look expensive but are actually assembled from assorted glasses: wines and tumblers, single and double. The table is set for the appetizer course, Shrimp Quiche served with white wine. The salad bowl adds a note of colour instead of a centrepiece—the contents will be served later, so it does double-duty.

When wine is to be served, only wine glasses need be put on the table and water omitted. (Provided you know the guests well enough to know that they will drink wine. If not, have a pitcher of iced water on a side table.)

A salad saves cooking pots. Wash the greens earlier in the day and have the bottle of dressing on the counter to add to the salad just before taking the bowl into the dining area.

The coffee problem. Serve instant coffee, or have a drip pot ready with the ground coffee and a kettle of water warming on the stove. Before bringing in the dessert bring the kettle to the boil and pour the water into the coffeepot. Coffee need not be served immediately after dinner.

Remove the main course dishes but leave the dessert plates if there's a separate dining room. If there are more than six and you host alone ask a guest, one only, to help. A joint effort is essential, otherwise the clearing takes too long, and guests may begin to move things to the kitchen adding to chaos, or feel that the host is working too hard.

If there's no dining room the plates must be cleared at the end of the meal. No one enjoys sitting around with messy dishes. Use a tray and remove all evidence of the meal.

Don't jump up immediately you have finished eating. Sit and enjoy the conversation. At an appropriate break, perhaps as wine is poured, get up quietly and take two dinner plates at a time into the kitchen. Scrape all the leavings into the large plastic bag. Return for the remaining dishes and finally remove the salt and peppers. Meanwhile, it is the host's job to keep the conversation going. (Let it be known that you don't want guests jumping up to help. It is a nice gesture, but be firm. When you go out to dinner you don't want to clear tables, and besides, too many people getting up disturbs the party and ends with smashed crockery.)

When the table is cleared bring in the dessert. If it is a showpiece that is divided it can be served from where you are sitting with the guests passing their plates. Or, you can put a dessert plate in front of every guest and pass the showpiece for self-service. Depending on the dessert, the flatware may already be on the table English-style or a spoon is put on each dessert plate as it is put in front of the guest. If you have single-serving parfaits bring them in on a small tray and place one in front of each guest putting it on the plate with the spoon to the right. Serve from the left. Again you enjoy the dessert and continue the conversation. At an appropriate moment, the hostess suggests leaving the table. The host snuffs the candles as the last guest leaves.

After a short time in the living room, leave for the kitchen and either percolate the coffee or make a pot of instant coffee. Place it on a tray, set earlier in the day with demi-tasse cups, liqueur glasses and bottles if desired, and a small container of mints. It was once a rule that after-dinner coffee was served black. A small jug of cream saves steps if a guest prefers white coffee. When the tray is complete return to the living room and the host will bring in the tray. Serve coffee black, allow guests to add their own cream and sugar. The host brings out the liqueurs and serves to those who wish them.

There's no point in pretending you can host and wait at the same time; to give a semblance of smoothness, service and food must be simplified so that the party-giver is with the guests as much as possible.

A Note on Carving

The old rule said that carving should be practised in private before being performed in public. Tools should be very sharp, and for poultry a pair of shears is a worthwhile investment. Know where the bones are in order to avoid them, and know the way the grain goes; slicing across it increases tenderness. It is much easier to carve a roast that is "cool," so allow it to set for ten minutes before attempting to carve.

If carving is a problem, there are two solutions: carve and slice in the kitchen and keep the platter and contents warm; or select a menu that avoids intricate carving. Borrow or buy a cookery book that gives diagrammatic instructions. Practise.

Help Wanted

Of course, we would all love to give parties with a splendid capable cook turning out masterpieces in the kitchen, a houseman to open the door, a housemaid to help the women guests, and an experienced waiter to serve. It needn't be just a dream, you can get help to lighten the load if you don't want to accommodate the party to simplicity, and if you have the money to hire experienced help.

Where do you look? Many towns have agencies that supply party help, and wine and liquor outlets usually know where such people can be found. No matter what the recommendation, ask for references, and follow them up.

If you can't get professional help, look around and consider reliable older children or neighbourly teenagers for help in circulating hors d'oeuvres. And they can do great service in the kitchen. If you have a young family, hire your baby-sitter to come and take charge of the children through the party preparation and the party. The baby-sitter should feed the children and put them to bed, and keep them entertained and invisible. You may want the children to say hello at the outset, but after that, they should disappear.

A party may be the first occasion for having paid help in the home, and the question arises: how to treat the help, how to react, how to ask them to carry out your orders. These are capable people being paid to do a job. Explain what you want, tell them how you want things run. Don't keep changing your mind and don't encourage them to chatter to the guests or participate. In fact, this should be made clear before the hiring. Treat help with respect and dignity. Yours will not be their first party, so after explanations, relax and let them do their job.

And If You Don't Have a Dining Area...

Too many apartment developers design places for living without room for a dining table. Of course, this doesn't mean you move—or have an excuse for not entertaining. Party-giving can be in variety: a small stand-up cocktail party; a buffet set out on the coffee or kitchen table; even a dinner party. If you plan a menu around an oven dinner (a casserole plus either an oven dessert or purchased pastry so that the kitchen is not mussed) eat at the kitchen table. Keep the feeling light and informal by using heavy pottery, textured and checked or flowered linens. Similarly, a sit-down dinner in the tiniest living space can be accomplished with a good sturdy card table. Many department and party stores sell plywood circular tops that turn the square mundane card table into a glamorous circular table. Visit the yard-goods department for a make-it-yourself circular cloth, or splurge at one of the linen shops. Circular cloths are somewhat more expensive but they are good-looking. Most attractive are the heavy "skirts" of felt with a deep fringe. Top them with a sheer square or circular cloth.

Living Alone

There's absolutely no excuse for a live-alone in an apartment to avoid entertaining. If money is no object there are restaurants; but even so, friends do enjoy the warmth, comfort and friendliness that comes with home entertaining.

If your apartment is small and has no dining area, then set up a card table or serve trays on laps, or invest in a nest of TV tables. Keep the menu simple and don't feel you can't use commercially prepared salads, desserts, soups, etcetera.

If you work, set up the table the night before so guests don't feel they have to plunge in and work. When you come home, pour a drink and talk with your guests. After a short while, move quietly into the kitchen and begin the meal.

Sample Menus

Appetizers (either smoked salmon on lettuce or
    avocado and ready-cooked shrimp)
Broiled Chicken Pieces with Barbecue Sauce
Green Salad
Garlic Bread
Pastry

Consommé with Sherry
English Mixed Grill
Spinach Salad
French Bread
Strawberries

Take-Out, Bring Home Without Guilt

You can bring home a meal in a plastic bag, a box, or a can and then soup up its palatability. You have to reheat in most cases anyway, so why not add the small extras that make the food "home-made" when you are making a time/money trade-off.

PIZZA: Order the size you want but choose only the basics. When you get home and before reheating add pepperoni, fresh mushrooms, green pepper, et cetera. This way you get the basic makings and add the luxurious touches (and get more) for less.

And a variation you can't buy: spread a pizza with 1/2 cup tomato sauce, top with drained canned clams, top them with melting cheese (mozzarella is an excellent choice) and bake in a 400° oven for about 8 minutes.

CHICKEN: Before your guests tire of the finger-licking flavour, you can ring the changes on everything from the bread to the coleslaw as well as the chicken. See the recipies for Hunter's Chicken and Spanish Chicken.

Guests Arriving

You can have an official door-opener, such as an older child. The host and hostess can share, or it is no great problem if the door is left unlatched. Show the women to a bedroom where they can leave wraps. Have the men hang theirs in the hall closet. (A woman does not hang up a man's overcoat.) Greet the guests warmly, make introductions, and then offer a drink. When you give a large party, you just won't have the time to introduce everyone to everyone else. But at a small party it is an unbreakable rule that the host must introduce all the guests to each other.

At a large gathering you are hosting never leave a newly arrived guest until there is a third person to speak with; then as host, you may slip away. The easiest way is to take the guest over to a small group, introduce them all round, try to mention something about common interests. Always keep an eye on the fulsome bore or the shy guest who is lost and take a moment to steer them to another group.

Tips

□ There can never be too many ashtrays.
□ There can never be too many glasses.
□ There can never be too much ice.
□ Always keep on hand a supply of extra forks—they have a habit of being dropped.
□ If you give one or two very large parties a year, rent everything. If you give more big parties, that is, for thirty or more, consider buying very inexpensive plates and glasses.
□ If you give big parties be prepared to do a house refurbishing afterwards. For some reason a crowd will treat a home as if it were a public hall. Cigarettes will often be grounded into fine china, ashes will hit the rug and glasses will be put on finely polished furniture, olive pits end up in the houseplants. Because of the spills, burns, and ring marks on furniture, an outdoor entertainment is one way to avoid this. However, if you do have damage don't try to remove stains, burns and other major accidents yourself. Get professional help. Call the rug cleaners immediately; they will clean spills and cut match and plug any holes. Furniture with damp rings can sometimes be helped by rubbing with cigarette ash (it's a mild abrasive); if this doesn't work, phone for repairs.
□ If the party goes flat, make one of the coffee drinks, for example, Irish Coffee. Serve it, and let the guests go. Later, hold a post mortem with yourself; were you too anxious; was the guest mix incorrect; was the physical layout of the rooms used difficult to get people together or moving? Don't feel sorry for yourself; try again with a different set of friends and a different type of party.
□ If the food fails, make no apologies. Simply serve. Parsley is a godsend for covering a variety of disasters. Use it in sprigs and chopped. Paprika is helpful too. Keep a standby shelf: you can always extend the meal by beginning with a hot and hearty soup.
□ Keep a supply of headache pills, needles and thread on hand, as well as paper napkins, towels, bandaids: you can never tell what a guest will need.
□ Never try to emulate the haute cuisine restaurants. Unless you bring in caterers or a chef, you can't do it. Serve what you like, do it well, and enjoy your own party. Guests would rather have coffee and sandwiches with a relaxed host than a seven-course meal with a nervous wreck.
□ Closing off a party (a successful one, of course), isn't difficult but requires firmness. Serve a final cup of coffee and say this is the one for the road because tomorrow is a busy day. It isn't rude and your guests should get the hint. If they don't, be bolder and say you have an early day. This is not rudeness, especially since people are now more honest with each other.
□ Smoke gets in your eyes? Here's a way to get rid of smoke in a stuffy room that seems almost too simple. Just put a big bowl of white vinegar and leave it overnight. It absorbs the smoke like magic.
□ Keep everybody happy. When you throw a good party, you need to please all tastes. So you'll find that a small investment in citrus-

flavoured mixes are popular at any party, alone or with gin, vodka or rum.

☐ You'll probably run short of refrigerator space, so fill a pail with ice and keep a dozen extra cans of mix cold. For a really big party, use the bath half full of crushed ice. Cold mixes make good parties better.

☐ You can always take it back. When you're buying liquor for a party, don't be too careful. In most provinces unopened bottles can be returned for a refund, so long as the seal is unbroken. So don't spoil the party by running short just because you're afraid of being stuck with liquor you don't really need.

More Calming Tips

Inexperienced hosts are often terrified of an evening of "just conversation"; they feel they must do something, even if it is only to empty ashtrays, turn on TV, twiddle with the knobs of the record-player, or rearrange chairs. There is no need for this nervous activity. It spreads to the guests. You have asked people who have some common thread of interest. If the evening gets off to a slow start, don't twiddle, and don't keep pouring drinks. Relax and encourage an extravert to talk about himself, his activities and interests. People are at their best when talking about themselves and that gets things going. Conversation develops opinions and is not the same as chit-chat conversation which does little except fill time. Generally, chatterboxes ramble on because they are ill at ease.

Contemporary manners on what constitutes party conversation are drastically different from a few years ago. It was once thought that politics, religion, illness, money and sex were not fit to talk about; to some extent this still holds true. However, a political discussion (provided it doesn't become personal or a war) is permissible. A good host watches and listens and is ready to change the conversation should there be danger of contention. Even religion is not taboo. Of course, no one would attack anyone personally concerning opinions. If the host relaxes, and the mood has been light, the group will develop conversation that is both interesting and comfortable. If it doesn't, then quick, get the Scrabble board, the backgammon and the cards! Or serve a nightcap and coffee, and go back to square one.

A party that is held in the room which contains the TV set can be a bust. If a guest insists on turning it on, that's the end of conversation. On the other hand, if you plan a TV-watching party, then four to six people are the maximum. And what can be done about the guest who turns the set on? Quietly, but firmly, turn the set off and start conversation.

What can be done about problem drinkers? The obvious answer is either not to invite them, or not to serve alcohol. Since this deprives both parties there are some alternatives. The host is in control of the party and should time the pre-dinner social time so that one drink is served. During the dinner, if the host is aware of a problem, wine should not be allowed to flow and refills not offered. If all goes well, the final control is to serve after-dinner demi-tasse without accompanying liqueurs. Since this is somewhat of a strain, invite those who might cause embarrassment to occasions where liquor is generally not served: brunch, afternoon tea.

Stop the Panic

Never show panic. No matter what happens, and almost everything can, simply behave as if it is all part of the routine. Don't apologize for a sodden cake, a boring guest, or a late meal; just do better next time. Nothing is more tedious than a Lady Macbeth act complete with tears and wringing of hands. Equally boring is the host who keeps on explaining and apologizing.

☐ Not ready when the guests arrive? A cardinal sin—but make them comfortable, offer some refreshment, disappear, and hurry back as quickly and as calmly as possible.

☐ The roast is tough or otherwise not up to scratch. Carve it as though there was nothing wrong, but change your butcher or recipe for the next occasion.

☐ The cake has fallen. Either break it into pieces and turn it into trifle (a matter of minutes with instant puddings and cream products), or cover the top and the hollow liberally with whipped cream.

☐ Something has burned? Most towns have take-out shops that deliver everything from Chinese food to fish and chips. You are only Yellow Pages away from rescue.

☐ A guest spills food or drink over himself and the rug. While your instinct is to preserve the rug (it is usually newly cleaned or a light colour), remember the guest first. Enquire if there is a scald. Then reassure the guest that no harm has been done. If clothes are wet, suggest the loan of a garment. Do this as quickly and as unobtrusively as possible. No need to tackle the stained garment—that's the guest's affair. In any event it is best sent to the cleaners the next day. After all this return to the guests calm and smiling. Blot up the spill on the rug. After the guests have departed check if a damp cloth will remove the stain but don't soak the area because that compounds the trouble. If the stain won't move, or you aren't sure about your next step, call the carpet cleaner the next morning.

☐ If an article is broken, the guest will probably be terribly embarrassed, so don't compound the situation by giving the long history of how the smashed item was brought from Scotland by a remote ancestor. Collect the pieces quietly and reassure the guest. Then return to the table and refill a plate or cup for the guest.

☐ A guest who is taken ill suddenly should be shown to a study or a bedroom and allowed to lie in a darkened room. Ascertain if the illness is a passing one or if it is the return of a known problem. Offer to call the doctor, then return to the others. The guest should feel well enough to rejoin the party quietly within fifteen minutes. If not he should ask for a taxi to be called and leave quietly.

Homeward Bound

When the first guests start to make for home, express your regret but don't press them to stay. It doesn't mean they didn't enjoy themselves, they may have their own reasons. Tell them how much you enjoyed having them and see them to the door. Remain by the door until they are off the premises, down the path or the hallway if it is an apartment. With a small group it is mannerly to see guests to the elevator, provided it is done quietly.

Are there rules for ending an evening? Not really, but as the party dies end it quickly, and remember the neighbours. If the party is a late one, keep the outside shouts of pleasure to a minimum. And hope your guests won't wake the neighbours by racing and revving their cars.

Before going to bed, sit and relax for a few minutes. Guests have been known to return for a forgotten slipper or purse. Before going to bed, be sure that all perishables are refrigerated, liquor bottles are stoppered, there are no burning cigarettes, and the fire is dead. If you have the energy, the more you can clear now, the nicer the morning will be. Rinse the glasses and set aside. Scrape off any leftover food and leave the dishes in a sinkful of hot suds. Put the linen in the laundry basket.

The Unexpected Guest

There is one similarity between the unexpected guest and the impromptu party: the possibility of panic. But this doesn't have to be, particularly if the same procedures for impromptu entertaining (see p. 63) are followed, making use of a party shelf and always having the ingredients on hand to make a simple meal. But the most important ingredient is a warm and friendly welcome that belies that first feeling of irritation.

The unexpected guest usually comes from work or travel, is often tired and wants to become part of the family warmth—otherwise there are hotels! The most common case is: "I brought-Joe-from-the-office"—and graciousness is a requisite! Of course, it is nice to be given fair warning, but sometimes this is difficult, especially if the meeting itself has been unexpected in the airport or in a store.

What to do? Give a warm welcome and settle down in the living room for a short time. The host will offer a drink which can range from vegetable juice to liquor. When these are served, slip out to the kitchen and put some cheese and crackers on a server and return and join the group for a short while. This relaxes you and avoids any semblance of panic. If you've planned a quick casserole, you will have turned on the oven while in the kitchen, and perhaps put water to boil for cooking noodles if that's to be the base. Mix the casserole, heat in the oven and rejoin the group while the mixture heats.

What you serve the guest depends on what you have on hand; sometimes the family dinner can merely be extended, sometimes it requires a completely new main course. (Save what you had planned and refrigerate as soon as cooked.) Extenders aren't difficult to manage. If it was to have been a hamburger dinner, break up the patties, add some tomato paste diluted with wine and serve over noodles for an Italian dinner. Or put together a quick casserole from creamed soup, quick cooking rice, plus canned fish, meat or chicken. Improvise with scrambled eggs, eggs Benedict, omelets or a soufflé. Desserts are a simple matter if the freezer has ice cream or a frozen cake, or if the refrigerator has fruit.

Set the table with the china, light the candles, and make the unexpected into a happy event. The guest has come to enjoy friends and the warmth of a happy home. When the meal is over, serve coffee in the living room and join in the conversation. Don't rush off and fix the dishes. This embarrasses the guest who is likely to be reminded that his presence has disturbed the household. There's time enough for the dishes when the evening is over.

Hot Breads

Light the fire, place a selection of hot breads, whipped butter, and preserves on the table and ask over friends and neighbours for a cosy friendly informal get together at any hour of the day. In the morning and the evening serve hot tea or coffee; at noon, or after a skating party, a mug of soup makes the snack heartier.

Summer Brunch (*Overleaf*)

What is nicer than a summer's day? A summer brunch party over the weekend. Keep your chores to the minimum by using spongeable plastic placemats and paper napkins. The place settings are cool and low-key to play up the colours of the fruits and meats.

The menu is blended fruit juice, broiled back bacon with herbed tomato slices, croissants, and preserves. End the meal with strawberries for dipping into sour cream and brown sugar and of course, lashings of freshly brewed coffee.

The Patio Picnic *(Overleaf)*

A simple outdoor meal that requires no cooking and very little clean-up time. The tableware is plastic, wood, and paper in bright clean colours. Plastic flowerpots and bowls make excellent containers for napkins, breadsticks, vegetables, and pickles, and no host can have too many baskets—for breads, cookies, and nibbles.

The meal can be assembled in minutes with a platter of cold meats, a generous selection of cheese, assorted breads and rolls, salad ingredients, and fresh fruit.

Sangria

Sangria is a cool not-too-sweet red wine-based drink that makes a delicious party punch. (See p. 132 for recipe.) Serve it with raw vegetable appetizers, and a main course—hot or cold. Or, serve icy Sangria with plain cake and shortbread cookies under the lawn umbrella in the late afternoon.

3
The Setting

How to Build a Table-Setting Cache

Entertaining has broken away from the old formulas. It is no longer necessary to set the table with double-damask, but it is still nice if you own it. Similarly, stainless flatware easily replaces silver, but if you have silver you'll want to show it off. One of the excitements of entertaining is using unusual possessions and making the buffet, table or coffee tray look just a little different. It takes more imagination than money. When you browse in an antique show, or look over a bazaar, buy whatever pleases you in the way of tableware, but also buy with an end use in mind. For example, a set of punch cups can be used to serve chocolate mousse or a custard-type dessert, tall champagne flute glasses do double duty for parfaits, and souvenir baskets can be used to hold napkins, plants, or hot coffee cake. Variety and versatility are the criteria in selecting multipurpose accessories in these days when storage is at a premium.

The only dishes that need match are dinner plates; and even with these, many hosts mix and match. Combining two four-place settings gives colour and variety to an informal buffet, patio party or brunch. Cups and saucers can be of different patterns, dessert plates can show off a colourful souvenir or antique collection, and bake-and-serve dishes cut the dish washing.

China

First Choice

10-inch dinner plates—nine to thirteen in number depending on whether you plan to keep parties to eights or twelves. The odd plate is your breakage insurance! (Open stock can be a snare and a delusion: it only means you can buy the china or glass one piece at a time. It is not a guarantee that you will be able to buy that particular pattern ever after. If it doesn't sell, if the manufacturer goes out of business, if styles change, you can be out of luck. So when buying open stock, buy as much as you want, as quickly as possible.)

Next Choice

6-inch plates—used for bread and butter, salad, hors d'oeuvres, as a base for a sherbet glass, etcetera. Use for tea and coffee parties
8-inch plates—useful for dessert, or small luncheon servings
Bowls—deep enough to serve soup, fruit, some salads; also use as finger bowls
Cups and saucers—tea size and demi-tasse

Glassware

First Choice

Stemmed water goblets
Stemmed wine glasses—large tulip shape for all-purpose use (see also p. 111).
Small tumblers or old-fashioned glasses—for short drinks, juice, some desserts
Large tumblers—for iced coffee, long drinks
Stemmed glass—for serving ice-cream; will double as a champagne glass

Next Choice

Sherry glasses—of a size sufficient to serve aperitif wines and cocktails

If You Wish

Glass plates—to match ice-cream glass, (the glass can be served on an attractive bread and butter plate)
punch cups
brandy glasses
seafood glasses
beer mugs

Flatware

First Choice

Large knives and forks
Teaspoons—in large and small size
Dessert-size spoons
Dessert-size forks
Salad forks
Butter spreaders

Next Choice

Soup spoons
Small luncheon knives and forks
Serving spoons and forks

Glasses with many uses. (Left to right) All-purpose 9-ounce glass is fine for any wine, red or white, still or sparkling; tulip-shaped champagne glass might also be used for aperitifs with soda; classic 12-ounce Bordeaux glass can serve other wines or mixed drinks; tapering 10$^1/_2$-ounce Burgundy glass might also be used for a Bloody Mary or a cold vichyssoise; rounded 6-ounce sherry glass can double as a cocktail glass; fragile 6$^1/_2$-ounce champagne flute might also serve fruit juice; chimney-shaped 5-ounce glass also serves liqueurs or straight whiskies; large tumbler is great for long drinks; smaller tumbler takes any mixed drink; slender tumbler is ideal for fruit punches, iced tea or coffee; the squat old fashioned glass serves any drink on the rocks.

As You Can and If You Wish

Carving set
Steak knives
Seafood forks
Ladle — for soup, punch, stews, sauces
Small ladle — for gravy or sauces (a small serving
spoon is a good substitute)
Demi-tasse spoons
Grape scissors
Nutcrackers
Pastry forks
Salts and salt spoons
Cake server
Pie cutter
Sugar tongs

Nice Accessories

Wine carafes
Wine stand
Decanters
Ice bucket
A series of round or oval serving platters
Wooden board for carving and for cheese
Vegetable dishes (covered) or substitute large
bowls
Cake plate
Cake stand and/or comport (helps to make an
attractive centrepiece)
Baskets for wine, bread

Table Linens

Table linen now means any fabric or material that
can be used for cloths and napkins, from damask
to towelling—or even a not too fluffy patchwork
quilt. Choose whatever looks fresh, lies flat, and
is easily cleaned. Shapes of mats can be oblong,
oval or round. The latter make a table look un-
crowded, while a cloth seems to make the table
look larger. If you eat and serve from a beautiful
bare polished tabletop without a cloth or mats the
setting appears to be bigger and uncluttered. But
be careful with hot plates and icy cold glasses
—they mark wood!

For variety, try plain mats on a flowered cloth,
or turnabout: use napkins as colour accents. Long
runners used either side of the table ring the
changes, as do Indian bedspreads. Or you can
buy striped fabric and hem the edges. Add a
fringe for dressy elegance.

Napkins

Paper or cloth? The tendency is to move towards
paper because these throw-away napkins save
ironing and come in such a variety of colours,
patterns, thickness and softness, and range in
size from tiny cocktail napkins to the generous
dinner size.

However some of us like to show off our
food, silver, china and table by using cloth, and
for some occasions, such as an anniversary or
wedding dinner, cloth is more appropriate. In
any case, cloth is not such a bother to iron because the double-damask is rarely used, and
there are crease-resistant materials available. The
home-sewer can whip up a magnificent collection of table linens with little cost in time or
money.

If you have beautiful double-damask napkins, iron them damp. Iron first on the wrong
side, then on the right. When smooth and ready
to fold, iron with a medium-warm temperature
and "polish" the surface with the heel of the iron
to bring up the pattern.

Are there right and wrong ways to fold napkins? No, although generally they are folded very
simply today. However, if you want to play and
fold them into different shapes, it is your choice.
The usual way to fold a napkin is to assume that
the fabric is already folded twice to make a
square. Fold it again to form a rectangle with the
fold to the right and the open corner at lower left.
For variation the napkin may be ironed flat, without being creased. The cloth is then rolled and
tucked into the glass so that the two long "ears"
stand up. If you want to fold napkins in fan and
envelopes shapes there are many books available
from the library that give instructions on this.
And, on a quiet day, the head waiter at your local
club or fine restaurant will teach you.

China and Silver at the Ready

Of course if you own lovely china and silver you will want to use these possessions, and they are easiest to use if always kept clean and at the ready.

After using china, if it isn't possible to wash the dishes immediately, fill the sink with water and let them soak. This prevents staining. Carefully washed and stacked, with a paper napkin between plates to prevent scratching, all is ready at a moment's notice.

When used regularly silver needs little care —in fact, the more it is used the better it looks. The tiny wear scratches give it a patina. However, sometimes silver needs freshening and a quick rub with a specially impregnated duster does wonders. The glow lasts longer if silver is polished occasionally with a tarnish-preventive polish; it costs more but is well worth it. Always store silver in tarnish-resistent bags or chests. One important tip: if open salts are used, never leave the spoons in the salt. The silver will corrode and there is no remedy.

Paper, Plastic and Throw-aways

There once was a time when people believed that not only did all the tableware have to match but ownership in the dozens was a requirement before a party could be held. Nothing is further from the truth today.

Paper and plastic from glasses to tablecloths are particularly attractive, with patterns ranging from the cottage-informal to near linen. And there are shapes, sizes and qualities for all purposes. Disposables make light work of clean-up, and save breakages, and allow for the feeding of more people. They are excellent for children's parties, barbecues, picnics and other outdoor fun sessions. Indoors, they are great for large buffet suppers, neighbourhood after-the-rate payers'-meeting refreshments, church socials and so on. The surfaces and finishes of these throw-away utensils allow for the serving of hot and cold food and beverages with no danger of collapsed and soggy plates. Knives, forks and spoons are also available, so a host need only offer the loan of the house for a church supper or a school meeting. And in these days of environmental concern, many throw-aways can be used again, if desired. And fine quality enamel and plastic plates are now very much at home with contemporary furnishings.

And don't forget paper tablecloths, napkins that come in cloth quality, and above all guest towels; the latter save hours of washing and ironing. What's more, guests really use these towels knowing they don't make work.

A large plastic bag, the size used for garbage, or even the huge garden size, is an invaluable adjunct to the kitchen for all types of entertaining. Put it in a corner, or sling the corners between two chairs and throw the debris, drink cans, bottle tops, ashtrays, dinner leavings into the sack. When the party is over, close the top with a twist'em and the bag is ready to go outside for collection.

To Rent or to Own?

Short of a large coffee urn, extra chairs, coat-rack, glasses? An awning for the patio, a punch bowl, additional bridge tables? Renting makes good sense and is economical if you don't plan to use these items regularly. A patio awning takes a lot of storage space, so do a punch bowl and several dozen glasses. In that case it's easier, cheaper, and more convenient to rent.

But before you rent and spend money, explore the freebies. Many supermarkets offer the loan of a coffee urn, wine merchants will loan or sell wine glasses at low cost. If you have to rent remember charges are based on the individual items plus the length of time rented; incidentally you are also responsible for the wear and tear while they are on your premises. Phone several rental companies and have a look at the items to be supplied before signing. It is important to examine the quality and condition of rented items, particularly flatware, china and glass.

If you rent, get a detailed written list and

description along with firm price quotes. When you unpack, check off, to be sure everything you ordered is there and that everything tallies with the list sent by the rental company. You may be required to sign a contract and to give a deposit.

Useful Extras to Own

If you can't borrow from family and friends, consider some of the following for birthday and Christmas gift lists. They aren't mandatory or necessary but, depending on your favourite type of entertainment and its frequency, many can be very useful.

—chafing dishes with water pans and burners (remember to replace your supply of candle warmers and sterno)
—salad servers—the one-hand type are good for buffet tables
—a huge salad bowl
—mix and match serving mats need only be wiped clean, heat-proof mats, trivets, tiles to go under hot dishes
—wooden boards for carving, for bread, delicatessen, cheese, cake
—coffee mugs—saves saucers at informals
—bun baskets with cotton liners, or plug-in types that keep breads warm for hours
—salt and pepper mills
—trays of all sizes for serving lap meals, and to take the place of plates
—inexpensive stackable ashtrays and glasses
—large-size electric coffee urn
—large-size coffee carafes for serving
—electric trays and warmers
—sturdy non-tippable candlesticks and a supply of candles
—a very large casserole
—electric "crock pots" (for soup or chili)
—onion soup pots
—clay bakers in assorted sizes
—large scallop shells
—ovenproof dishes for crêpes and eggs
—poultry shears
    and especially for barbecues:

—sturdy tongs
—large apron
—heavy heatproof gauntlets
—wooden trays to hold meats
—covered cake and butter dishes
—unbreakable tableware

Dressing the Table

At festive occasions such as Christmas, Thanksgiving and Easter nearly everyone takes the time, and uses imagination to create a special table setting. At other times most of us make do with some candles and perhaps some flowers. And yet it seems a pity to spend time on preparing a delicious meal, asking friends, and then leave the table looking as if there wasn't time to organize it.

It doesn't take money, but it does take time and imagination. Your home, the markets, small import stores are filled with the makings for unusual yet suitable table settings. One way to come up with decorating ideas is to consider the food to be served. Is it a super party stew? Then consider scrubbed new potatoes, or mushrooms set in a dish or wicker tray. If it is to be fish, then pots of parsley, a pyramid of lemons or an arrangement of both on a wooden tray. While the purist wine lovers usually avoid flowers with strong scents, African violets massed in pots can be delightful, especially when surrounded by matching candles. Heady plants and flowers such as hyacinths, freesia or carnations should be used only when the food is also powerful—for example, a rice table or curry dinner, or when no wine is being served.

Items from personal collections can serve as foundations for table decoration: oriental lacquer boxes or bowls, shells, toby jugs, copper moulds (see below). An element of fun is needed to achieve success. The failures happen when people are too serious about the occasion and their possessions. Many are so in love with what they call "my silver, my china" that they are unable to let these possessions become the elegant accessories.

A successful table maintains a balance between the simple and the ornate. If the dinner service is extravagant in pattern, use restraint with everything else from table setting, to flatware, linens, glasses, etcetera. Tables loaded with every elaborate household treasure fight for attention. If in doubt, always remove what seems in excess. And because the table decorations and place settings are put into place before the food, it is easy enough to forget that the meal will bring other colours, shapes and textures. Allow for this when planning in order to get a visual balance.

Decorations for the dining or coffee table need not be expensive, and the most delightful are generally the low-cost items used with flair. Libraries have books on flower arranging and decorating, and there's always the florist if money is no object. Apart from formal entertaining, such as weddings or very special occasions, most hosts readily learn the knack of making their own decorations at little cost or effort.

CANDLES are probably the most festive and the easiest to manage. Candles can be combined with flowers, whether the arrangement is informal or "set." And they are charming on their own. You don't need to own silver or crystal candlesticks; there are interesting and inexpensive ones available from gift and candle shops. And these shops sell a soft wax or putty that anchors the candle into position so that goblets, saucers, glasses and other containers can be used successfully. Candles come in so many colours, shapes and sizes that nothing more need be said, except that Votive candles in their glass containers are often overlooked. They can be used among figurines, clustered around a green potted plant, and used to outline the edge of a pool or the base of a tree.

VEGETABLES—a bonus, first you use them for decoration, then the next day you cook and eat! Fill a tureen (if it's deep, put in layers or crunched up tissue before filling), bowl tray or comport with small cabbages, broccoli, egg plant or tiny turnips. Fill a large wicker tray with Oasis and toothpick white or brown mushrooms into position,

adding ferns, parsley or trailing vines to fill in the cracks.

FRUIT can be arranged directly on the table or on comports. Pyramid oranges, lemons, apples or pears, holding them together with toothpicks. Mix them, match them and if you can arrange without toothpicks, use the fruit for dessert. Bunches of different colours and varieties of grapes look beautiful. And in the fall and winter don't overlook bowls of red tomatoes, small squash and gourds as well as pottery filled with almonds, Brazil nuts and walnuts. Fake fruit made of wood or straw can be fun. And fruits, either real or artificial, can be spray-painted as shown in the illustration opposite, p. 32. (Be sure, however, that children aren't lured to nibble.)

GREEN THUMBS—Show off flowering houseplants or forced bulbs by centring them down the table in a massed arrangement. (Put a runner beneath to prevent a scratched table.) Or lift a clump of flowering chives from the herb garden and pot temporarily. Use potted herbs in their earthenware pots to make a clustered centrepiece, or a single pot as a side-table decoration. The gentle warmth from candles will bring out their scent. Tiny growing plants are always delightful and these can be massed on a tray or flat wicker dish effectively. Rosemary, parsley and mint make a pleasant combination of greens, texture and shape. (Be sure to return them to the windowsill or garden the day after the party.)

COLLECTIONS. With imagination just about every collection from wine bottles to feathers and shells can be turned into show-off table decorations. Use figurines singly, in twos, or clustered. Similarly, early glass goblets can be shown off as is, or filled with small nosegays. Old pottery such as ink wells, preserve jars and bottles can be grouped and filled with flowers, feathers or branches with berries (but without leaves, which wilt). A shell collection offers many uses: the big conch shells filled with small flowers and other shells clustered around. A napkin ring collection will show off bright napkins or beautifully embroidered or lace-edged linens. Don't forget feathers: peacock feathers and game-bird feathers have glorious colours and can be used alone in tall vases or mixed with dried flowers.

The Looks of the Table

Times have changed. Fifty years ago etiquette books devoted at least a dozen pages to the folding of napkins. In addition, the tables were remarkable with their pyramids and standards of flowers so that guests were unable to talk across the table. If that wasn't enough the linen cloth was sprinkled with flowerheads, and the many candles or individual electric lamps had silk shades. Today simplicity, which adds up to elegance, is the keynote. Although we want the tables to look pretty, we do this with careful selection and precision placing of flatware and glasses. A few years ago it would have been unthinkable to use place mats for any but the most informal meals: today we may eat directly off a beautifully hand-rubbed antique table.

Flatware is chosen to reflect personal taste and is always arranged about one inch from the edge of the table, knives to the right, forks to the left (except for oyster forks which are placed on the extreme right and are gradually becoming something of an oddity). Flatware is set out in the order it is to be used, working from the outside in towards the plate. The knife blade faces the plate.

Generally dessert plates and silver are presented later. Glassware is placed at the head of the knife, wine glasses to the right of the water glass. However, many wine lovers will omit the water goblet.

Lunch or Informal Supper

No tablecloth is necessary; use place mats and napkins folded very simply. Meat fork is on the outside, salad fork next. However, if the salad is served first, reverse the forks. To the right of the plate a soup spoon, knife. Dessert spoon and fork can be placed above the plate or brought in later with the dessert plate. Glasses above the

knife point, and a bread-and-butter plate with spreader above the fork.

Place-setting for a lunch

Dinner

Again dinner and salad fork on the left. There is no need for a bread-and-butter plate unless the menu includes hot rolls. If the first course is in position when the guests are seated then the napkin to the left; if not, then the napkin on a service plate which can be used as the base for a soup plate. Or the napkin goes between the utensils on the cloth, mat, or wood. Napkins are folded simply, and paper is never used for a formal occasion.

Place-setting for a dinner

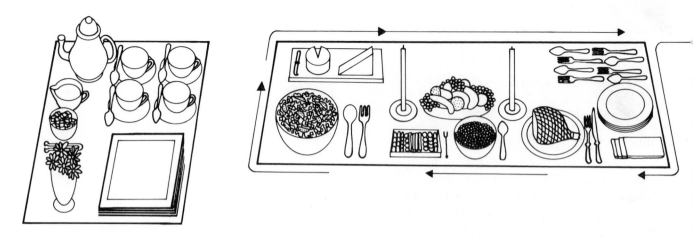

Table Settings—Buffet

In buffet service guests help themselves, although the host may want to help them to the hot dish or the salad. On formal buffet occasions caterers will ask a maid to assist the guests. It is generally more convenient to serve from a table around which the guests walk. After the guests have walked round the table and helped themselves they can take the plate, silver and napkin to a second table that is set with small trays and the beverage. They put their plate on the tray, help themselves to tea or coffee and carry the tray to the place designated for eating, which is done lap-style or on small tables set with cloths, salts, ashtrays and centrepiece. Alternatively, the guests take the filled plate, flatware and napkin and go to the eating room. The choice again is either at small tables or lap-style. If the latter is used, the food must be fork or finger foods.

When space is at a premium, push the table against the wall or beneath a window. Decoration can be a combination of fruit to be used as dessert placed at the back of the table. Guests always begin with the stack of plates. Some hosts place the flatware rolled in a napkin beside the plates. Others find it easier for the guest if the napkin and flatware is picked up after the food is selected. Food should be easy to serve from the platters; if not, then the host assists. Large serving spoons and forks should accompany every dish. If the guests are seated at small tables, the carrying of napkins and flatware can be eliminated.

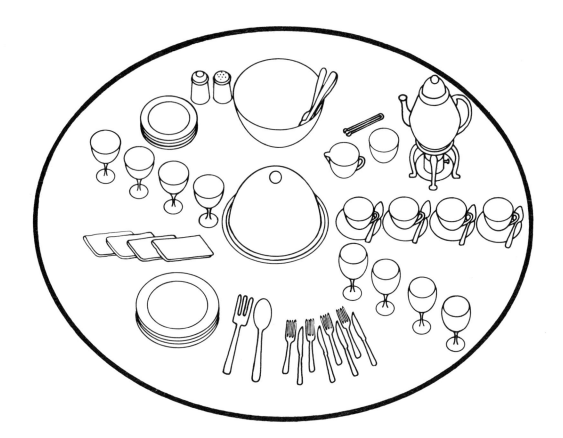

Here a round table is shown with a setting for a buffet supper. Round tables look best when silver and other items in the arrangement radiate from the centre. A buffet should not be too crowded. Additional serving tables may hold everything else if the main table is not large enough.

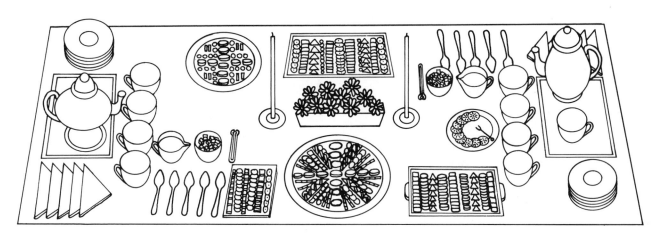

A formal tea table

Wine at buffet meals should be set out on a separate table, if possible. Put the glasses on a tray and fill them two-thirds full. Guests can help themselves if the host is too busy to pour and serve. Uncorked bottles on the wine table indicate that guests are welcome to refill. If there is help, either host, selected guest, or waiter, the filled wine glasses can be passed on a tray to the guests after they have seated themselves with their food. This is a more elaborate service—but it does save spills which easily happen when guests walk with plates, flatware, and napkins, as well as a filled glass.

A formal tea table allows the ultimate in detail; lovely china, silver, table linen and flowers. Tea may be served at one end, coffee at the other. The tea end has lemon, sugar and milk, the coffee, cream and sugar. If there's the alternative of a punch, it is usual to put this on a separate table for ease of serving. Arrange cups uniformly, avoiding stacking. Similar plates of sandwiches, cakes and sweetmeats on either side of the table facilitate service. Decorate with candles if it is late in the day and getting dark, or flowers or a centrepiece, which may vary from a celebration cake to an arrangement of fruit.

Where Does Everybody Sit?

Once there was a formal ruling on seating at the dining table. Men and women alternated, husbands did not sit next to wives unless they were recently married, and so on. All this is now more or less disregarded, because the party may include an uneven number of people and the sexes may not be evenly distributed. The old style of two-by-two reflected the past and it led to cruelty. While an "extra" man was always a gift to a hostess, a widowed or single woman, let alone a divorcee, was dropped as inconvenient or perhaps asked to afternoon tea. Today hosts plan the seating with other thoughts in mind. If two people have interests in common, seat them side by side or, if the table is narrow, opposite each other.

The standard arrangement is for the host to sit at one end of the table, the hostess at the other—usually the kitchen end. Today, there may be one host, and for convenience that person asks a member of the opposite sex to assist. For example, a woman may ask a male guest to pour the wine. If a man is carving, he may ask a woman guest to be hostess and serve the accompaniments, although today it is simpler and quicker to have these passed by other guests.

Conventionally, the guests are seated around the table, man, woman, man, with mn on both sides of the hostess, women on both sides of the host. With six or ten guests, this works out fine. But with eight the formula doesn't work. So one man—the guest of honour, if there is one—takes his place opposite the host, and the hostess moves to his left.

Today, if you have an equal number of guests of both sexes and you have a long or oval table, there's a return to the ancient custom of seating women on one side of the table, men on the other. It keeps the conversation going back and forth, and the men like it.

If you have a guest of honour or a house guest for whom the party is being given, that person takes the honour seat. For a man it is the hostess's right, for a woman, the host's right. It was once customary, and still is in some areas, to give the seat of honour to a clergyman and his wife, to the oldest couple (but be careful here!) or to the new bride.

When you want guests to sit at a particular place and, even though you've written down your plan, there's a last-minute fluster, use a handwritten place card at each setting.

4
A Guide to Parties

There are many different types of party—as many different types as there are hosts! This book can only offer suggestions based on some tried and tested parties as well as the most popular at the moment. But a good party depends on the host's pre-party preparation and planning skill. There can be a party with a reason, such as a graduation reception, or a party for no reason except that the garden is perfect, or the host hasn't had a party for a while. Only imagination is needed.

Old Favourites and New Variations

The Breakfast Party

It's not quite as mad as it sounds! Consider a breakfast party—the hour can vary—for entertaining and feeding out-of-town guests and bridesmaids and attendants before a wedding, or for friends who enjoy early morning sports such as swimming, golf, sailing. Call your club committee meeting for a breakfast—many club women have been too busy getting the family settled and off to have indulged in breakfast. And consider it as a way of entertaining business wives from out of town attending a convention. If it is at all possible ask them to your house. Out of town guests love to visit a home and it is so much warmer than a hotel. (If the guests are at a hotel ask friends to run a car pick-up for you.) However, if your home is too small or you have too little time, then do entertain but go to the hotel. For this type of group, reserve a private room in the convention hotel and see the catering man-

ager regarding the food several weeks ahead of the event. It's a nice touch to have the fresh flowers arranged so that each guest leaves with a flower.

Time: invite for as early as you dare or up to 10:30 a.m. (later it becomes a brunch and is more substantial). Be sure there is plenty of seating.

MENU: The basics of breakfast: hot coffee and/or tea, and hot rolls or coffee cake. Add fresh fruit or fruit juice, butter and a selection of jams. It's also nice to add a main dish that can keep well over hot water or on a hot tray, such as scrambled eggs, back bacon or sausages.

The Coffee Break

The mid-morning coffee break is now an institution. It can be just fun and a chance to meet friends and neighbours, or it can be part of a study session or a committee meeting. It's strictly informal. But, casual as it may be, the hostess wants the surroundings as pleasant as possible. If it's in the kitchen, there should be no leftover dishes or other breakfast reminders lying around; in the living room the ashtrays should be fresh and old newspapers whisked away. No need for decorations, but a growing plant is always fresh and lovely, and so is a roll basket filled with oranges and lemons.

THE MENU: Coffee, hot and strong, or ice cold in summer. Serve hot buttered toast, English muffins, crumpets, cinnamon toast, hot rolls or warm croissants. The only other additions: a pot of butter and some preserves. The idea of a coffee break is simplicity. Keep the food that way too. Never fall into the trap of competition and begin to outshine your neighbours' coffee parties. If you do you will find the party and the friends give up!

Brunch

Tell your guests to dress casually and arrive around 11 o'clock, so they'll be relaxed and hungry. Serve outdoors on patio or balcony if the weather allows. Have the drink ingredients set out, and let guests mix their own concoctions.

Menus

Fruit Juices (with vodka if you like)
Crackers with Spreads
Eggs, sausages, tomatoes,
  mushrooms
Toast   Coffee

Fresh Fruit Salad
Scrambled Eggs
Sautéed Chicken Livers sprinkled with Madeira
Danish Pastry   Hot Biscuits
Preserves   Coffee

Melon with Crystallized Ginger
Scrambled Eggs   Bacon
Croissants   Butter   Preserves
Coffee

Assorted Juices
Pancakes   Sausages   Bacon
Maple Syrup
Coffee   Coffee Cake

Orange Juice
Shirred Eggs with Mushrooms
Croissants   Brioches, Muffins
Butter   Preserves   Coffee

Lunch Party

This is given anytime from one o'clock to half past two, at home or in a restaurant. An at-home lunch party is a convenient time for women to entertain women friends, a club committee, the bridge club. The hour makes time to give the house a quick tidying, the children are either napping or on their way to school—all of which adds up to a popular form of entertaining among women. It is a more personal invitation than being asked to morning coffee or for tea. A lunch can celebrate an occasion, such as Valentine's Day, or a birthday, or just a get-together.

THE MENU: Lunch can begin with an aperitif or sherry, and the menu should be simple and easy to serve. It can be avocado filled with seafood and covered with a homemade Hollandaise and broiled, or served cold with a mayonnaise-type dressing, a puff pastry shell filled with seafood or chicken, or a fresh fruit salad plate. But whatever the choice, select a menu that requires the least amount of time for cooking and serving in order to have adequate time to be with friends and to allow sufficient time for the meeting or bridge to follow.

Luncheon Menus

Sole Poached in Vermouth
Green Grapes   Parsley Rice
Lettuce Salad
Pears and Cheese
White Wine

Poached Cold Salmon
Green Mayonnaise
French Bread
Tossed Salad
Strawberries   Sour Cream   Brown Sugar
Sugar cookies

Make-your-own Sandwich Lunch
Platters of sliced chicken, smoked turkey,
    ham, cheese, hard-cooked eggs, crisp bacon
Mayonnaise   Mustard   Soft Butter
Assorted Breads
Sliced Fresh Fruit   Zabaglione

The Tea

Tea for two or twenty or two hundred: it doesn't matter, the formula is the same. Tea is selected and the leaves or bags are steeped in boiling water. And, of course, the container has been warmed with hot water prior to the making of tea. If you have a crowd from fifteen up, rent a tea urn.

How to Serve

When it's a small group of a dozen or less, the tea service is put on a tray or a cart, or on a table beside the hostess. The tea service consists of cups and saucers with spoons, the teapot, a hot water pot, sugar, milk, cream and lemon slices. And if you enjoy specially blended loose tea—a tea strainer. Also provide small plates with napkins and forks if any of the food should be gooey. The hostess pours tea, adds milk or lemon at the guest's direction, puts the sugar requested on the saucer and places the cup and saucer on the napkined plate.

When the party is large this individual service is not possible and a buffet is the best (see p.51). At very large teas or receptions it is customary to ask friends to help in pouring. There should be several pourers so that no one need serve for more than a half hour. At all times someone should be near the table to see that supplies of beverage and food are replenished. If there is no help, ask a friend to do this, and again, have relief for the watcher!

What Kind of Food?

Tea food should be only what can be picked up in the fingers, unless it is a small group and guests are seated. Sandwiches, of course, both open faced and closed, but never more than two-bites in size. Add fruit and nut bread and tiny hot biscuits. Pound and fruit cake are easy to handle, so are petit fours. Candied orange peel and tiny cookies round out the selection. Of course, the bigger the crowd, the greater the choices.

The Cocktail Party

You love them, or you hate them. But sooner or later you may want to give one because you have been to a number, for business reasons, or even because you enjoy a crowded party where you are surrounded by lots of people you know. Any crowd requires planning. You must check over the number of people you can entertain at a stand-up party without a crush. Of course, if the weather is fine you can count on the outdoors—but don't rely on fine weather! In any case, the best cocktail parties are planned so there is somewhat of a crush. Having surveyed the scene and made a mental note to alter the furniture arrangements (see below), make a list of names. Then figure out the food and drink; you can never have too much and unopened bottles can be returned. If it is a large party, figure costs too. Base the budget on a medium-priced brand of liquor, but remember some of the most popular foods, such as shrimp, pâté, and smoked goodies are expensive.

If the group is large and you want to be free to enjoy your own party, you will need professional help. In any event, a professional barman will save you liquor, serve correctly, and keep an

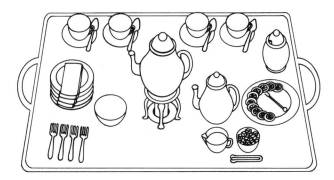

eye on things generally. Or, you can avoid mixing drinks and save on hiring help by having a punch bowl, or two. Keep the punch flavourful, not too sweet (the problem with most punches), and remember that the melting ice dilutes the mixture. You can't meet, greet, introduce, and serve food and liquor all on your own.

Moving the Guests Around

Getting people to move, to circulate and sometimes even to talk with each other at a cocktail party, reception, or other similar gathering isn't easy. There really aren't any tried and true rules, but from experience the following advice may help.

If you can, have help when there are more than one dozen people. While the host and hostess are not expected to introduce everybody, they are then free to wander, able to greet and make introductions to the first dozen or so people. Then after the party is underway, they move among groups introducing and taking guests from one group to another. Ask three or four friends to act as sub-hosts. They introduce, get

conversation going, and keep a roving eye for wallflowers, bores and the over-exuberant.

The arrangement of the furniture can help keep the party moving. Remove most of the chairs, or if the home is large enough to have several reception rooms, keep chairs in the furthest room, usually the library. If possible set up one bar in the centre of the movement, between two rooms, and if the crowd is large a second bar, for the second drink, at the far side of the furthest room. Separate the food table from the bar so people will have to move. Have waitresses circulate food in the less busy room and have the hosts gently walk and talk people into another room. A host at a cocktail party has to really be a working host, keeping conversation and people moving. It is a far different role than the dinner party or tea host.

Even if you have only a small house or apartment you can have a large cocktail party. Rearranging the furniture is the basic step. Study the sketches of the way in which an apartment without a bedroom has been transformed to hold up to forty people; many of the ideas can be

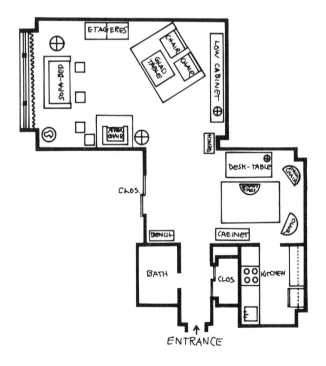

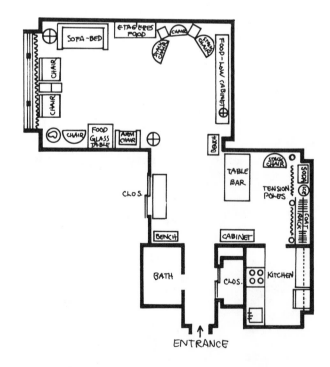

applied to your home. The effect may seem startling when the room is empty, but once the place is full of people it will seem quite different.

The Cocktail-Buffet Party

Newer than the old stand-up cocktail party, which is losing ground because so many people use it to pay off social obligations, is the cocktail-buffet.

To this party are invited a smaller number of people. (Never invite problem drinkers or talkers—save them for dinner parties.) Guests are invited around 6:30 or 7:00 p.m., an hour or so later than the conventional cocktail hour. Cocktails, drinks, hors d'oeuvres are served first. Later in the evening there's a buffet supper, or the buffet can be set up throughout the evening, thus avoiding the pernickety canapé-making. The cocktail-buffet is a little different from the regular buffet in that the meal is simpler, the party is shorter, and it can be a drop-in affair. The only requirements for decoration are flowers and candles.

THE MENU: This type of party begins with a good bar. You don't need every kind of liquor but what you have should be good quality and plentiful. Have a selection of what your crowd likes, then add sherry, ginger ale, and another soft drink choice. Have the bar set up so you don't have to run back and forth if you are without help. After the first drink you can suggest guests pour, but this is somewhat of a mistake with a large crowd. Or ask a friend to supervise the bar. This is no chore if it is set up in the living room and the "bartender" is not hidden from the party. Order plenty of ice, and before the party, cut lemon peel, slice lemons, oranges and limes. The simplest way of serving drinks is the punch bowl, and if the crowd is large don't offer mixed drink cocktails. The English custom of having sherry or a wine party is also easy to handle, since there is no mixing.

The food can be very simple—loaves of crusty bread, butter, cheese and olives, accompanied by icy-cold vegetables. If you want canapés, consider some of the frozen ones that need only a hot oven. If you wish, add platters of cold sliced ham, smoked turkey, and other delicatessen.

The cocktail-buffet can be as simple or as elaborate as you wish. It can be timed so that guests drop in after work or late afternoon, drink and snack and then leave for other activities or the hour can be set so that guests arrive after a weekend outdoors and drink and sup for the evening.

The Dinner Party

The old favourite, the dinner party, is detailed in Chapter 2. Whether sit-down or buffet, it remains one of the easiest ways to entertain. Today there doesn't have to be the terror of rigid formal etiquette and, what's more, a host who hasn't cooking facilities or doesn't want to cook can offer a delicious dinner without home cooking (see p. 35). The dinner party has endless variations, from the serve yourself to the travelling party that has guests eating each course at the home of a different host.

Dinner Menus

Mushroom Soup   Cheese Straws
Chicken Casserole
Buttered Noodles
Salad
Orange Slices in Cointreau

Crab Bisque
Mixed Grill
Jacket Potatoes   Green Peas
Cheese Cake   Fruit Sauce

Liver Pâté
Chicken and Mushrooms
Wild Rice Casserole
Tossed Salad
Chocolate Cream

Consommé with Sherry
Chicken in Red Wine
Pilaf Rice
Spinach
Brandy Alexander Pie

Borscht
Cold Poached Salmon
Mayonnaise   Green Peas
Minted New Potatoes
Fresh Fruits   Cheese

Gazpacho
Paella   Watercress
Syllabub   Poundcake

Crudités   Pâté
Spaghetti and Meat Sauce
Tossed Green Salad
Lemon Sherbet   Cookies

Cheese Tray
Chicken Cacciatore
Rice   Marinated Artichokes
Bean Salad
Spumoni ice cream   Macaroons

Assorted Hors d'oeuvres
Roast Lamb
Baked Potatoes
Frenched Beans
Apple Tart   Whipped Cream

Assorted Cheeses   Crackers
Chili con Carne   Rye Bread
Salad   Fresh Fruit

Avocado
Cornish Hens
Noodles   Broccoli
Eclairs with Chocolate Sauce

Vegetable Soup
Roast Duckling
Potato Puffs   Salad
Mint Parfait

Potato Soup
Lamb Chops, Mushrooms, Kidneys
Spinach and Lettuce Salad
Chocolate Roll

Lasagna
Green Salad   Italian Bread
Cheese and Crackers
Hot Brandied Fruit

Consommé
Broiled Steak
Green Salad
Cheese and Crackers

Buffet Dinners and Suppers

Planning a buffet for a very large crowd is often easier than arranging a sit-down dinner for eight or more. For one thing the timing isn't crucial. In fact there need be no timing if the complete meal is cold—remove everything from the refrigerator just before the guests arrive. And today, with the variety of warmers, hot trays, chafing dishes and candle warmers, even hot food is no problem.

If you worry that the salad will slowly sog, put the salad bowl on the table and serve dressings separately. Or to make it all seem more (and that's the secret of buffets, a kind of fool-the-eye approach), put the different salad ingredients in separate bowls. The guests mix and choose their own combinations.

A buffet meal is made from favourite foods, hot or cold or a combination. Select them with an eye to colour and texture contrasts and serve them in colourful containers. There's only one rule for buffet parties: unless there's room for everyone to sit and use both knife and fork, serve only fork and finger foods.

For some reason unknown, guests eat more at a buffet, so calculate your usual portion size then add more to each dish. And for the main dish, whether it is spaghetti and sauce, chicken and noodles, or beef stew and herbed rice, calculate on at least one half more. There is nothing as disappointing as coming to the buffet table late or at the end of the line and finding the main dish empty. If you are serving a very large crowd, you will find it easier to have several containers of the main course that can be brought from the kitchen as the guests empty the one on the table.

When you are sure that guests have had sufficient of the main course, you can direct them to a separate table for dessert and coffee. Or you can collect plates and serve dessert from a table or wagon in the living room.

If you are coping with a crowd without help, keep an eye on the buffet table. When the service is over and you see perishable foods are left over, quietly remove them to the kitchen and place in the refrigerator. Later, when you have time, put the food into shallow pans so that it will cool quickly; reheat and use within a day or two.

The Fondu Party

There are two kinds of fondu, one is a mixture of melted cheese. Guests sit around the chafing dish in which the mixture gently bubbles and every guest has a long-handled fork to spear a small chunk of French bread to dip it into the cheese. Finally the crusty residue is lifted out and divided among guests—it is considered a delicacy.

The fun of the Swiss fondu is that the person who dips bread into the cheese and loses it pays a forfeit, usually a kiss. Serve a chilled white wine, and supply plenty of napkins. Cheese fondu can be made at home quite easily and it can also be bought ready to use in cans.

The other type of fondu party is the cooking of shrimp or tender chunks of steak in boiling oil. This type of cooking is fun, but can be dangerous and no more than four guests should be seated around the fondu pot, which should be placed on a tray. Guests take turns in spearing food and holding it in the oil until cooked, then dipping into a selection of sauces. Food to be cooked includes mushrooms, chicken, liver pieces, slices of lamb kidney, scallops, eggplant and tiny sausages. Sauces range from barbecue, mustard of various strengths, plum and soy sauces.

For all occasions keep the numbers low around the pot because fire is needed and there is a hazard. The safest is the Swiss Fondu party and a great idea if some of the guests are taking off on a European trip. For one dozen people, set up three separate tables with a fondu pot in the middle of each (on a tray to catch spills). Add a bread basket filled with crusty cubes. Each guest needs a plate and a long-handled fork. Extra forks are needed to get out dropped or overcooked pieces.

A variation of fondu is the dessert-dipping party. Sweet or semi-sweet chocolate is melted over warm water until thick and creamy. The container is transferred to a chafing dish and set over a water bowl, or over the low heat of a candle-warmer. If desired add 2 tablespoons of Kirsch or 1/4 cup of Cointreau to the chocolate mixture. Guests spear dried maraschino cherries, orange sections, banana and pineapple chunks into the hot chocolate. Serve plain cookies or ladyfingers and plenty of black coffee.

The Wine and Cheese Party

Serve a choice of red wines including a Burgundy, an appetizer wine such as Vermouth (dry and sweet), St. Raphael, and medium or dry sherry. You can offer a red table wine such as a Bordeaux, but try to avoid the very sweet wines—although this is a personal choice. Set out trays of assorted crackers, plain and salted, as well as those with sesame seeds. Most wine drinkers feel that onion and other flavours interfere with the business of tasting the wine and cheese. However, almost all wine and crackers will go with cheese. The rule is: the stronger the cheese, the more robust the wine. Red wines should be served at room temperature, provided the day isn't at 30 degrees Celsius. Appetizer wines should be cool but not chilled, although some like to drink these wines on the rocks. And, of course, cheese. Choose three or four from the various types.

Mild: brick, cheddar, Swiss, Colby, Port Salut, Lancashire, Brie. *Cream:* farmer's cream cheese, as well as soft cheeses rolled in grape seeds or flavoured with Kirsch, herbs, walnuts, etcetera. *Sharp:* Limburger, Oka, Tilsit, Camembert, Blue, old Cheddar, Stilton.

Serve cheese at room temperature. Remove from the refrigerator one or two hours before serving. Place on trays with a sharp knife, a slicer knife and butter spreader or scoop for the soft types. If you wish, add bowls of fruit. Apples, pears, grapes and cherries go well with all cheeses. And nuts, shelled or unshelled, are excellent with both wine and cheese.

How Much to Buy?

This depends on your guests, the type of wine and cheese, and the time of day. But count on serving from six to eight ounces per person up to half a bottle, when it comes to wine, less for the appetizer wines. For cheese, count on four ounces per person, but buy larger amounts of known favourites such as cheddar, Oka, Swiss and Gouda.

The Supper Party

A supper party can be played up or down; it can be quiet and simple, or large and formal. A Sun-

day night invitation to supper, by tradition, implies informality and a relaxed, cosy evening. It generally starts early, between six and seven, and ends no later than ten. It is a suitable party for inviting parents with older children, or for mixing the generations.

A late supper party follows some other event such as theatre, concert, movies or sports. It can be very formal, it is often very late, and the atmosphere is more frivolous than "family."

MENUS: A Sunday night supper party may have wine and/or drinks and the menu is usually planned around one main dish, either a chafing dish preparation such as scrambled eggs, or crêpes with a savoury filling, or perhaps a substantial casserole based on noodles and rice. Other easy alternatives are hot chili served from a soup tureen, lasagna, spaghetti and meat balls, or chicken pie. Add a salad and follow with a simple dessert and coffee.

A late festive supper requires a slightly different menu and an efficient hostess. Everything must be prepared in advance, and ready to heat quickly and serve with the minimum of last-minute kitchen effort because the hostess will have been at the earlier event, and guests develop enormous, but finicky, appetites late in the evening. Have a tray of canapé-makings ready: smoked fish, cheeses, thinly sliced ham, so the guests can make their own while the host pours drinks and the hostess assembles the supper. The menu could feature crepes ready to be glazed under the broiler, scrambled eggs and sausages, or a casserole if you have the kind of oven that turns itself on and cooks while everyone is away. Other variations include a hot soup, followed by a platter of cold meats and assorted breads.

The After-Dinner Party

This can be given any time after 8:30 p.m. It has the minimum of problems: the house is in order, the young children are in bed. There is a party atmosphere, but it is informal. There's no need to provide lashings of refreshments and you can invite from two to fifty or more, depending on the occasion. A good way for the family teenagers to entertain on Friday nights or during the school holidays; or it can be a neighbourhood group get-together, a drop-in to decorate the Christmas tree, an adult birthday reception, or just a meeting of friends. It can be an evening of relaxation and chatter, or a games night. It can be a simple party for busy hosts at which a drink is followed by coffee, tea and cookies; or an elaborate evening with flowers, candles, a selection of cheeses, breads, pastries, beverages, and separate rooms for conversation and card players. The after-dinner party can be an inexpensive way of entertaining, it can have a theme, and it may verge on the formal. It is the most versatile of parties.

If you have food, serve it late, buffet style from the dining-room table or from a wheeled cart. And unless the crowd is large, provide plenty of seating. At a late hour people want to sit and relax.

Serve coffee, either just before the guests leave or during the evening. In addition to the basic coffee, it is nice to offer tea for those who prefer it. An added touch is to have some caffeine-free coffee. Accompaniments will be milk, cream and lemon.

An elegant touch is to serve coffee with coloured coffee sugar or brown sugar, as well as whipped cream. Liqueurs can be offered for separate sipping, or guests can add them to their coffee. Liqueur preferences are personal but good for sipping with coffee are: Tia Maria, Creme de Cacao, Drambuie, Cognac. Or serve Canadian Coffee.

Serve individual pastries, fruit tarts, fruit cake, pound cake, or a dessert such as Black Forest cake or pineapple mousse.

If you wish, drinks can be served soon after arrival. With these pass tiny sandwiches, nuts or dry nibbles. Later in the evening, and before the guests leave offer delicatessen make-your-own-sandwiches and simple dessert for the sweet-toothed, with tea and coffee.

On a summer evening offer a chilled punch with bowls of fresh fruit. If the punch is not too sweet offer cheeses. With a sweet punch serve a plain cookie, or, unhulled strawberries with bowls of granulated or fruit sugar, and a bowl of whipped or sour cream (or a mixture of the creams) for dipping.

For very festive occasions serve an elaborate dessert such as cold chocolate soufflé, or ice-cream eclairs with a brandied chocolate sauce, accompanied by sparkling wine or champagne.

Housewarmings

Housewarmings get friends together and at the same time allow them to satisfy their curiosity about your new home. It also allows you to show off! Housewarmings are usually informal and are given by the home-owner. Circumstances dictate how soon after moving the party is scheduled. If you wait until everything is perfect, part of the fun is lost, and you may never get around to a memorable housewarming. As many guests as can be comfortably entertained are invited, and friends usually bring inexpensive gifts: things for the house such as flowers, potted plants, playing cards, wine, gourmet foods—nice luxurious extras which are needed and useful, but which do not conflict with the owner's colour schemes or taste in furnishings.

Refreshments can range from sherry and some nibbles, coffee, and a warm streusel-topped coffee-cake, to a more elaborate offering including a buffet. There is no need for entertainment: talk and exchange of good wishes are sufficient. But the new home should be very tidy because your guests will want to see *everything*. You can tour the place together, or you can suggest they look around themselves.

Some housewarmings are given as a "surprise" party by friends. This has some disadvantages if it is a true surprise and even if the friends come armed with gifts, food, wine. The owner may be surprised at an inconvenient time, so that "half-a-surprise" often works with a friend calling to ask if anyone will be home on a specific hour of a specific day.

The Impromptu Party

Some of the best parties aren't planned—they happen. And there's no party that's quite as much fun as the impromptu one. It could happen after a movie, or it's Sunday and you feel like company. No matter what or how, it's a great way to meet old friends and make new ones with the minimum of fuss. But it's Sunday, it's late at night and the stores are closed. This shouldn't be a problem. First there are the standby appliances: refrigerator and freezer plus your pantry. In addition you have a secret basic emergency shelf of goodies squirrelled away: cans, preserved foods, drinks, mixes, nibbles. Just remember to replenish stocks after the party.

There's no way of knowing what constitutes a well-stocked store cupboard, freezer or refrigerator. We all have different ideas about that and different ways of entertaining. But it's a good idea to keep the ingredients for at least one main casserole and one dessert and also sufficient nibbles and canned goods to make a trayful of snacks. Plan supplies with six people in mind.

Or, if you want to make life very easy indeed, as close as the phone is a world of home delivery that brings everything from piping hot pizza to Chinese egg rolls.

For pantry shelf hints see p. 139.

Bring Your Own

This is a popular party in some areas where the implications are understood, otherwise it is a good quick way to lose friends! An invitation that comes with the contraction: B.Y.O.B. means bring your own bottle. It is also etiquette to leave the bottle and remaining contents with the host. It is a cheap way to entertain, and to build a cellar, but it is like a pyramid club—there are losers and you mustn't feel resentment at leaving the dregs when you go home.

Another, and nicer version of the B.Y.O.B., is the Bring Your Own—or an update on the Pot-luck Supper. And it is an easy way to have an informal get together. The host calls friends and asks them to bring their favourite dish and from the collection an impromptu buffet supper is arranged. You can leave it very impromptu and take a chance that you will get a selection of main dishes, casseroles as well as salads and dessert. But you may end up serving six noodle-tuna casseroles and four chocolate cakes. A better way is to ask guests and suggest the offering: "Why don't you bring the makings for your superb Caesar Salad?", etc. Then the food forms a varied menu, work is saved and all the contributors bring their finest and most successful foods. It also enables those who don't cook, or who are too busy, to bring goodies from the pastry shop and delicatessen.

The Music Evening

Or Sunday afternoon, for that matter. Get music lovers together to spend a few hours listening to some favourite records. Be sure they all like the same type of music! You just can't mix the Rock with the Classics. Music buffs will cease to talk while the music plays, but you can have conversation and discussion during "intermission" and a good time to pass a preferred drink. Don't play record after record, let them want to come again. An hour to an hour and a half is sufficient. Then serve refreshments and resume discussion until the party breaks up.

Singalong

People like to sing regardless of their ability. An hour or two of "old-time songs" or carolling is enjoyed by a mixed age group. If you don't play the piano or can't lead, either ask a musical friend to take over or hire a local amateur musician to get the ball rolling. With musical friends ask them beforehand if they will lead or play, don't spring it on them when they arrive at the party that you expect help. If they make their living as professional musicians, it's best to discuss a fee. Regardless of who leads the group, have a program consultation ahead of time. Hand out typed song sheets to the guests. Begin with a drink if you wish. Serving mulled wine is pleasantly traditional. End the party with tea, coffee, and sandwiches with tiny cakes or bar cookies.

Home Movies

If you are interested in film-making and have friends with similar hobbies, ask them over for a movie night. But have a rehearsal before the party to be sure that the equipment is in good shape and to check the film and time it. Keep the running time no longer than one and one half hours. Serve refreshments after the movie, but it's fun to have bags of popcorn to pass around during the performance. This is a party only for those with like interests. Try to avoid showing endless footage of family antics, unless the audience is family. Above all, don't apologize for any shortcomings in the movie. If the movie is that bad, leave it in its can and rent one.

Big Game Hearty Snack

Set up individual trays in the kitchen. Before the game begins a heat a potful of homemade vegetable, minestrone or onion soup. Before serving add a jigger of red wine or Madeira to each cup. Put a plate on each tray with sliced buttered rye bread, a devilled egg, sliced ham and salami, plus a bunch of grapes. At the break in the game, guests file through the kitchen, fill soup cups and trot off with the tray.

Fun and Games

Many people, while offering guests refreshment that can run from a simple supper to a cocktail-buffet, build the party around some type of entertainment. It can be a general participation in games such as bridge to groups playing Scrabble, War Games, or piecing jigsaws. There are those who enjoy parlour games such as charades and guessing games. Other parties are built around a particular celebration, dancing, listening to music, watching a TV special. If you want to have

an evening of entertainment or a special celebration, plan it, but let your guests know what it is. Everyone likes to be aware of what will take place, and even to be warned if the evening is for serious bridge or for uninhibited party games.

You can't bludgeon people into having fun playing games; you need a group of ready-to-go enthusiasts. Behind every game-lover lies the discovery of skill. The games you like best are those you play best. That is why the best game evenings are those where everyone present can be expected to be reasonably good. Obscure games aren't fun; they allow one or two people to show off, but they bore the rest and sooner or later impatience leads to a premature end to the evening. Mean games based on pseudo-psychology leading to personal remarks are even worse, and so are games that show people to be poorly informed or clumsy.

Good party games come in sizes. Some are for small parties, others work best with large groups. There's nothing like a good game to get people to meet, to get a terrific party going, but they must not be overdone. One or two are sufficient for an evening; and knowing when to stop is very important.

Success depends on enthusiastic players and adequate preparation. Setting the stage may require the hostess to do nothing more taxing than having sufficient pencils on hand, but it may also mean several hours spent in "hiding" many small objects in plain sight, or writing out a "Treasure Hunt" set of clues. And if you have asked a crowd you'll want them to meet, mix, and have fun, fast. There are many tricks for "getting to know you". Many of the party games in the next section can be used as ice-breakers or mixers. Among the easiest: write the names of characters on small cards, for example, Cinderella, Prince, Oberon, Titania, etc. Pin the cards to the backs of guests and send them off to find their partners. Or, use simple, homemade jig-saws. You can start by sending out the invitations "jig-sawed". When the guests arrive, have enough two-piece puzzles prepared so that each guest gets one piece on arrival, usually one-half of each pair goes to a woman and the other to a man. Each then checks every other guest until he finds the matching piece.

Party Games

CHARADES: Props and preparations: list eight to twelve familiar phrases or quotations to be acted out by teams of players. Object: for each team to guess, as quickly as possible, all the phrases from the actors' pantomime.

Action: divide guests into two teams; send teams into separate rooms. The compiler of the list is in H.Q. between the two. The game begins by giving the first phrase to one player from each team. Each player returns to his team and pantomimes the phrase for them. When a team has guessed, the player who solved it runs to the list-keeper for a new assignment, which he acts out. The play is repeated, much like a relay race, until one team completes its list. There are variations: teams make a list for each other, or teams can be in the same room and act out in turn. This eliminates the list-keeper so all can play.

HIDING THINGS IN SIGHT is really a children's game but many adults enjoy it. You need something like twenty small objects, plus a copy of the list and a pencil for all the players. You hide the objects in advance. The rule is that the players must be able to see each thing on the list without moving or touching anything in the room. You have to be a camouflage expert: an aspirin in a plant pot or in the centre of a white flower, a gold ring on a lamp finial, and so on.

DRESS-UPS: Use cartons or containers of fabric, feathers and all kinds of accessories, plus pins and scissors. Players work either in pairs as designer and model, or alone. The prizes are for the handsomest, and most grotesque, the most sporting costume, etcetera.

IMPROBABLE CONVERSATIONS: Two players leave the room to decide on their identities: for example, Queen Victoria talking with Mickey Spillane. When they return to the others, they hold a brief conversation larded with cues. The audience asks

The Formal Dinner

Elegant in its simplicity but still showing off your nicest possessions. The placemats are small enough to reveal plenty of polished wood which makes the silver gleam and reflects the candlelight. The centrepieces use a silver cream and sugar or other small pieces of silverware filled with simple flowers.

The soup tureen has consommé with sherry and a sliced lemon garnish. The wine has been poured so that it will continue to breathe and will perfect by the time the entree is served.

leading questions until the characters are revealed.

THE CHIN GAME: Divide guests into two teams and line them up. Under the chin of the first person in each line, tuck an apple or orange. That person must transfer it to beneath the chin of the next person in line without using his hands. (If he drops the apple, he picks it up and starts over again.) The team that first gets its apple to the end of the line is the winner.

WHO AM I? For this game, prepare slips of paper bearing the names of famous persons and pin one to the back of each guest as he arrives. The guest must then find out his identity by asking questions of others—questions such as "Am I alive?" "Am I a real person?" "Do I live in Canada?" and so on. All questions can only be answered "Yes" or "No," and only one question may be asked of any one person at a time. Winners are the first five people to guess their assumed identities—and no peeking in mirrors!

ALPHABET: Select one guest and give him a letter of the alphabet (omit J, K, O and Z). A time-keeper with a watch with a second hand calls out a starting signal. The player then names as many words, starting with the given letter, as he can in sixty seconds. The host keeps score and writes down the total. Each guest has a turn with a different letter (repeat some letters, if you run out). The winner is the person with the highest score.

CATEGORIES: A somewhat similar game, in which each player is given a pencil and a piece of ruled paper which he divides into columns. Each column is marked with the name of a category—such as flowers, fruit, vegetables, animals, minerals. When everyone is ready, start calling out letters of the alphabet. Each player tries to write an appropriate word beginning with that letter in each of his category columns within the time allowed. The winner is the player with the biggest total in all categories.

SCREEN TEST: In this game everyone is given a chance to show what a great actor he (or she) could have been on the silent screen.

Spanish Buffet Supper

A simple but elegant meal with all the preparation done beforehand, and everything from the soup to the dessert set out so that the guests can help themselves.

The colour scheme of red and gold with a hint of brown evokes the colours of a sunny Spanish village. The appetizer salad-soup, Gaspacho, is served from an oversize brandy snifter, or from a punch bowl, and is surrounded by bowls of vegetable garnish. The mixture of seafood and rice, Paella, comes directly from the oven to the table. Dessert is an ice-cold lemony flavoured cream.

Before the guests arrive, make up slips of paper, each bearing the name of an emotion —fear, jealousy, love, suspicion, envy and so on. Also copy all the names on a master list.

To play the game, each guest selects a slip and acts out the emotion named—with gestures and expressions only, no words. The master list is given to the guest chosen as "director." With the help of this list, he must then guess which emotion is being portrayed. Most of the time the director, the actor who is "on" and the other players are broken up with laughter, so no score is kept. But then that's not the object of the game!

PASS IT ON: The players are divided into two lines, far enough apart so that whispered words cannot be overheard. Then a written message (the same one) is shown to the leader of each team. He is given a few minutes to memorize it; then he repeats it verbally to the next player, who in turn passes it on to the next one in line, and so on. When the message reaches the last player, he writes it down. The final versions submitted by both teams are then compared with the original message, and the one that resembles it most closely is declared the winner. As with "Screen Test," there is more hilarity than competition to this game; often the final message on both sides is ludicrously different from the original.

GHOSTS: Almost everyone has played this game since he first learned to spell, but the more words your guests know, the more fun it is. Each player takes turns calling out a letter, with a definite word in mind and the object of trapping someone else into ending it—at which point that person is penalized one point and becomes the "G" of "G-H-O-S-T." (A five-point loser becomes a full G-H-O-S-T and is out of the game.) Thus the wary player faced with E-X-P-O-S does not add E, thus ending the word. Instead, he adds I, which can build toward "EXPOSING" or "EXPOSITION," or T, with "EXPOSTULATE" or "EXPOSTULATION" in mind. The player who collects the fewest points for ending words wins. (In some versions of the game, players are per-

mitted to add a letter either before or after the letters already assembled.)

CHAIN SPELLING: The guests are divided into two teams; two persons (one from each team) play at a time. The first player says a word. The second player must reply with a word that starts with the last letter of the first word. The round continues until a player cannot think of a word beginning with the last letter of the previous word. (Words may not be repeated.) To make it more difficult the word category may be limited to animals, plants or insects—for example, horse, elephant, tiger, rat, toad.

REMEMBERING CONTESTS: The remembering contest has no age limits and is a fine game for picnics or other parties where both adults and children are present. Beforehand, prepare several of the following displays, carefully counting the items in each and recording the totals:

A bottle of peanuts
Ball of twine
A cookie
Can of nails
Money
Book (players remember title, author, publisher)
Newspaper page (players remember headline)

Give each player a piece of paper and a pencil and ask him to record his remembrance of the units. Closest guess wins a prize.

There are hundreds of parlour games. Every group that fancies them has favourites, but for those in doubt, the library can come up with compendiums.

The Barn Dance

Unless you have a barn or a large, clean garage, this is for the recreation room or basement. Remove everything except a few chairs against the wall and set up a bar. Dress the room with fall leaves, pumpkins, gourds, and light the place with lanterns, or hurricane lamps. Ask the guests to come in jeans and "country style" clothes. If you splurge, hire a professional square dance caller and a fiddler. If not, get plenty of dance records and m.c. yourself. At one end of the room set up a trestle table covered with a checked cloth or paper tablecloth and serve country food.

MENU: Baked ham, coleslaw, spareribs, cold fried chicken, chili. Corn muffins, sourdough bread, salads of all kinds: green, macaroni, potato. Take your choice, keep it plentiful and simple. Use paper plates, napkins, glasses and there's no muss.

Costume Party

Many adults love a dress-up party. Choose a theme, and tie the invitations, decorations and prizes to it. There are thousands of ideas: Movie Stars; That Wonderful Year: The Year 2000, and so on. A party starter is guessing who or what each guest represents. Award prizes for the best costumes, the best guessers, the worst guessers. This is an evening for a buffet supper to be followed by games, such as charades and word games, as well as dancing. Or stage the costume party on Mardi Gras, and set the mood with paper flowers, streamers and balloons and whistles. Guests can come masked which makes guessing longer and more fun.

Hawaiian Luau

This kind of a party is given in the recreation room, patio, basement or beach. Use lots of green crêpe "grass," pineapples, fishing nets, flowers, and of course, paper leis. Get Hawaiian records going, have hula contests and settle down to sent-in Polynesian food, or have a selection of chicken and almonds, fried shrimps, salads, roast pork, and easy dessert of fresh fruit marinated in liqueur. Or get out the hibachis and cook chicken livers wrapped in bacon, miniature egg rolls from the frozen food counter, wieners and sausages dipped in crumb-coating mixes.

Treasure Hunt

You must have friends who like games, and you must take the time for the preparation. Timing: a cottage weekend with friends "around the lake" or a long summer evening at home.

Hide treasures—small gifts at the end of a trail of clues. Make up tricky and misleading clues. There may be at least a dozen clues and if you are setting the guests up in teams you'll need separate clues for each. Pair people off and set a time limit. In addition to the prize, have one for the first home, another for the boobies.

Scavenger Hunt

A variation of the treasure hunt, it doesn't require the host to work as hard. It can be played all over the neighbourhood, provided you know your neighbours—and ask them. You hand the guests a list of things to find, somehow, somewhere, without breaking the law. The requests must be difficult but not impossible: an old style 78 r.p.m. record, a 1940 one cent piece, a blue tie, a red garter. The trick is to list things that are unusual and out of date. And a time limit must be set, say two hours, else your party will have vanished.

The Bridge Party

Bridge and other card games are good mixers. When giving a card party, hosts can play it safe by counting themselves out, which leaves them free to fill in for last-minute regrets, and enables them to circulate and to check on refreshments, empty ashtrays, and so on.

For serious bridge a small party is best with only guests who enjoy playing seriously. To keep the atmosphere light and gay, have a few prizes that are inexpensive and for laughs. At an evening bridge don't insist that guests play so late they are exhausted; set a time limit for play. Most players prefer to quit at a reasonable hour. Then serve some late-evening refreshments.

In choosing guests select those who enjoy the game and are of an equal skill. Most players are good sports and will be on their best social be-haviour, but try to avoid poor losers who play for keeps and who call attention to other guest's mistakes. Invite them to another type of party!

A bridge party can range from a foursome to as many tables as you have space for comfortably. Arrange the room with the tables set up with card decks, score pad, pencils and ashtrays. If you serve nuts or candy keep the bowls small, the ashtrays large, and try to keep the tables unclut-tered. Wherever possible use comfortable straight-backed chairs.

MENU: If refreshments are served prior to playing, set the card tables, if you don't have extra room, with linen and silver. Remove after the meal and put the card covers on the tables with the card decks, etcetera. Keep the menu light because guests will either sit for two or three hours, or will have been sitting. During the game have water and other cold drinks available.

Card Etiquette

Always state frankly whether you are a good, middling, or rabid player, so that the others can decide whether to risk you. If you play very poorly, either take lessons to improve or accept card party invitations on the understanding that the host knows your rating.

Card playing has its own nerve-racking man-nerisms: the slow player, the one who drums on the table, the chair teeterer, the whooper who enjoys the other partners' defeat, the poor loser and the inquest opener.

If cards are to be played for money, the host should say so when issuing the invitation. If a guest prefers not to play for money an awkward situation and one of discomfort is created. Play-ing for money can create problems and many hosts on principle state at the beginning, "We don't play for stakes."

Should you play for stakes, be prepared to lose and to pay off the losses immediately, pref-erably in cash. If you can't afford to lose, don't play for money.

Outdoor Entertaining

Picnics

The confirmed picnicker begins by purchasing one hamper—a basket that is light and equipped with strong handles. Then he equips it with flat-ware, plates, cups, vacuum bottles, salts and peppers, corkscrew, bottle opener, can opener —and never, never snitches this equip-ment for other occasions. On returning from a picnic the equipment is washed and replaced, and each time a large plastic garbage bag and a box of napkins is tucked in ready for the next outing. Picnic hampers can be purchased ready equipped, but these are usually quite expensive and often have a combination of accessories that may not be as useful as chosen items. In addition to the hamper, a cooler chest is a must if foods other than a sandwich are to be eaten. From then on, add whatever makes a picnic more comfort-able for you and your guests: a sunshade, col-oured blankets or car rugs, a hibachi or small barbecue (don't forget to keep a bag of charcoal and fire lighters packed with this equipment). A variety of vacuum bottles in different sizes and some with wide necks allow for a wide variety of foods. Be sure never to fill a vacuum bottle with a carbonated beverage—it will explode disastrously.

Packing the Picnic Hamper

It's an art, learned by experience, to pack a picnic with the kind of food that makes everyone pleased they came. There's nothing quite as un-appetizing as a curled peanut butter sandwich dripping melted jelly! Choose foods that travel well: cold chicken cut in portions or cold veal and ham pies. And don't forget the mustard, pickles and relishes. Potato salad travelling in a glass jar and whole tomatoes combine on the spot with lettuce leaves brought separately in a damp towel. And there are all kinds of good things that can travel in vacuum jugs and bottles: hot sherried consommé, spaghetti and meat sauce, chowder, chili con carne, stew.

Warning: anything mixed with mayonnaise and anything creamy such as devilled eggs, chicken salad, fruit flans, egg salad sandwiches, must be kept very cold. Put them in a vacuum container or surround with an ice packing in the cooler chest.

Picnic Meals

A picnic can be any meal that's portable, from simple cheese sandwich to a splendid fête champêtre that includes everything from crusty French bread and pâté to strawberries marinated in Cointreau plus iced bottles of wine. However, organization for all outdoor meals is a must. The planning is as minute as for an indoor dinner party, perhaps more so, because if the forks or the salt are forgotten there's no going home. Many practised picnic-givers have a permanent list of necessities written on a plastic covered sheet and kept in the main hamper.

Providing comfort is important at picnics. An extra sun hat, sun tan lotion, and insect repellent are good to take along—but pack them separately from the food! Blankets give comfort and if you have older people going, or want more comfort than a blanket, consider some cushions and folding chairs. Keep the napkins as big as you can and terry guest towels are ideal—they sop and mop up and are so easy to wash. Plastic cutlery is useful, though not particularly attractive; but if you take stainless, be sure to have a count before going home. Paper plates are great, but some prefer the more permanent feel of quality plastic.

Picnic Hints

□ For a convenient picnic sandwich, slice a large loaf horizontally four times, layer with different cooked meats (chicken, ham, salami) with mayonnaise. Wrap in plastic wrap to keep fresh; simply slice vertically to serve.

□ If you're looking for ways to stretch the budget, heavy-up the potato salad. It's cheap, easy and everyone loves it.

□ Pack wet washcloths in plastic for cleaning sticky hands, or tuck in commercially packaged moist towelettes.

□ Make sure cold foods are cold, hot foods hot. Use coolers with ice or canned cold; wrap hot foods in layers of newspaper.

□ If you're planning to have a fire, bring marinated beef cubes in plastic container, a few skewers, and barbecue your own shish kebabs.

Menu
Crackers and Dips
Potato Salad
Assorted breads and rolls
Cold cuts (in sandwiches, or spread on a platter, with relishes)
Fresh or Marinated Vegetables
Cake and Cookies
Fresh Fruit and Cheese

Outdoor All-Ages Parties

It's fun to have hot, satisfying but simple refreshments after cross-country skiing, sleighing, snowmobiling, walking. The air is crisp, appetites are enormous and no one wants to wait. This is the time for instant foods as well as the variety of Thermos jars and bottles if the service is out of doors. If you bring guests into the house, the same service will do. No fuss, but simple hot foods such as soup, hot chocolate, large sandwiches with thick fillings, raisins, apples and fruit cake. If the weather is very cold, beware of alcohol; it seems to work much quicker when guests are cold and tired.

A Winter Car Picnic

This is a great way to stoke up after cross-country walking, driving, or even sedentary antiquing. Pack the Thermos with hot soup (for some reason tomato soup seems to keep much hotter). Pack sandwiches of thinly sliced cold beef and horse radish butter, fresh fruit, plain chocolate bars, nuts and raisins. You'll generate enough energy to go on for several more hours!

Food for Sport

Food for outdoor eating should be hearty and portable. Take along the makings, the ready-mades and pack in a camp stove. Then whether you work on the tailgate or a picnic table, food is ready in minutes.

Menu

Spaghetti or Ravioli (take cans, can opener and a
  deep pot)
Grated Cheese
Crusty Bread
Green Bean Salad
Fresh Fruit   Brownies
Thermos Coffee or Tea

Champagne Strawberries (combine sugar, berries,
  then drop in champagne-filled goblets)
Scrambled Eggs, Bacon, Sausages
Asparagus Spears (marinated)
Croissants Muffins   Preserves
Coffee   Tea

Eating Outdoors at Night

If you have the garden, the equipment, and the weather there's nothing as pleasant as a mid-summer supper or dinner party under the stars. But while the moon is romantic, it generally doesn't co-operate by lighting the table, and good lighting at night is essential in order to avoid accidents. Low-intensity illumination hung in the trees or from the eaves is ideal and can also be used all year round to play up the night landscape. When you use outdoor lights they are more effective if you extinguish or dim as far as possible all the house lights to lessen competition. Pathways and steps should be well lighted because the shadows play strange tricks with the eyes. And, of course, an outdoor cooking and serving area must be well lit, unless you plan to cook indoors and serve outdoors.

To add gaiety, use outdoor Christmas lights strung through the trees and around the porch or house eaves. Votive lights set on the edge of a terrace or among a display of potted plants add to the party atmosphere.

Barbecues

The barbecue is one of the easiest ways to entertain, it can be used summer and winter, indoors (be sure the barbecue is set in the fireplace and the damper is open) and out. The equipment can vary from a small tabletop hibachi to a charcoal-fired barbecue to an elaborate gas-fired outdoor cooker. A barbecue is always informal and paper or durable plastic is both sensible and attractive. Fingers, forks, and lots of napkins are the only other requirements. In keeping with the informality food should be simple but plentiful: keep to stews, chowders, steaks, chicken, hamburgers, shish kabobs, with simple green salads, hot bread, corn in the husk and roasted potatoes. Desserts should also be simple, so they can be eaten out of the hand—fresh fruit, fruitcake, brownies, butter tarts.

Guests like to watch the cooking and in this way the cook is not cut off from the party. In outdoor meal planning and cooking, never experiment. This form of cooking is unpredictable until you are experienced. Only a trial run and practice can tell you the cooking time, the fire heat, how to cope with dripping fat, the wind, and so on.

Barbecue Hints

Have two pairs of tongs—one for the coals and one for the food.

Soak hickory or apple chips in water for twenty minutes, then sprinkle a few over the coals for a subtle smoked flavour in the meat.

Control kibitzers who help you by stirring up the fire. They mean well, but two firemasters is one too many.

Menu

Appetizers (canapes and pickles)
Salads (green, potato, macaroni)
Meats (hamburger, steaks, roast chops, wieners)
Relishes and Sauces
Vegetables to roast (corn, potatoes, onions)
Dessert (fresh fruit or fruit pie)

The Steak Story

Most common steaks for barbecuing are: rib, T-bone, club, sirloin, and filet. Just ask your butcher to suggest the cut that suits your purpose and your pocket book.

- Score edges of meat so steak won't curl.
- Little bubbles on top of meat means its ready to turn.
- Broil second side a bit less than the first.
- Don't salt uncooked meat or it'll lose its juice and flavour.
- Try the other barbecue favourites, lamb, pork chops, and shish kebabs.

Outdoor Barbecue Timetable

Beefsteak	(total minutes)
1 inch thick, rare	8 to 12
medium	12 to 15
well done	up to 20
1½ inches thick, rare	10 to 14
medium	14 to 18
well done	up to 25
2 inches thick, rare	18 to 30
medium	25 to 35
well done	up to 60
Lamb, chops, steaks	
1 inch thick	12 to 18
2 inches thick	15 to 25
Chicken, split	25 to 45
Ham steaks	
¾ inch thick	25 to 30
1 inch thick	30 to 35
Hamburgers	10 to 12
Frankfurters	6 to 8

The Cook Out

If you are cooking over charcoal or briquets don't make the mistake of starting to cook before the fire is really ready. Those off-putting meals of blackened food that's raw inside comes from this over-eagerness. The delicious charcoal flavour comes from cooking over a small rosy bed of coals that looks almost finished; in fact they should look ash-grey and only glow red at night. Once the fire is started and has died to the right heat, follow the barbecue's instructions for placement of grill—usually high up to begin, gradually lowered for the final cooking.

Trim off as much fat as possible from meats so the drippings won't cause a flare-up. Use the cut-off fat speared on a fork to quickly grease the rack. If you are using chicken parts cook them on aluminum trays, otherwise you may lose wings falling through grill bars. Most meats should be removed from the refrigerator one hour ahead of cooking, apart from hamburgers which should go straight from the cold to the fire. Fish is usually too tender to cook on the grill, so wrap in foil or place on a foil tray.

Brochette or Stick Cookery

Small manageable pieces of meat and vegetables are threaded on metal skewers or slim green sticks and broiled over high heat and turned constantly. Because of the heat, the food is best when some moisture is added, such as wrapping chicken livers in bacon, and alternating tomato wedges and green pepper chunks with the meat. Marinating the meat not only adds flavour, it supplies the moisture. (Marinade is simply oil, vinegar, spices, salt and pepper. For speed use a commercial oil-and-vinegar or Italian-type salad dressing.) Select from beef and lamb chunks, scallops, chicken livers, tomatoes, green peppers, onions, pineapple chunks.

Cooking With Foil

Foil adds convenience to open-air cooking. Wrap corn or potatoes in foil and bury them in the ashes; or put them on top of the grill and turn once or twice. Lay fresh or frozen vegetables on a double sheet of foil, season, add some butter, and bring the foil up over the food, securing all the corners with a double, or druggist, fold. Place on grill and turn once or twice using tongs.

If you haven't saved foil pans from commercial pies, buns, TV dinners, make pans from heavy-duty double foil, mitring the corners so you can cook hamburgers and chicken parts. Bread, buns and biscuits can be buttered, seasoned with herbs and garlic and wrapped in foil. Heat them at the back of the grill.

If you put foil under the charcoal you will get a hotter fire, as the heat will be reflected upwards and the cleaning job will be simplified.

Menu using foil
Drinks: Vegetable or Fruit Juices
Hamburgers
Corn on the Cob   Butter   Relishes
Buttered Buns
Hot Apple Turnovers

Alfresco: Let's Eat Outside on Trays

Eating outdoors is very relaxing and doesn't have to be a picnic, merely less formal than indoor meals. Actually it is much the same as a tray supper, and an outdoor meal is great for family, friends for breakfast, lunch or dinner. You can serve the trays with everything in place, or let the guests tote their own outdoors. Be sure the trays are deep enough to avoid tipping glasses, adequate in size to hold the meal and light enough to carry comfortably.

Menu Suggestions

Clam or Tomato Juice or Bloody Mary
Crackers   Raw Vegetables
Chicken Salad   Hot Biscuits
Fresh Berries with Cream and Sugar
Shortbread Cookies

Marinated Bean and Mushroom Salad
Meats Balls   Rice
Herb-Buttered French Bread
Strawberry Shortcake

Frankfurters
Baked Beans
Rye Bread
Mixed Salad
Apple Betty and Whipped Cream

Eat with the Fingers
Chicken in the Basket
Potato Puffs
Devilled Eggs   Hot Buttered Biscuits
Raw Vegetables (tomato wedges, celery, carrot
   sticks, cauliflower rosettes)
Mince Tarts or Fresh Fruit

Pool Parties

Pool parties are increasingly popular, but they require organization and strict rules to ensure that all have fun and there are no accidents. If you have teen-agers and a pool, you will almost automatically be hosting pool parties. But they are also a good way to entertain adult friends on summer days and evenings. With smaller children you must be even more careful with the enforcement of the rules. For all ages keep the numbers down.

For day-time parties you can adapt most buffet or snack menus with light foods. Try the Salad Bar (see p. 148). For more elaborate occasions in the late afternoon or evening you might serve food around a theme.

Mediterranean Pool Party

Sangria
Raw Oysters with Lemon and Seafood Sauce
Fresh Green Vegetables with Yogurt Dip

Honey Garlic Ribs
Brown Rice
Greek or Italian Bread
Assorted Cheeses   Fresh Fruit

Caribbean Pool Party

Rum Punch
Baked Whole Fish (Red Snapper)
Chicken Curry with Condiments
Rice and Red Peas
Fresh Fruit

When you have a pool party, do not serve any alcoholic beverages while there is swimming. Serve food and drinks away from the pool area. If you do snack around the pool use only unbreakable utensils.

Do not operate a pool unless your insurance is in full effect and be very strict about uninvited swimmers; they can add to legal problems. If you are a new pool owner you may tend to be generous with it. Letting friends and neighbours use it is a mistake and a responsibility. Make it understood, use is by invitation only.

If you are planning a pool party, whether it is a day or night event, tell your neighbours so they are warned about increased noise. On other occasions keep the noise around the pool to a minimum. If you have a big splashy pool party for friends, it is a nice gesture to make up for any inconvenience to ask the neighbours in for a pool party shortly after.
□ Keep the pool gate locked and each user should be required to lock the gate whenever leaving the area.
□ Do not permit children to swim unsupervised, or anyone to swim alone.
□ Require very young children to stay at the shallow end and to wear approved life preservers, and always have a swimmer watching the action at that end.

□ Prohibit running, jumping and general rough-housing.
□ Forbid unorthodox use of diving boards and slides.

Feeding a Crowd

If you have a large home and are prepared to have the furniture removed, or, have a garden and do not mind the expense of erecting a marquee then a crowd party can be organized. Some apartment buildings have a large party or games room that you can arrange to use. However, most people find that renting a hall saves wear and tear. But, regardless of your choice, the organization is the same.

It can be a fun party that you give for your club, the neighbours, the Home and School, or it can be a big fund-raising for the church or club. Whatever the event, the general ideas can be applied to all kinds of crowd parties. A light snack can be served to fifty people, but beyond that number and if you wish to serve a meal, planning and the delegation of authority and chores is a must.

Fund-raising occasions begin with a committee. Sound organization and efficient teamwork by all members spell success. If you, as chairman, find a committee member riding along, you will have the unenviable task of replacing that person. Do it—kindly but firmly. Don't cover by taking on the additional job yourself. Your responsibility is assigning specific jobs and seeing that things get done on time. A chairman of the organizing committee must sit down and appoint people to head up subsidiary groups to plan, budget, and eventually bring off the function. Use tact and commonsense in choosing people: someone with a flair for decoration should obviously be in charge of these; a good administrator with knowledge of figures should handle the budget. Never pick friends because they are friends. An early start is a must. Set the budget from the beginning, pick the committee, assign duties. Delegate work evenly and separately, and having assigned duties, don't interfere. Hold regular meetings so that you get up-to-date information (a nice occasion for a coffee or luncheon party); and as the day draws closer and the group gets busier, a soup and sandwich meal will suffice to keep everyone in the picture.

Committees

Depending on the size and scope of the proposed entertainment the number of committees or workers will vary, however, the following are merely guides:

Accommodation—makes the arrangements for space, utensils, flatware, crockery, glasses and staff as needed.

Treasurer—supervises the budget.

Ticket and Sales

Prizes—obtains prizes and arranges draws at the function.

Publicity—if a public event, contacts local newspapers, radio, TV. Handles mailings, posters, and arranges for printing of same. If it is a members-only event, arranges for notices in club newsletter, sets up a phone committee to get members out.

Food and Liquor—decides on type and quantity to serve. Handles food budget, does ordering and receiving.

Music and/or entertainment—if outside entertainment is required obtains quotes, contracts from talent agency. If the entertainment is put on by members, obtains props, costumes, etcetera.

Secretary—keeps records of all meetings and accounts of who is doing what, keeps notes of deadlines and constantly reminds.

Decorations—arranges the buying, renting or making of decorations for the room, tables, hallways, their installation and their removal.

Clean-up—either arranges for commercial clean-up after the party or gets it done among the members.

Early Planning

Early planning is absolutely essential. For formal banquets and dances, six months of planning isn't too much. What comes first, the food or the budget? Actually both; you can't ask the public to pay for a meal they wouldn't eat at home! But it would be folly to do a show-off spread that left little or no profit.

When Should It Be Held

Always remember large numbers of people are busy at Christmas, the long weekends, Easter, Thanksgiving, and during the summer months. That means the fall and late winter are the most popular months for banquets. Once you've set the date, announce it as soon as possible so that members will put it into their schedule. And if it's a large public fund-raising event, find out what other groups are planning so that you don't compete or conflict.

Themes

Generally the choice of a theme will help in choosing food, decorations, entertainment, and even the location. Many circumstances, as well as personal preference, determine the choice of theme. For example:
□ Is there a special event involved, such as Hallow'een or the club's fiftieth anniversary?
□ Will it be held in or outdoors?
□ Who will attend—members only or adults in general? Will there be children, singles, families?
□ What time of day—morning, afternoon, evening, late night?

Accommodation

The accommodation you have access to will also determine the type of activity. If you plan a sit-down dinner for one hundred and fifty, don't choose a location that will serve fifty at a buffet. On the other hand, an oversized hall gives a cold feeling and unused space is expensive. And as warm and personal as an at-home crowd party can be, too small rooms leave an uncomfortable cramped feeling which will affect the guests' dispositions. Having decided on a location, whether home, rented or club rooms, check on the number of tables and chairs. Will there be sufficient linen and crockery? How many people can be accommodated? (Note: it is particularly important to check fire regulations if you are using decorations and candles.) Is the kitchen and refrigeration space adequate? Who does the preparation—will club members be asked to donate, can the club staff do the catering, or will an outside caterer be required? Is there a microphone for entertainment or speaker, and a lectern for announcements? Is there sufficient insurance on the building, whether it is a rented hall or your own clubhouse? If the party is in your home, speak to your insurance agent regarding breakage or losses you or your guests may sustain. At the same time, check with the police on the parking situation on your street. Around a rented hall, and at a club, you may want parking attendants.

Liquor

When holding a public function it is important to know what licences and permits are required. The laws regarding the serving of liquor vary from municipality to municipality and from province to province. Provincial liquor authorities or wine and liquor sellers can give you advice. They will tell you such things as whether liquor can be served in the area, whether it can be served outdoors, whether you can order in bulk, and the cost of any permits.

Other Regulations

If you plan to have a draw, to light outdoor fires for a barbecue, or to have booths to sell goods you may need permits. Carnival games, Monte Carlo nights, and street parades may also need permits. Check with your municipality before planning. Contact should be made with provincial authorities if you are charging admission or selling, drawing or auctioning, because taxes may be applicable. Don't risk fines, and don't risk losing the profits!

Deciding the Menu

Will it be hot or cold or a combination?

If hot, consider old standbys such as casseroles and scalloped potatoes. Who will bring and/or make them?

Are there any dietary laws to be observed?

Is this a luncheon, dinner, or a late-night supper?

Is the goup well-known for certain specialities?

If this is to be a sit-down meal you will want to start with a vegetable juice and salad (easier than soup), a main dish plus one other vegetable if the main dish is a casserole containing rice or pasta, and a dessert and beverage.

When making a selection remember that the food will have to arrive at the selected home or hall by a designated time if the group is catering, and in all cases, it will have to stand around while being served. So choose dishes that will not lose their appeal. Also choose popular items; for example, spinach and mushroom salad is liked only by some people, the more general taste is for a mixed green salad. A lot of people don't like fish, others are allergic to seafood, and elaborate moulded desserts generally don't stand up to heat and look messy once serving begins.

If you plan a sit-down meal, work out the number of servers, courses and guests. A rule of thumb is that it takes about three quarters to one minute per course, per person, per server. This means that with a hundred people and five waitresses it will take fifteen minutes between the time the first and last are served. Multiply this for each course. That's why crowd parties are usually self-serve.

Buffets

The buffet has many advantages when it comes to serving large numbers unless, of course, there is a head table, speakers, or guests of honour. However, even this can be overcome if all the guests are seated, grace is said and an announcement is made that the head table guests will begin by moving to the buffet with the other tables following in a designated order. A buffet moves fast if there are two or more identical tables set up, and each table is arranged for traffic on either side.

Smorgasbord

This the most elaborate, most complicated, and generally the most financially successful meal that can be given. Everybody loves the groaning board with its tremendous mixture. But this type of club or community meal takes the largest amount of planning, action and coordination. Most of the food is brought from members' or neighbours' homes: the meal is made up of relatively small servings of a very large number of things. And every category—cold meats, hot meats, fish, relishes, salads, desserts, cheese, bread—must be adequately represented. Generally you need half the usual serving of say, meatballs and noodles, because of the other goodies; but you can count on needing twice the amount of dessert. Table-carved meats can be dispensed with, and any community meat markets or delicatessen will slice the home-cooked meats.

With so many dishes coming to the party the kitchen staff has to be alert and very organized. A timetable should be worked out and hot dishes kept in hot ovens until they go on warmers on the smorgasbord table. However, the party can be simplified if all the main dishes are cold, and the need for something hot is satisfied by serving hot bouillon in mugs at the begining, and plenty of tea and coffee at the end of the meal.

Smorgasbord Suggestion Choice

Cold Meats—two or more
  Sliced Roast Meat—Ham, Beef, Turkey, Chicken
  Assorted Cold Cuts
  Sliced Boiled Ham or Tongue
  Liver Pâté

Hot Meats—two or more
  Meat Balls
  Kidneys and Mushrooms
  Savory Cabbage Rolls
  Chicken Fricassee
  Beef Stew

Fish
  Herring in Sour Cream
  Sardines
  Anchovies
  Creamed Seafood

Hot Dishes—two or more
  Baked Beans
  Scalloped Potatoes
  Macaroni and Cheese
  Pilaff
  Chile con Carne

Relishes—three or more
  Olives
  Corn Relish
  Mustard Pickles
  Pickled Beets
  Cucumbers in Sour Cream
  Cranberry Sauce or Jelly
  Marinated Mushrooms
  Pickled Onions
  Pickled Cucumber
  Devilled Eggs

Fruits—two or more
  Canned Fruits
  Fresh Fruits in Season
  Fruit Kebabs

Breads—three or more
  Dark Rye Bread
  Pumpernickel
  Rye Wafers
  Melba Toast
  Hard Rolls
  Bread Sticks
  Muffins

Cheese—three or more
  Edam
  Cheddar
  Blue
  Cottage
  Swiss

Salads—two or more
  Potato Salad
  Macaroni Salad
  Stuffed Celery
  Sliced Tomatoes
  Marinated Vegetable Salad
  Coleslaw
  Rice Salad
  Egg Salad
  Tuna Fish Salad
  Herring Salad
  Shrimp Salad
  Salmon Salad
  Jellied Salads

Desserts—one or more
  Chocolate Cake
  Coffee Ring
  Cookies
  Ice Cream
  Fruit Pies
  Chiffon Pies

The Budget

When it comes to catering for a large group the forgotten extras can add up to a great deal of money, so that pre-planning with everything itemized and costed is a must. Every detail must be considered (things that you take for granted at small home parties) such as linens, glasses, napkins, washing supplies, garbage bags, even salts and peppers. And, of course, flower arrangements, although if you are cutting costs, one for the head table is sufficient.

Food Contributions

These can certainly cut costs. But your contributors have to be contacted, and you must have those who are reliable and will really turn up at the designated hour with a casserole of lasagna for fifteen! If the membership are going to donate food, make up a list of who might be asked, and what they will provide.

Incidentally, at these neighbourhood parties take advantage of the kind offers of friends willing to supply casseroles, pies, baked goods and salads. List the foods so that the table doesn't groan with nothing but angel cake. Don't feel bashful in asking the best lasagna-maker in the area to contribute, and it is correct to ask the laggards what they intend to contribute.

Nowadays, with many women holding two jobs, purchased foods are also acceptable and delicious. If you are making up a full meal, rather than a smorgasbord, then provide full recipes and precise instructions as to quantities to make. At the same time give the delivery time and place. A member of the committee should be appointed to receive the food, to telephone reminders, and to see that all returnable containers to be returned. (Nail polish is a good label and while oven heat won't remove it, nail polisher remover will.) Adhesive tape with the name in indelible pencil is another way to mark containers. And rather than having to wash and return the next day, at the end of the festivity slide the dish into a plastic bag and send it home with the owner.

How Much? How Many?

The following guidelines will serve approximately fifty.

FOOD	QUANTITY
Meat	
Ground, stew, cold cuts, etc.	11 lbs.
Cuts with little bone (pork, lamb or veal cutlets)	15 lbs
Cuts with medium amount of bone (steaks and chops)	21 lbs
Cuts with bone (short-ribs, spareribs)	38 lbs.
Poultry	
Roast turkey (drawn)	40 lbs.
Roast chicken (drawn)	30 lbs.
Fried chicken	12-13 lbs.
Cooked and cubed chicken	each 5 lb. chicken yields about 4 cups cut up meat and 3-4 cups stock
Chicken à la king	4-5 lb. chickens
Fish	
Fish fillets	17 lbs.
Whole stuffed fish	29 lbs.
Fish steaks	25 lbs.
Soup	12 qts.
Vegetables	
Potatoes:	
mashed	13 lbs. potatoes, 30 oz. milk, 1/2 lb. butter or margarine, 5 tsp. salt, cup onion flakes
scalloped	13 lbs. potatoes 3 qts. white sauce (3/4 lb. butter, 3/4 cup flour, 2 1/2 qts. milk, 5 tsp. salt, 1 tsp. pepper, 1/2 tsp. nutmeg)
french fried	13 lbs. potatoes (pre-cut)
potato chips (dry)	6 lbs.
potato salad	12 lbs. potatoes (diced) 6 cups mayonnaise

FOOD	QUANTITY
Peas, beans, carrots, beets, etc. (canned)	20 oz. or just under 1/2-cup servings)
Carrots, turnips, parsnips, beets (fresh)	10 lbs.
Rice	8 cups uncooked (if using pre-cooked instant rice, read package directions)

Sandwiches (one per person)

Bread	4-5 loaves
Butter or margarine	2¹/₂ lbs.
Filling or spread	12 cups

Salad

Lettuce for the base	12 firm heads
Tomatoes, celery, cucumbers	50 oz. of each (weight)
Dressing	40 oz. (liquid)
Fruit salad	280 oz. (7 qts.)
Chicken salad	8 qts. (20 lbs. chicken, 4 qts. celery, 1 cup French dressing, 4 cups mayonnaise)
Coleslaw	6 lbs. cabbage, 1¹/₂ lbs. grated carrots, 1 qt. mayonnaise, 1¹/₂ cups chopped green peppers, 2 tbs. sugar, 2 tbs. salt

Olives (3 per person) — 96 oz.

Celery — 7-8 bunches

Desserts

Ice cream and sherbet	9 qts.
Pie	9-10 inch pies
Cake	5 large 2-layer cakes
Fruit cocktail	5 qts. (200 oz.)
Whipped cream topping	1 qt. whipping cream (35%) yields 2 tbsp. whipped cream per person

Beverages

Coffee	1¹/₄ lbs.
Tea	25 tea bags
Cream for coffee	1 qt.
Sugar (cubed)	1¹/₂ lbs.

Four feet between tables should be allowed for servers to move. The main aisle should be wider if space permits. (The four feet allows the server eighteen inches when all are seated and each guest twenty to twenty-four inches of table space.) Serving stations spotted through the room are convenient for the placing of trays, and for extra water, silver, butter, and so on. Professional waitresses know they are assigned regular stations and are responsible for their own tables; each should have a copy of the menu. Place cards are only necessary for a head table.

Home-style Club Party

This type of arrangement has many advantages. The familiar family routine of passing bread, et-cetera, is a conversational starter; the number of staff is cut and reliance is placed on the hostess who sits at the head of the table. Even so, it is helpful to have a few waitresses for serving coffee and bringing bread. Usually the table is set for twelve, and the committee member presides. While she keeps conversation going she sees that everybody is served. She may either serve from a family-size casserole brought to her, or waitresses may serve. To save time the hostess can have beside her a stand with a tray. Empty dishes are passed, she stacks them and the waitress whisks them away.

Buying Food for a Crowd

There are a number of excellent books on feeding crowds available in the public libraries. Most clubs who do large catered get-togethers will find them useful.

Buying Food

One person should do the buying, having worked out the amounts (see below), and orders should be placed at least two weeks in advance. The person placing the orders should be available at the time of delivery to check off quality and quantity.

Tropical Poolside Party

Masses of used candles, those assorted odds and ends from other parties, together with flowers and fruit give an illusion of the warm tropics. Everything is casual, the napkins are made of a bright print fabric, the cloth has a plastic coating for easy clean-up, and the food doesn't require last minute fussing. (For the menu, see p. 73.) If you don't have a pool, set up a table in the garden, or dim the lights and have a Caribbean party indoors—the atmosphere and illusion are easy to achieve.

Safety Checks

There are problems in buying for a crowd because of spoilage. Therefore adequate refrigerator and freezer space must be lined up either at the hall or in members' homes. Fresh fish if not used immediately must be frozen, and frozen fish must not be allowed to thaw until it is cooked. Hamburger should be kept frozen, but it is not necessary to thaw meat before cooking; simply allow additional cooking time and check when the meat is done with a meat thermometer. Fresh vegetables should not be frozen and perishables such as lettuce should go in crispers. Bread, rolls and most cakes can be frozen.

Menu Suggestions

Celery and Olives
Tomato or Vegetable Juice
Baked Ham, Pineapple Slice
Mashed Potatoes   Corn
Rolls and Butter
Ice Cream with Fruit Sauce

Bouillon   Celery Stuffed with Cheese
Chile con Carne
French Bread
Tossed Salad
Fruit Cup
Brownies

Fruit Cup
Meat Balls and Noodles
Pickled Beets   Coleslaw
Rolls and Butter
Ice Cream   Assorted Cookies

Tomato Juice
Roast Turkey, Cranberry Sauce
Herbed Stuffing
Whipped Potatoes   Beans with Almonds
Hot Rolls
Apple Pie and Cheese

A Mediterranean Buffet Party

On those warm lazy summer days when there's an "R" in the month set out an oyster buffet around the pool or patio. The table settings show that plastic can be beautiful because everything apart from the wooden cutting board and the terry cloth napkins is unbreakable plastic. The food is prepared ahead: oysters with lemon or a sharp tomato dip, spicy spareribs, raw vegetables with a yogurt dip, herbed rice, plus a variety of sharp and mild European cheeses and fruit.

Pea Soup   Celery and Olives
Meat Loaf   Mushroom Sauce
Mashed Potatoes   Green Salad
Applesauce and Brownies

Holiday Fare

We all have our own family, neighbourhood, area, regional, and religious customs. It is these slight differences that make each family's celebration unique and special. Today, when so many of us live and work away from each other, holidays have a special significance. It is sometimes the only time we can meet and we look forward to, and later savour, our own special way of celebrating Thanksgiving, Christmas, birthdays—all the festivals and feasts. We have a warm nostalgia for Grandmother's pies or sugar cookies, and while we may not want them for adult fare, they remain a pleasant memory. What we do in our contemporary entertaining makes the memories for our future years, and glimpses will remain with some tiny moppet asked to share a supper by the pool on the first of July or to receive a chocolate egg at Easter. And if we are far from home on these occasions, it is time to start new traditions based on the half-remembered family customs.

Alone at holiday time? Don't let it be a time of depression; far better to think ahead of people who would like to share and enjoy the holidays with others. You don't need to have a twelve-foot tree in order to give a pre-Christmas party—try a bare branch hung with baubles. The secret of holiday entertaining is like all other entertainment—reach out and invite. Once you have asked, you will find the occasion is twice as much fun when shared.

If your background or religion is different from that of your friends and neighbours, you will make the occasion even more interesting should you show them how you celebrate and let them join you. It starts a "turn-and-turn-about"—and that's what partying is all about. For the holiday seasons try one or two of

these menus, especially those that provide variations from the traditional offerings.

Christmas Tree Trimming

Eggnog
Wine   Cheese   Crackers
Fruit Cake

Holiday Buffet

French Onion Soup
Tourtière
Green Salad
Fruit Cup
Cookies

New Year's Dinner

Baked Ham
Cinnamon Sweet Potatoes
Green Salad
Log Cake

Christmas Dinner

Consommé Royale
Roast Turkey   Cranberry Sauce
Whipped Potatoes   Baked Squash
Plum Pudding   Hard Sauce
Mince Pies   Fruit and Nuts

Dinner Party

Tomato Bisque
Roast Duckling   Orange Sauce
Wild or White Rice
Green Salad
Chocolate Mousse

Christmas Eve Dinner

Onion Soup
Tourtière
Spinach and Mushroom Salad
Hot Rolls
Mince Tarts
Whipped Cream
Shortbreads, Fruit, Cheese

Holiday Party (tree trimming, asking in the neighbours, any evening festivity)

Choice of Wines (a red and a white, two
    different reds, or apertifis)
Cheese   Fruit   French bread
Poundcake, Fruitcake

A Winter Dinner

Vegetable Juice
Baked Ham
Sweet Potatoes or Yams   Tossed Salad
Broccoli and Lemon Butter
Lemon Curd Tarts

After-the-Festivities Open House

After coping with excited children on holiday and the build-up to Christmas Day is it possible to think about a casual party? Yes, indeed, and some the nicest are held at this time. There's something magical and relaxing for the guests about getting out of their home. It's a happy time and it is the kind of party hostesses love —informal. If you have family staying, in-laws, grandparents, small children, open house is a lovely way for them to meet friends and neighbours and for young and old to mix. Time? From early afternoon through to after dinner.

And it is practical too. You prepare everything ahead (don't forget to send the guests cards a month ahead), put the refreshments on a big table, let everybody mingle and help themselves. It is a great time to entertain: the house is decorated so you need only replace the burned-down candles. There are Christmas gifts of wine, cheese and candy that can be added to the spread. You've probably used a family heirloom cloth for the holiday meal and it is going to need laundering, so you may as well give it further mileage at the second party. But cut down the remaining laundry by using bright holiday-patterned paper napkins.

The food to serve is always important and the choice depends on the time of the day and the ages of the guests. Remember most of them have had their fill of rich foods and drink, elaborate garnishes and hostess show-off concoctions. Make everything simple, but warm and friendly.

Drinks are a matter of choice and family tradition. You can set up a coffee urn and offer the alternative of a brisk, cool not too sweet punch; you can offer straight drinks, eggnog, or tea. Keep the food easy to handle with the fingers; then you'll have less crumbs on the rugs and can dispense with a great many plates. And keep the amounts, variety and sizes small. There is a natural tendency to over-eat, and by the end of the year, after a month of conventional partying, guests are somewhat jaded and have a guilty conscience when it comes to calories. They are looking for good company rather than a meal.

Simple foods are the easiest and most popular. Set out cheese and surround the board with baskets of crisp crackers. Add bowls of olives, pickles and comports of grapes that give colour as centrepieces but are also great accompaniments to cheese. Bowls of fresh vegetables make a good low-calorie relish. Cut them into small bite-size pieces and place them beside a bowl of a sharp tangy dip. If the time makes you feel a more substantial offering is needed, set out platters of thinly sliced delicatessen meats. And, if you can face it, a turkey casserole is tasty, substantial and does save freezer storage! There will be fewer family grumbles if turkey and other leftovers aren't served day after day during the following week!

Round out the table with some hot mince pies, and the remaining shortbreads and cookies. Remember everybody loves to taste somebody else's fruitcake.

New Year's Eve

This is probably the worst night of the year for entertaining. It is difficult to make a success of gaiety because everyone is trying too hard to have a good time. Invitations are accepted, often out of desperation because there is a fear that one doesn't want to be at home, alone. People have a compulsion to go out, to go to a series of parties, some are apt to walk out on your party to be on time for another one somewhere else. The best New Year's Eve parties are those with guests who are loved—close friends who want to spend a happy evening.

If, having faced all the problems, you still want a New Year's Eve party, it's best to keep things informal unless you have settled for the small dinner and know your guests will stay. Even then, consider dinner beginning with drinks and snacks at 8 to 8:30 p.m. First it gives your guests time to relax in their homes after the day's work; also, unless dinner starts reasonably late and is served slowly with plenty of relaxation, you'll find your guests incapable of seeing in the New Year.

Special Events

Anniversary Parties

Wedding anniversary parties are usually intimate celebrations that include close friends and family, and sometimes members of the original wedding party. Parties are given for another couple, or friends are invited to help the hosts celebrate their anniversary. (Of course the anniversary or special events in one's life other than marriage can be and are celebrated.) Anniversary gifts are optional, and expensive ones are usually given only on special milestone dates. Today there is the growing custom of giving one gift from all the guests, amusing gifts rather than elaborate offerings, or remembering the hosts' favourite charity. However, if you are giving a party for yourself it is not correct to say "no gifts" on the invitations, since it assumes there will be gifts! When an anniversary party is given for others, particularly a Golden Wedding reception, then it is permissable to suggest no gifts but telegrams, cards and flowers, or a charity.

The anniversary party takes many forms. It can be a dinner, an open house, a tea, a cocktail party, a buffet supper or an after-dinner reception. Themes using the flowers used for the wedding are nice sentimental reminders, and special colours such as silver for the twenty-fifth and gold for the fiftieth, make sparkling tables. On these special occasions it is customary to have a guest book for all to sign as a permanent record of the occasion. If photographs are taken, these are later added to the book. And if the party and the mood suggest it, the former best man or a close friend will toast the celebrants.

Wedding Symbols

Tradition has decreed that each anniversary has a special symbol which can be incorporated into gift giving, the table decorations, invitations and used as part of the general theme. In addition to the old one that begins with paper and can include everything from a carton of household paper towels to rare or new books, the various gift and jewelry organizations have come up with a contemporary list which has more commercial overtones than the traditional list. The choice is yours.

THE TENTH is the first of the really big anniversaries to be celebrated with a large party. It can be fun to ask friends and relatives to come as they may have dressed on that day. Ten years is not long enough to make clothing impossible to find, yet long enough to make the style changes amusing. Because it is traditionally the "tin" anniversary it is amenable for informal decoration. Have the meal served on new foil or tin pie pans (the former can be tossed out and the latter can be given as favours), use new tin cake and loaf pans to hold flowers, mints, nuts. A square tin grater makes a hurrican shade for candles and looks like an old-time lantern.

THE FIFTEENTH anniversary is the crystal one and its formality is an opportunity for a lovely table making use of as much glass as possible. Use white or pastel linens to show off heirloom or contemporary glass used for candlesticks, flower arrangements, fruit. Use tiny bud vases filled with a wedding flower as a guest gift.

THE SILVER WEDDING anniversary is the big one. This is the time to use silver without appearing ostentatious. If you want to splurge you can give guests favours of anniversary cake packed in a silver box. An afternoon tea reception is a nice way to mix a lot of guests and feel there is a celebration. Adult children act as hosts, and an open house is held. If you can afford it, hire musicians to play 25-year-old songs, or get out the old records. Usually the table is made to look gorgeous with a white lace cloth over foil and the flowers should be white with touches of silver. The white anniversary cake is as elaborate as a wedding cake but usually without tiers. The easiest way to serve refreshments is to ask close friends to take turns at serving tea and coffee. If there is a punch bowl, it is on a separate table. The refreshments are on a buffet table or sideboard and range from canapés and tiny sandwiches to petits fours and fancy cookies. It is a good time to have a waitress to help pass the food trays and leave the hosts free to meet friends.

THE GOLDEN WEDDING anniversary is very special. If you are fortunate enough to have parents celebrating their fiftieth wedding anniversary you will want to give them the most beautiful party ever, with all their children, grandchildren, relatives and friends on hand to honour them. The numbers invited depend, of course, on the health of the celebrants.

An afternoon tea reception is the most usual, and once again, the table reflects the occasion. Decorations can include a lace cloth over a gold undercloth, yellow and white flowers. If the party is late day, then candles can be used. And, of course, a white wedding anniversary cake decorated with yellow rosebuds. Once again, ask friends to take turns at serving the hot tea and coffee. If there's a punch bowl or a toast in champagne have a waitress to pass the glasses just prior to the short toast.

This party must be carefully scheduled so that the guests of honour are not fatigued. Invitation, therefore, should make the time very clear: for example, "from four to six," so that guests know when to come, and when to leave. If the couple gets tired, then one of the family should escort them through the guests, stopping briefly as they go, and let them retire and rest.

Because there will be many older people present provide sufficient chairs so they may sit. And if there is room, provide a number of small tables for sitting at. This can be done if one of the rooms or the sun porch is cleared of furniture.

I Remember Party

Select a year or an occasion that is full of meaning to you: for instance, the year you were born, graduated, or returned to the city. It's easy to make a fun party from the invitations onwards, you can follow the theme through with the dress of that year, the music and use the headlines as decoration. And if you feel extravagant, rent a movie from that year.

Birthday Parties

The surprise and fun of a birthday party isn't the exclusive privilege of small children. Everybody enjoys a party, and a party with a reason is always successful—in fact the atmosphere is a gala one so it can't help but be a success. A birthday party for adults can be celebrated in a variety of ways: a simple at-home get together, or a travelling party with each course at a different home, or a costume party. But be sure the celebrant enjoys that kind of party. Nowadays the celebrant often gives the party asking friends to participate in the occasion.

Gifts for adults are optional, but packages make it seem more like a birthday. Unless the guests are family and very close friends, specify on the invitations amusing small gifts. When this is done, the gift from the host should be in the same category so that guests are not embarrassed. Or the host can specify no gifts and provide one gift for the guest of honour. What about joint gifts? These should be restricted to family or special club groups. Sometimes it is permissible for friends to buy a gift jointly, when all of them know the celebrant very well, and when the latter is known to have a special hobby or interest such as collecting stamps, coins, porcelain or plants. On such an occassion it is practical for friends to contribute to one special gift.

All birthdays need a cake, but it need not be the traditional chocolate layer requested by five-year-olds. For adults it can range from a cold soufflé to Baked Alaska. It should come discreetly decorated with one candle and served with champagne or other sparkling wine.

In choosing decorations for an adult birthday party, the colour of the birthstone and symbolic flowers for each month are easy guides to colour schemes. Another help is the zodiac symbols.

YEAR	OLD LIST	NEW LIST
1st	Paper	Clocks
2nd	Cotton	China
3rd	Leather	Crystal and glass
4th	Fruits and flowers	Electrical appliances
5th	Wood	Silver
6th	Sugar and candy	Wood
7th	Wool or copper and brass	Desk, pen and pencil sets
8th	Bronze or pottery	Linen and lace
9th	Pottery or willow	Leather
10th	Tin or aluminum	Diamond jewelry
11th	Steel	Fashion jewelry and accessories
12th	Silk and linen	Pearls or coloured gems
13th	Lace	Textiles, furs
14th	Ivory	Gold Jewelry
15th	Crystal	Watches
20th	China	Platinum
25th	Silver	Sterling
30th	Pearl	Diamond
35th	Coral	Jade
40th	Ruby	Ruby
45th	Sapphire	Sapphire
50th	Golden	Golden
55th	Emerald	Emerald
60th		Diamond jubilee
75th	Diamond jubilee	

The Christening Party

A christening party is formal in the sense that it is a sacramental day. It is a pleasant custom to entertain godparents, relatives, the officiating clergyman and his wife, as well as close friends. The hour of the party can be anytime after the ceremony, and since most of the guests want to see the baby, if you can pick a time that isn't set aside for napping or crying! A brunch or buffet luncheon immediately following a morning service is appropriate; so is an afternoon party with tea, coffee and/or champagne.

The mother of the baby usually has her hands full, and it is nice for close friends to offer to arrange the reception. Since this is a formal occasion, the table should be festive with flowers. An old and charming custom is to have the top layer of the wedding cake re-iced as a centrepiece, later cut and served. Or a white christening cake is ordered and forms part of the menu. Usually a godfather gives the toasting champagne but if he doesn't offer, have some ordered and iced. Another nice tradition is to have potted greenery and to plant a tree or shrub in honour of the occasion.

Children's Parties

Parties are usually given for birthdays, but don't forget such occasions as the end of school, the

MONTH	BIRTHSTONE	FLOWER
January	Garnet	Carnation or Snowdrop
February	Amethyst	Violet or Primrose
March	Aquamarine	Jonquil
April	Diamond	Sweet Pea or Daisy
May	Emerald	Lily of Valley or Hawthorne
June	Pearl or Moonstone	Rose or Honeysuckle
July	Ruby	Larkspur or Water Lily
August	Sardonyx or Peridot	Poppy or Gladiolus
September	Sapphire	Aster or Morning Glory
October	Opal or Tourmaline	Calendula or Cosmos
November	Topaz	Chrysanthemum
December	Turquoise or Lapis Lazuli	Narcissus or Holly

PERIOD	ZODIAC SIGN
January 20 – February 18	Aquarius
February 19 – March 20	Pisces
March 21 – April 20	Aries
April 21 – May 20	Taurus
May 21 – June 20	Gemini
June 21 – July 22	Cancer
July 23 – August 22	Leo
August 23 – September 22	Virgo
September 23 – October 22	Libra
October 23 – November 22	Scorpio
November 23 – December 21	Sagittarius
December 22 – January 19	Capricorn

Fondu *(Overleaf)*

The decorations are houseplants and green fruits and the latter will be the dessert served in small baskets. The wicker theme is carried through the generous supply of crusty French bread in baskets, and the plates sit in wicker holders rather than on place mats. The paper napkins and the goblets for the white wine are generous in size, and the fondu pot is on a protective stand placed on matting so that the bare wood table is protected.

The Formal English Tea

A beautiful table set with the finest family china and table linen set off by an informal flower arrangement in an heirloom container. Tea and sherry are served, hot buttered scones, fruit and pound cake as well as assorted pastries. A lovely party to introduce a visitor, for a family celebration, an adult's birthday—even a christening. A tea party is not exclusively for women, men enjoy them too, especially if the food is ample and it is a weekend afternoon. Guests help themselves to sherry, the hostess pours tea, and the guests seat themselves in small groups around the room, which has tables set out for perching plates, and settle in for conversation.

The Elegant Picnic

It's great fun, but organization is a must to be sure that all the items are packed securely and will fit into the baskets and hampers. It's even more fun if you invite a small group, wear costume, and take along the guitars.

The meal is eaten from fine china with silver accessories, and crystal glasses, set out on a lace cloth put over a car rug or blanket. The napkins look like heirlooms but are men's hankerchiefs trimmed with inexpensive lace then starched.

The menu includes pâté and melba toast, lobster tails with lemon and mayonnaise, Rock Cornish hens, breads, avocado with lime, cheese, and fruit. Served a cold white wine or champagne.

Kindergarten Entertaining *(Overleaf)*

A birthday party for the four- to six-year-old group with ice cream and cake to be served after preliminaries of hot dogs, but it could also be served as a dessert party at mid-afternoon.

The pirate motif is carried through from hats and chocolate "pieces of eight" to the birthday cake which is a chocolate loaf cake decorated with Lifesaver portholes and black paper sails made from extra hats and secured by drinking straw masts.

The napkins are inexpensive gingham yard goods in which the chocolates can be tied for the take-home loot. The napkin can be used later as a bandana. The party food is set on a plastic cloth for minimum clean-ups, and the ice cream can be served in glass or plastic glasses.

Kids' Barbecue

An ideal party for the eleven- to fourteen-year-old group — the food is hearty, yummy, and the high spirits are dissipated outdoors. There are plenty of iced soft drinks, lollipop pickles, and lots of crunchy raw vegetables. The main attraction is the barbecued meat ball shishkebobs that slip into submarine buns. Dessert is rich chocolate cake plus marshmallows for toasting over the hibachi. The napkins are large so that no plates are necessary, the cups disposable, and the clean-up minimal. Simplicity adds up to fun!

beginning of school, a visiting friend, buying and cutting a Christmas tree, the Easter egg hunt, making Valentines and Hallow'een.

Birthday parties can be a disappointing chaos or a happy occasion that becomes a delightful memory as time passes. The secret lies in planning, and especially planning with an eye to the sensitivities not only of the small host but of the guests.

The party starts early, and the rule of thumb is no more guests than the age of the birthday child. If you invite more children than you can handle, bedlam is the result; and if the birthday child is shy, this guest of honour may be ignored by the other guests! Young guests should be in the same age group, never more than a year apart. The time can be a noon lunch, early afternoon from say 3 p.m. to 4:30, or a 5 p.m. supper to bedtime. For the kindergarten set the simpler the party, food, games, and arrangements in general, the better. Keep it small, keep it short. What makes it a party are the favours, the decorations, the cake, and the loot that goes home.

Invitations in the mail delight children, but more important, they advise mothers where, when, and how long. Be quite specific about the time the party begins and ends. (If you want to be really specific, you can arrange to deliver the guests at the end of the party.) In setting the time, allow about an hour for present opening and play, half an hour for the meal. Where practical, an outdoor party allows for energy to be dispersed outside the house.

ENTERTAINMENT: The crux of the party is the entertainment. Younger children like extension of kindergarten games and old-timers such as musical chairs, pin the tail on the donkey, hide and go seek. Older children enjoy outings to a bowling alley, or to see the firehall, a train ride, and the circus, but games are still enjoyed (see p. 64).

FAVOURS AND GIFTS: With small children when the birthday child has opened the parcels, let all the guests pick a prize from unwrapped dime store selections (skipping ropes, whistles, crayons and pads). For the very young, offer no choices. Give the same favour to each child. When they leave have bags ready with a selection of cereal-box premiums, some candy, a cupcake iced like the birthday cake, and so on. If you give balloons, hand them out just at the leaving-taking and count on needing half as many again because of the high popping rate! Be sure the balloons are all the same shape.

FOOD: Serve it indoors or out. It's fun to find boxed lunches growing on a tree. Use disposable containers wherever possible and keep to familiar foods that the children like. Hot dogs, hamburgers, cold fried chicken seem to be liked by most, as are tiny sandwiches. Have lots of vegetable sticks. Give a choice of milk (either plain or chocolate) or orange juice. Then the cake. The best children's parties have simple food. Very young children are so excited they hardly eat; older children come on like the locusts.

Some Games for Children

Fish Pond

Best liked by the three- to six-year-olds. Drape a blanket across and over a table or doorway so that someone can hide behind. Each child takes a turn in fishing with a yardstick to which has been tied a length of string and a "bull-dog" paper clip. Each child chants:

Fishy, fishy in the pond
Make this pole a magic wand.
Fishy, fishy pull the line.
The gift you put on it is MINE.

The hidden fish attaches a small, wrapped parcel.

This is the Way

This old favourite is loved by pre-schoolers who enjoy the miming.

This is the way the ladies ride,
This is the way the gentlemen ride,
This is the way the huntsmen ride,
This is the way the soldiers march . . .

And if you end with "This is the way we walk to the birthday supper," you will get them to the table without confusion.

Musical Bag

A variation on musical chairs. A large shopping bag is filled with an assortment of clothing from hats to ties and passed round the circle. When the music stops, whoever is holding the bag must pull out an item and put it on. When the bag is empty give prizes to all: for the child with the most items, the child with the least, the child with the red belt, the child with the cloth flowers.

Round Games

Small children love to sing and dance. "Ring-a-ring of roses" and "Sally go round the sun" give rhythm and action, help even the shyest guest to participate and keep exuberance in bounds.

There are many excellent books specializing in parties and entertainment, obtainable from book shops and libraries.

From Engagement to Wedding

The Engagement Party

An engagement in the family calls for a party. It can be a party after the engagement has been announced, or a surprise party to announce the forthcoming marriage. A party isn't a necessity, but it is a lovely, traditional, and joyous custom to introduce the newly engaged couple to family and friends. The family of the bride-to-be gives the party, and the groom's parents should be there as well as close relatives and friends of the family and the newly engaged. The party is usually a late afternoon or an evening entertainment, and the guest list is selected from close friends. It is not the time to invite casual acquaintances or to pay off old social debts. At a formal party the engaged girl and her mother receive the guests or the engaged couple may receive with the girl's parents.

It is traditional to have the prospective bride's father propose a toast to the couple and it signals his welcome to the young man.

THE MENU: This depends on the kind of party, but it should be pretty with the best family possessions brought into use. Fancy sandwiches and petits fours are ideal, with a choice of beverages including a punch bowl. It is customary for glasses of champagne or sparkling wine to be passed prior to the toast, which is timed to take place shortly after all the guests have arrived.

The Shower

A shower is planned to celebrate a forthcoming happy event: a wedding, a baby or a housewarming. They're the sign of affection and well-wishing towards the guest of honour from her nearest and dearest friends. It is not a party to be given by or for nodding acquaintances, and at its best it is small.

Almost any kind of party can be the background for a shower, from a morning coffee party to an evening event. It is both a sentimental expression of affection and a practical material expression too. However, it is now acceptable to have men present at an evening shower, except for the baby shower. But there is no reason why they shouldn't be asked. However it is best to check with the mother-to-be before inviting.

Whether the party is a surprise is up to the hostess, but it is a good idea to check with the guest of honour's family. And friends should check with each other. If there is to be one shower with very super gifts, then it becomes an imposition if there are many expensive showers. There is an unfortunate growth of stress on the material, rather than the traditional sentiment which lead to many small showers at which the gifts are inexpensive and useful; for example a kitchen shower with small items from canned goods, oven mitts to a cookery book or a dish towel. Today there is a tendency to gift with small appliances and this means that guests will not want to attend too many similar showers. Indeed, the shower gift should not be confused with a wedding gift.

Protocol

The shower has its own protocol which should be followed:

□ A shower is never given by a member of the family, but is arranged by close friends.

□ A shower should not force guests to buy expensive presents.

□ Guests should not be asked to give money towards one big item unless it is an intimate group, such as graduates of the same class, a club, the office.

□ Check beforehand on surprise showers.

□ If you accept an invitation (which is up to you) you must bring a gift.

□ If you regret, follow local custom about whether you send a gift. This also depends on the closeness to the recipient.

Entertainment

Since the presentation of gifts is the reason for the party it is the focus and the chief entertainment. The hostess should think of something other than the umbrella. A basket to carry away the loot can make a pretty centrepiece and be useful when the party is over; or have ready some cardboard cartons covered with paper.

THE MENU: Casual, simple food that can be eaten with the fingers should be offered. The service can be seated, buffet or teatable depending on the time, type of party, local custom and number of people. Since the present-opening is a long ceremony, which gets underway as soon as all are present, seating should be provided for all.

Weddings

Of all the family events, one of the most cherished is the wedding, with its glamour, tradition and celebration both before and after the ceremony.

Once many brides were married in their homes and the celebration was held there. With the shrinking of houses and the fact that many now live in apartments, it's not always possible to do this. So clubs, restaurants, hotels and cater-

ers, as well as services that undertake to manage everything from the invitations to the souvenir boxes for cake, have come into being. The Yellow Pages list a variety of services but, like all services, check out references; usually the most popular places and services are booked months ahead of the day.

However, with increasing informality there is a return to the small reception and greeting of very close relatives and friends at the place of the ceremony, as well as a tendency to limit the guest list and to have a reception at home.

If there's to be a wedding, first study the book of etiquette to see what may be involved and then decide on the number and type of reception. The reason for the reception is to give those closest to the couple an opportunity to see them and to give personal good wishes. The time of the reception depends on the time of the ceremony and that depends on religion, local custom and personal choice. A wedding breakfast and a wedding supper are pretty much the same as far as food is concerned, but the difference in expenditures may be enormous. In general, there are three basics: a ceremony, a toast to the bride by the best man, and a wedding cake.

Can a Wedding Party Be Given at Home?

Yes indeed, and the home wedding is growing in popularity. Some people like to give the provision of food, flowers and drink over to a professional caterer or service. Others want to keep it within the "family." If the guest list is manageable, if the parents, a friend or even the bride can undertake it, then it can be a memorable occasion. After checking space, consider a menu. Choose one that can be made ahead, will keep, is simple and suitable, whether there are five guests or five hundred, whether the time is noon, or evening. It could be:

Menus

Small Sandwiches
Olives   Relishes

Petit Fours   Nuts
Wedding Cake
Champagne

Canapés
Olives   Relishes
Wedding Cake
Sparkling Punch

Sometimes the work may be split between caterer and home with the latter supplying the cake, plates and glasses, and the caterer supplying sandwiches, and such items as wine, coffee, nuts, mints and table decorations. For a simple menu the caterer isn't too expensive for sandwiches, and it is nice if a variety of breads, shapes and fillings are used. If you plan a do-it-yourself, order a week ahead long sandwich loaves and if possible get some sliced extra thin. Check if the baker will slice some loaves the long way for pinwheels, rolled sandwiches and other fancy shapes.

If you are going to slice the bread yourself, get the carving knife or bread knife professionally honed ahead of time. Sandwiches should be packed in foil-lined, foil-covered baking pans, one kind to a pan. Refrigerate until time to serve—you may have to borrow refrigerator space from a neighbour.

No hostess can serve a meal unaided to a number of guests, particularly if she is part of the wedding party. But with assistance from friends and neighbours, up to thirty people can be served, whether the wedding breakfast consists of a buffet-type fork meal or a simple sandwich reception.

While colour is used extensively at buffet and dinner tables, traditionally the wedding reception table is white and lavish with the family silver. The wedding cake is white-frosted, although it may be garnished with fresh flowers, green leaves or silver dragees. If the table is crowded, set the cake apart on a table of its own. (For second marriages a cake is sometimes used but the traditional top decoration of bells, bride-and-groom, is omitted. Instead use a small posy of fresh flowers.)

Can the wedding cake be made and decorated at home? All things are possible. You can learn to use a pastry tube and practise, always keeping in mind that simplicity is best for the amateur. Or you can bake your cake and ice it simply with a white frosting, decorating with fresh flowers. The professional bakers' cake is sensational, and some will ice your home-baked cake. Costs, time and the type of cake (usually a rich fruit cake) should be discussed. The cake is baked well ahead of the party so that it will age, and it is packed into an airtight container or wrapped in foil and plastic-wrap to keep it moist, with an occasional addition of brandy to mellow the flavour and keep the moistness just right.

Cutting the Cake

The idea is to cut the cake but keep it sightly. Generally the bride and groom cut the first piece and then the caterer or a close friend takes over. An old custom, if it is a layered cake, is to save the top layer for the bride. This is packed and put away for her first party, anniversary or baby.

Wedding Parties

There are a number of traditional parties given before a wedding. However, a word of caution: too many parties or parties too closely scheduled can be exhausting to everyone concerned.

The Bridesmaids' Party

If there are a number of bridesmaids they often band together to give a party (not a shower for the bride) a week before the wedding. This may be a luncheon, tea, dinner or even a cocktail party. The guest list may include only the bridesmaids and attendants; or the groom, best man and ushers may be included, all with respective spouses.

Party for Out-of-Town Guests

At a wedding where a number of out-of-town guests are expected a party is often planned by the family or friends of the bride for those guests before an afternoon or evening wedding. Occasionally it might be a dinner following an early wedding reception.

Bridal Teas

An old tradition is for a close friend of the bride's family to give a tea to honour the bride-to-be. These are usually all-feminine parties. It is standard to have close friends and relatives taking turns at pouring tea and coffee and helping to serve. It is a way of involving friends who have no other part to play in the wedding. The service is reasonably formal. If late in the day, candles are on the tables, but the attraction is usually the centrepiece on the table. And there is no receiving line unless the numbers are large or if the groom's mother is not known to the gathering.

The Bachelor Dinner

Two or three nights before the wedding—never the night before—it is customary for the groom to give a bachelor dinner to his best man, ushers and his closest friends. This can be held in his appartment but is usually held in a private dining room or a restaurant or club. This dinner by tradition includes a toast to the bride. The groom and guests rise, the toast is simple "to the bride". The glasses are drained. Formerly it was customary to snap the slender stems of the glasses so that no lesser toast would be drunk from the glass. Some restaurants, knowing this custom of honouring the bride, are willing to provide inexpensive glasses and bill the host for the breakage. However, this is a regional custom, and it is well to discuss this with the restaurant before the party!

The Rehearsal Dinner

It is usual to have the rehearsal the day before the wedding and to follow it with a dinner, which is customarily given by the groom's parents. However, a close friend of either family or a relative may ask to entertain. If the party is in a home it is usual to have a cocktail-buffet party (see p. 57) but if the numbers are too large, then the party is held in a private room at a restaurant or club. The simple seating arrangement then is to have the host and hostess at the head and foot of the table with the bride and groom together along one side.

A rehearsal dinner need not be elaborate, and it is the hostess alone who determines the invitation list and the size of the party. But all members of the wedding party, including both sets of parents, the clergyman and his wife, must be included. It makes the dinner more enjoyable if the spouses of the wedding party are included. If spouses and fiancés of attendants can't be included they should not feel slighted over this minor issue. If the hostess wishes, out-of-town guests often enjoy participating in pre-wedding festivities. However, a large party should be avoided as the rehearsal is tiring and the following day will be a long one.

A custom that is being revived with so many weddings consisting of a ceremony and a simple greeting of guests afterwards, is to use the rehearsal or night-before-the-wedding dinner for the cake cutting. This party is usually a simple buffet and the cake and a beverage, champagne if possible. The first piece of cake is cut by the bride and groom, just as it would be at the wedding reception. The advantage of this party is that it is friendlier and more intimate and a perfect substitute when there is to be no elaborate wedding breakfast.

The Wedding Breakfast

The wedding breakfast is actually a luncheon and traditionally of three courses. Guests are seated and the menu could be a seafood cocktail, consommé, or fresh fruit cup; seafood or chicken in a patty shell with a simple green salad, and petits fours and an iced dessert. Usually a white wine is served with the entree, and a champagne with the dessert and the wedding cake, which culminates the event.

When the breakfast is served as a buffet the first course is omitted, unless consommé is served in a cup. Usually the entree is something substantial yet light, such as poached salmon which can be eaten with a fork, or chicken Tetrazzini with salad and a dessert.

Today there is the return to serving the wedding breakfast at home. Even a small home can accommodate a large number of well-wishing friends—if the large pieces of furniture are removed and small tables and chairs are rented.

After the Party

After any party, whether a small get-together or the traditional family gatherings of Christmas and Easter, there's the problem of facing the big-clean-up, plus the saving of the left-over food.

For your sanity and for the feeling of tranquility that you must give guests, the major clean-up should be left until the next day. Some things can be done during the entertaining in order to give some order and preserve sanity. For example, a large plastic bag in the kitchen is a lifesaver. It keeps ashtrays clean and disposes of table debris. Gift wrapping turns the living room into a mess in no time, although small guests and family pets love to rush through it adding to the excitement, noise and clutter. This should be tidied, or else you won't be able to cope. Save all the gift cards for later thank-you notes. If you are the saving type, collect all the paper that's worth saving, together with ribbons and trims, and quietly put them in a closet. You will smooth, roll and sort them later. The remainders go into the kitchen debris bag or get added to the yule log.

The next day move through the house with a garbage bag in one hand and a duster mitt in the other, thus doing two jobs at once! Separate and flatten out cardboard boxes and tie in bundles for the garbage collection. Non-returnable bottles can go back into their cardboard cases or be loaded into a heavy-duty garbage bag.

Before the china, glass and silver are put away, check that the dish-washing has left them pristine clean. Double-check all metal flatware and trays. A quick rub now with a specially designed polish-duster will remove spots and stains, particularly those on fork tines. Leave this, and you'll have double work when the next party is organized. Check the interior of cups; if they've stood a long time with tea or coffee they may be stained. A soaking in a sink filled with warm water and a small amount of household bleach will remove the brown streaks. Rinse and dry well. Similarly, wooden boards used for cheese and bread may have been put into the dish water. Rub them lightly with corn oil, and polish with a clean cloth before storage. Wicker baskets can be cleaned by dipping quickly into sudsy water and running a dish brush over the basketry to loosen crumbs. Dry with a cloth and leave in an airy place until completely dry.

Save Special Foods

After a party there is a tendency to become slack about food storage. Not only does this spoil expensive tidbits but there is a real danger of food poisoning. As soon after serving as possible all creamed foods, meats, soft cheeses, pastry and custards should be refrigerated. You can get back to rewrapping them and storing them later. Leftover stuffing from poultry should be removed from the cavity as quickly as possible and both the meat and the dressing refrigerated. Later the dressing can be reheated and served with another meal, but it should be used within the next four days. Freezing isn't recommended, as the herbs and flavourings take on a different, and often unpleasant, taste.

Most of the leftovers can be used if correctly stored, and with those that don't respond to long storage—well, they're the base for another party in the next three weeks to a month. Caviar and similar spreads will keep if tightly covered and refrigerated for about three weeks. Pâté will keep for approximately ten days in the refrigerator, and about a month in the freezer, although the texture will not be as smooth. (However, you can dress it up and overcome this by garnishing with "Mimosa"—finely grated hardboiled egg sprinkled all over, then flecked with a sprinkle of parsley.)

Nuts go rancid quickly because of their fat, but if frozen, will keep any length of time. So shell them and bag them, chop as required. Shelled and refrigerated, they'll remain fresh for four to five months. Similarly coconut should be put into an airtight container and refrigerated.

Tomato paste should be removed from its can and put into a well-stoppered jar and will keep refrigerated about a week. Canned chestnuts, whether whole or creamed, should be similarly stored and will last the same length of time.

Separate crisp from soft cookies and store each separately in tightly lidded cookie jars and freeze. If not separated they will all turn soft. Remove from the freezer and thaw as needed. Most will last a year, as will frozen fruitcake. If you plan to use fruitcake regularly, pour some rum or brandy over the cake, then wrap securely in plastic wrap, overwrap with foil, then a tea towel, and store in a cool place. Or else place the foil-wrapped parcel in the freezer. It thaws quickly and cuts best when partially thawed.

Most soft cheeses such as Brie, Camembert and Boursin will keep refrigerated for about two weeks. The harder the cheese, the better and longer it keeps. Wrap in heavy-duty waxed paper and overwrap in foil, then refrigerate. Cheddars and other hard cheeses can be frozen, but the texture is affected and they tend to become dry and crumbly. If you freeze cheese, thaw it in the refrigerator and use immediately. Don't freeze, thaw and refreeze.

More Leftovers

There's usually a turkey—sometimes half a bird, sometimes the carcass only—and often there's a quantity of ham. The meat should be sliced, bagged and frozen. Ham should be used within two months or the salty flavour becomes accentuated. When slicing meats keep the large pieces separate for such casseroles as Tetrazzini. Some of these leftovers make excellent party fare the second time around. Bag the small slivers separately, using them for filling crêpes, as the sustenance base for homemade soup, or as a garnish for hot bouillon spiked with a spoonful of sherry per serving.

The very best of homemade soup starts with bones. Use the stripped turkey carcass and beef ribs as a base (but keep them separate!). Cover the bones and any small "useless" meat shreds, avoiding fat, with two quarts of cold water, add chopped carrots, onion, a handful of celery leaves, peppercorns and, if liked, a pinch of thyme. Simmer for three to four hours. Strain. Taste for seasoning. Avoid salting if you plan to freeze or use as a soup base later.

The ham bone should be used as quickly as possible as the flavouring base for pea soup.

Entertaining Outside the House

The basic concept of hospitality is the same whether the host entertains at home or away at a restaurant, hotel or club. But the effect and interpretation is somewhat different. There's no escaping from the fact that this is not the host's home, so special efforts must be made to counteract the impersonal environment. And all reminders that the entertainment is being paid for should be eliminated as far as possible.

Plans must be made in advance to know guests' acceptance, to make reservations for the theatre and restaurant, and, above all, measures should be taken to make sure that payment is not made in front of guests. Tickets are booked and paid for in advance, and it is permissible to use a credit card at a restaurant. But it should be done quickly and discreetly without stumbling over the gratuity which can be added to the account. Or the host can see the restaurant before the event and make private arrangements for payment. In fact, it is a good idea to visit the restaurant, particularly if the party is having dinner before a performance and time is important. Arrangements can be made to serve a specially selected menu. With a large group this saves embarrassment as guests dither over choices, and some will choose the least expensive item while the host may have some qualms when extroverts order à la carte everything from foie gras to Chateaubriand.

The host should arrive ahead of the guests and guests should try to be very prompt. When the host arrives, even though it has been decided to offer drinks in a bar or private reception room, the host announces his arrival to the head waiter and checks that the table is set up, has flowers and all is well. If the restaurant can't offer a private meeting place, the host goes to the table and leaves word with the head waiter to bring the guests as they arrive. However, a single man should not seat himself at the table and wait, he should be at the door until a guest arrives with whom he will sit at the table. While not necessary, a woman entertaining may find it more comfortable to wait for a guest to arrive before being seated.

Similarily, since guests don't give orders in their host's house, they should not do so in public places. Guests make their requests to the host, and trained waiters never question a guest directly. Unless the party is large, all orders for food should be relayed to the host who will give the order to the waiter. If in doubt, order a main course. The host can then suggest: ''Won't you have something to begin?''

At restaurants where there is dancing the male host will ask the most important older woman to dance first; he next asks each of the other women to dance, and dances with his partner last. Other men must ask their hostess and each other woman guest to dance at least once. No woman should be left alone at the table at any time; there should always be at least one man or one couple with her.

Business Entertaining

The demands put upon women to entertain on behalf of their husbands' business can seem beyond the call of duty. But the tension is lessened if it is done gracefully and the hostess realizes that she and her husband are learning this one together. It is the job of both the host and hostess to make these special guests feel comfortable and at home. Sometimes the hostess is at a disadvantage if she doesn't know the guests and their backgrounds as well as her husband. He should give her as much advance information about them as he can. Some business entertaining is done in the home, but today a great deal is done outside at clubs and restaurants. However, it is considered warmer and more personal to invite guests to the home. The choice depends on the business relationship.

Why business entertaining? For a variety of reasons; perhaps the most important is to get to know people. Rising executives know that progress means moves from one city to another, which in turn requires the making of new friends and meeting new business associates. Whether business is talked, depends on the occasion, but generally, it is good taste not to do so unless the meeting was called specifically for that purpose.

No matter how much you wish to advance the position of your spouse it is important to first know the entertaining protocol of the company involved. Some desire entertaining and socializing among staff of equal rank, others do not.

Business Guest Basics

Keep the planning and the meal relaxed. Don't aim for new highlights in gastronomy, or new levels in elegance to match the scale on which you think your guests live. Your guess about their lifestyle may be wrong, and the most successful host is the one who is herself and doesn't change personality to fit an occasion. Set the table with what you own, choose a menu you know you do especially well, relax and enjoy the occasion.

A small dinner gives a chance for everyone to

become better acquainted, which is the reason for the invitation. Whether you add friends is a delicate matter. Usually, it is better to have a first meeting alone. But if you want to leaven out the group or know the guests well, select friends with similar interests but not similar or competitive professions. Choose friends who like meeting new people, have a variety of interests and aren't boisterous or likely to monopolize the conversation.

Entertaining the Boss

Today the boss may be a woman and may not have a spouse, nevertheless the rule holds good: you do not invite first. Even after you have been entertained by a superior, it is a delicate matter whether you return the invitation. This is unlike pure social entertaining. You have to be sure that the social relationship is wanted before the invitation is returned. Of course, all rules have exceptions, and in small communities there is less emphasis on rank and much more on informality. However, when in doubt the best rule to follow is, don't.

The Office Party

This is sometimes a very sore subject. Some companies frown on them because of the problems they can bring about, others encourage them occasionally for the pleasant spirit they can engender. People who spend their working lives together do have something in common even if otherwise they are not homogeneous. So from time to time routine and caste are dispensed with for the office party, which is usually a Christmas party or a summer picnic.

Pitfalls

The big danger in the office party is the convivial drinking, which quickly lets down barriers and encourages familiarity. This doesn't always spell trouble, but it may. People lose their inhibitions and when it is back to business the following day, there can be embarrassment.

□ The host, who is usually the highest ranking person, is the keynote. Such a person must maintain dignity while being friendly.
□ The catering committee should ensure that there is plenty of appetizing food, and that the food arrives at the same time that the bar opens.
□ Make arrangements for an adequate supply of soft drinks, so that non-drinkers are not embarrassed.
□ Never refill a glass against someone's wishes, or urge another drink.
□ Establish beforehand definite hours for beginning and ending the get-together. Close the bar at that time but see that there is still some food.
□ The host should see that everyone leaves before leaving himself.

At an office function with spouses present there is usually more dignity but it has its own peculiar problems. This type of party can be awkward and dull because while the employees know each other, mates do not and there will be a shy group of employees as well as some who will come alone.

The host or a host committee should make it clear that is is not necessary to bring a partner.

Entertainment, such as a small group playing softly or a wandering guitarist, breaks the ice, relaxes the atmosphere, and the sound of the music covers any gaps in conversation and sets the party mood. However, avoid loud music or any suggestions for dancing unless the function is a dance.

At private parties name tags are not worn, but at this type of office party, knowing the name can prevent faux pas, and they also serve as a mass introduction and imply that everyone can talk and mix.

If it is an outdoor picnic affair, start off with games or fun races to help break the ice, or arrange for entertainment for the group. A Punch and Judy show or similar keeps children amused and involves the adults.

If the function is a dinner, have an executive and spouse at every table but allow the other guests to sit wherever they wish.

The woman executive who wants to entertain employees can consider a private dining room in a club or hotel which keeps the party on an impersonal basis. If she entertains in her home the party is more intimate and informal but she should steer the conversation away from office gossip.

The spouse of the host entertaining staff must put everyone at ease, but must remember it is not a personal party.

5
A Weekend in the Country

Making the House Guest Feel at Home

Making the house guests feel comfortable and wanted begins with the invitation. The longer ahead the guests know about the invitation, the easier it is for all to make arrangements, whether it be for city apartments to be closed, animals boarded or babysitters located. The more the guest knows about the weekend plans the more relaxed the occasion. Guests should be told the time to arrive and the time departure is expected. They should be told of the proposed activities so they know what clothes will be involved. While it is easier to tell men that sports clothes will be worn but there will be dinner at the golf club on Saturday night, women have more subtle shades of formality and a smart hostess gives a brief description of what she plans to wear.

Invitations

While an informal weekend invitation can be telephoned, a written note saves mistakes, sets the time and jogs memories.

Dear Mary:

Will you come down to stay with me at the lake on the weekend of July 24th? There will be an antique auction on Saturday morning, and in the evening I have asked a few friends to join us at the golf club for dinner. On Sunday, I have asked my neighbours the Browns to come for brunch.

While I am sure you remember your way to the cottage I am making sure you arrive safely by enclosing a map.

Come in time for a swim and informal supper on Friday night and stay for an early Sunday supper.

Life is informal, so plan to bring a swim suit but we will be a trifle more dressy on Saturday night. I plan to wear the long blue print dress you have admired.

Needless to say, Puppy is welcome. But would you mind bringing his favourite chow. I don't think the village store stocks much in the way of variety.

Jane

Activities With House Guests

Generally, there should be minimum organization. The idea is for all to relax. And the best weekends are those where the guests share the interests of the house and putter in the garden, swim and laze or wander off to the local farmers' market. But there are also rainy days when everyone is kept indoors. Books, records, puzzles, games and magazines are the answer. Not everyone wants to chatter. On the other hand most guests are happy to relax and idle away some time. It is generally the host who feels frantic and keeps apologizing for the weather —which doesn't help the situation one jot. When hosts feel a compulsion to stage constant entertainments which include the organizing of sightseeing expeditions, games, visits by neighbours, the guests tend to feel strain. A relaxed guest should feel free to go off for a sleep, a walk or a read or do nothing.

The House Guest

When a guest spends several days in someone else's house there are certain unique obligations. A guest becomes a member of the family, but still retains a special status. While the hosts make the guest feel at home, the guest never abuses the privilege and has to show a contented mood regardless of whether the hosts and other guests are boring or the weekend stormy. The most satisfactory arrangements are when the guests enjoy the kind of activities the host enjoys. And the happiest house guests are those whose habits and tastes are reasonably like your own.

Guest Rooms

Naturally they vary depending on the pocketbook, the location and style of living; however, they all have certain basics. Privacy, a door that shuts, a reading lamp with a good light, screens that have no holes, and blinds that give darkness. Guest rooms are more comfortable if there is an extra pillow and blanket. (Tell the guest where they are kept. Many have spent a sleepless night not knowing where to find the extras.) A small sewing kit is useful, a clock is essential, and some browsing books and up-to-date magazines are a pleasant luxury. A wastepaper basket is useful and so is a large ashtray, a box of tissues, and a plentiful supply of towels. If the area is subject to storms a working flashlight is useful, as is a candle and matches. If the closet has to be shared with the family, portion off a section for the visitor and supply sufficient hangers, including suit and pant types.

Organizing the Meals

No matter how informal the weekend, it is necessary (for peace of mind and sanity) to plan all the meals in advance. Write out a shopping list as well as menu plans. Do the shopping, stashing, and as much preparation as possible before the guests arrive.

Meals should be as simple as possible, but can still be delicious and elegant. But the cooking should be arranged so that there is no visible strain.

Breakfasts

If you don't have early morning plans, let the guests sleep, but also let them know the night before what is scheduled for the next day and whether or not there is a set time for the first meal of the day. There's nothing more sleep-destroying to a house guest than not to be sure about breakfast, when, or even whether it is served. And how should the guests come to the breakfast table? Completely dressed? In housecoats? There are many stories of house guests sneaking to the stairs to see if the hosts are preparing breakfast and how they are dressed.

Some hosts like to bring out electric equipment or old-fashioned iron pans to make pancakes or serve bacon, eggs and the trimmings. Some guests love breakfast, others can barely tackle coffee or fruit juice. (If that's the case, don't ever press food.) Do-it-yourself breakfasts are very practical if people get up and are hungry at different times. The table or trays can be set the night before. Assorted packages of cereal left on the counter or in the cupboard and the fridge filled with juices, eggs, plus frozen baked goods in the freezer. Organization is easy, if a card is propped against the toaster listing the foods available and their location.

Dinners

Friday night dinner is always informal and the handiest food is a casserole made and frozen in town, reheated on arrival in the country. Many small towns have excellent take-out service for cooked foods and it may be simpler to stop on the way and collect dinner.

Saturday dinner is usually the most important meal of the weekend. If the hosts don't take the guests out, it is the time when local friends are invited in to meet the house guests. The easiest meals include roasting poultry and meat (which gives leftovers for the following day), or barbecued foods if the weather is good. And all accompanied by salad, rolls and followed by fruit and cheese or ice cream and fruit. Vegetables can be cooked at the last minute but salads are probably the easiest way of serving vegetables. The mixture of greens can be prepared and placed in a refrigerated salad bowl earlier in the day and dressing added just before dinner.

Desserts need never be elaborate. Cheese and fruit are good any time, in any season. Pies, frozen and purchased or homemade, can be reheated and a selection of ice creams and a variety of sauces make endless desserts without cooking or spending too much time.

Plan a hearty Sunday brunch—it allows everyone to sleep later, laze in the sun and yet sends them back to town with a substantial meal. If they stay to the evening, it cuts out one meal! Consider scrambled eggs, bacon, sausages, and a variety of muffins, breads, rolls, fruit and cheese. This is the time when heating trays, chafing dishes and other gadgets come into their own.

Country Etiquette

At some time or other when a weekend with a house guest is planned, a neighbour will phone and ask the hosts to a party. Regardless of whether the party is a lawn social or a formal dinner, the hosts should not accept and take their house guests unless specifically invited to do so.

The way to tackle this situation (and to give the hostess an out) is to say, "Oh we would love to come, but we have Jenny and Jack, our friends from the bridge club, staying so we won't be able to come over on Saturday." Then if it suits the hostess she can suggest that the guests come. If not, the conversation end with, "We'll make it another time."

Weekend Hints

Never try new recipes—unless you decide to have a gourmet cooking weekend, inviting guests who also love to cook and experiment and who want to participate. A cooking group can be enjoyable fun, especially in the summer and early fall with the abundance of fruit and vegetables for

preserves and pickles. But you must know your guests' interests and capabilities. And you need a large kitchen.

Allow your children to help and the guests' children if they are part of the party. It's a good opportunity for children to learn good manners, hospitality and to be generally useful: all of which makes them feel part of the scene. With your own children, discuss the tasks with them in advance such as carrying bags, hanging coats, unloading cars, passing finger foods, checking that the ice trays are filled, and so on.

When you entertain older people, or those accustomed to a more formal way of living, there's an understandable desire to splurge and put on a show, if you can afford the money and the energy do it. But today, if the formal style is alien to your way of life, keep to your own style and your guests will be happy with your hospitality that's warm and welcoming. You will make older guests feel at home if you include others in their age group or with similar interests when asking over neighbours and friends for any at-home entertainment you may plan.

House Guests in the City

With guest rooms in apartments and houses almost non-existent the visitor who stays too long will tax hospitality and friendship. Sleeping arrangements may be makeshift and closet space at a premium which necessitates suitcase living. This can be difficult at any time; under such circumstances the guest must be as neat as possible, fall in with the household's normal routine, and keep the time of the visit to a minimum.

The Responsibilities of the House Guest

As with all other social occasions, the guest has the responsibility to be adaptable and to fit in with plans already made, as well as to be prompt for meals. In most weekend homes, guests should be responsible for making their own beds, keeping their rooms tidy, and keeping track of possessions so that packages don't have to be mailed or delivered later. When possible, house guests can help by setting the table or helping with the dishes or food preparation, but only after asking the hostess if she needs help. Basically, guests should be quick to offer assistance but understanding when the answer is no. However, in most homes volunteers for dishwashing, table-setting and even dog-walking are eagerly accepted.

House Guest Tips

□ Don't invite your hosts to a meal in a restaurant during the weekend; the hospitality is returned at a later date.

□ Don't telephone that you have arrived at the station, airport or bus terminal unless you have been asked to do so. Take a taxi.

□ Don't accept invitations from friends in the area. A host's house is never used as a springboard.

□ Don't accept an invitation from a friend who asks you to bring your hosts. If your friend and your hosts know each other, the friend should contact them.

□ Don't hesitate to discuss bath schedules and meal plans if facilities are limited.

□ Make up your own bed either before breakfast or immediately after. Before leaving ask the hostess whether she prefers you make up the bed, use clean sheets or strip it.

□ Send a thank-you note within a day of arriving home.

Hosts and House Gifts

It is a pleasant custom for a visitor to bring a gift which is technically given to the woman of the house, but with today's breaks in tradition and the fact that bachelors also entertain, gifts are selected for the host, house or children of the house or, if the guest is staying for any length of time, for all the people involved.

Choice need not be a problem and gifts do not have to be expensive. For women: a new book, or if she has a special interest such as china collect-ing, or gardening, then a piece for the collection, a book on it or a tool for it. Special books on cooking are always appreciated by both sexes, as are candles, plants and wine. Most hosts are happy to receive unusual foods such as fine chocolates, especially packed teas or imported spices or preserves. Ornaments and suchlike are risky unless you know the owner's taste very well.

6
Wines and Spirits

Wines

Wine is an ancient food with an alcoholic content of 14 per cent or less, which is promptly converted by the body into energy. However, the ceremonious serving of wine at banquets and on very special occasions has led many people to avoid buying wine or selecting it in restaurants for fear of making a blunder. More twaddle has been written about wine than any other food.

Should the wine be red or white, should it be sweet or dry, what kind of glasses, and at what temperature should it be served? It is a mistaken notion that the serving of wine is governed by rules of etiquette. The only rule is to drink what you like, when and how you want to. And if you are unsure about taste, flavour, sweetness or bitterness, buy a small bottle and try it. Many wines come in half bottles; admittedly they are more expensive than the whole bottle, but an excellent investment for taste-testing and a bonus for dining for two. Some liquors and liqueurs come in half sizes, and a good way to try an unfamiliar variety is to order the miniature bottle, available in some liquor outlets but always on hand in trains and planes. For salvaging real taste mistakes, see p. 110.

Rules Are for Breaking

1. Serve all red wines at room temperature, all whites chilled.

It depends on what you mean by room temperature. European rooms are cooler than Canadian dining rooms, so room temperature means approximately 60°F. which is slightly cool. Certainly some coolness (not icing) tends to cover up the deficiencies of some wines. The best way to overcome deficiencies, temperature and snobbery is to pour the wine into a claret-type jug or a decanter (so no one checks labels). For red wine do this two hours before serving to let the wine "breathe" and place the container between a storm door and the backdoor, or on the apartment balcony depending on the weather. White wines and rosé are uncorked just before serving or they wilt and die. Generally, white wines (and the rosé family) all taste better cold. But chilling isn't freezing; a wine chilled too long may as well be water. Depending on the outside temperature, it can sit in the snow for about half an hour if the refrigerator is bulging, else refrigerate it for three-quarters of an hour. Never consider a "quickie" cooling by using the freezer compartment.

2. Opened wine will spoil quickly.

Recork any left-over wine immediately and refrigerate (unless it's a sparkling type, then drink the leftovers). It will keep two or three days but it won't taste quite as good. Left any longer it will likely turn to vinegar.

3. Always store wine on its side.

Yes, this keeps the cork wet and helps it to swell (unless it is one of the screw-topped bottles); this prevents air from entering the bottle and oxidizing the wine. But for fortified wines such as sherry, port or Madeira this isn't necessary or recommended, as their higher alcohol content could eat away at the cork. There are wine racks in all price ranges and they are very decorative. However, avoid using your wine rack as a decorating accessory if the room is over 70°F. Put the rack in a cool closet if you don't have a cool storeroom.

4. Wines are low in alcohol content.

This is true, apart from the fortified wines. Therefore, serve sherry, Madeira and port in small glasses and in smaller quantities.

5. Filling glasses one-half or one-third full is just a tradition and is done to show off.

There's a very good reason to leave plenty of space in a glass. Wine, like food, has the taste and aroma mixed and the empty top of the glass traps the aroma.

6. Always serve white wine with fish and poultry, red wine with meats.

Today drink what you like with what you like to eat. Germany has no red wine to talk of, yet plenty of meat is eaten. Similarly, the fish stews and soups of the Mediterranean are cooked in red wine.

All About Wine One-upmanship

The skin of the grape hosts the natural yeasts that ferment the juice sugars to alcohol, and the grape skins also determine the colour of the wine. There are three: white wine can be made from any colour grape but the skins are removed at the beginning of fermentation; red wine results from fermenting the skins with the juice; and rosé is made by removing the skins halfway through the fermentation process.

There are imported wines and domestic wines. Neither qualification is a guarantee of superiority. Most domestic wines are standard (that is, the flavour is the same from year to year and there are no great vintage years). Imported wines can be standardized and many are; others are based on vintage year qualifications—on which hinges the price tag. There are mediocre and inferior wines in all categories. Only tasting and personal preference should select wines, and

snobbery must be avoided. Difficult—but it is amazing what a label will do for prejudice!

Table wines are the reds, whites and rosés that are served with food. There are also appetizer wines, known as aperitifs, meant to precede a meal (for example, the dry sherries) and dessert wines to close a meal, such as port. Champagne is considered the all-purpose wine appropriate before, during or after dinner, or without any food accompaniment. And wines are either still or sparkling depending on the effervescence, with champagne the ultimate in bubbles. There are many excellent books on wine put out by wine producers and importers, and a number written by wine experts. The former can be requested by mail and are usually free, the latter can be borrowed from public libraries or ordered from a bookstore.

It takes a long time to cultivate a knowledgable wine palate, but getting there is more than half the fun. Every wine has a distinctive aroma, known as the "bouquet." It forecasts to some extent its flavour. A soured wine smells sour and vinegary, a sound wine smells pleasant, "flowery," "brisk," "steely." Wine has an argot of its own and like taste, it can be aquired; but the beginner should not allow the jargon to deter him. Wine, unlike water, is savoured not swallowed. To fully enjoy wine a sip should be swirled to the back of the tongue where the greater number of taste buds are located. It is not necessary to accentuate this taste swirling so that it looks like a pantomime act to the guests.

Don't get worried about the "right" glass. There's a classic system of prescribed stemware but nowadays an all-purpose 9-ounce stemmed glass is satisfactory, and a 5-ounce for aperitifs and dessert wines is sufficient. If you want to add glasses, see p. 144 and buy the little-used glasses only with a second purpose in mind. Experts suggest that the conventional open champagne glass is not the best choice since it lets the sparkle escape. If you don't have a flute glass, use your 9-ounce tulip. If you have been given open champagne glasses (how many times a year do you use them?) consider using them for desserts or fruit cups. If you have champagne flutes, they can double as parfait glasses. The reverse is true, too, if you aren't a stickler because the latter glass is often somewhat thicker.

The classic-shaped wine glasses are not only practical and beautiful but they are immensely versatile because they can be used for much more than drinking. Rounded wine glasses double for seafood cocktails, sherbet, syllabub, for fresh fruit in wine. The huge classic Burgundy glasses or the almost useless over-size brandy snifters (inevitable among housewarming gifts), make excellent servers for cold soups such as vichyssoises (add a measure of vodka) for gazpacho or for jellied consommé. Sherry glasses and punch cups are excellent for syllabubs and zabaglione.

Set the table with the wine glass to the right and slightly lower than the knife and water glass. (Wine lovers never use a water glass in table setting, considering water suitable for washing the mouth, not for tasting!) If you are serving two wines at a meal, the glasses may be placed side by side, or one below the other. If you serve two wines, the lighter wine is served first, unless you serve a robust table wine followed by a dessert wine.

Open a bottle by cutting the foil or plastic seal well away from the lip, this ensures that the wine won't come in contact with the seal while being poured. After removing the seal, wipe the top with a napkin and withdraw the cork. An investment in a good corkscrew is a must. Wipe the opened bottle, especially inside the neck, to remove any flecks of cork.

To uncork sparkling wine, cut the foil at least an inch below the lip. Holding the loop, unwind and remove the wire, being careful not to jiggle the bottle. Hold the thumb over the cork, grasping the lower part of the bottle with the other hand. Angle the bottle to about 45 degrees. This means you are less likely to get a showy but wasteful overflow. Twist the bottle, NOT the

cork. Internal pressure will actually push the cork out. If it doesn't, rock gently from side to side. Once the cork pops, continue holding the bottle at the 45 degree angle for a few moments to give the internal and external pressures time to equalize.

Fill a table wine glass one-third to one-half full. Pour champagne slowly, allowing the froth to reach the rim of the glass. Wait a second, then finish by refilling until the glass is two-thirds full.

When the host opens a wine, he should pour a small amount in his own glass first, to sample before pouring for his guests. This allows detection of a soured wine and ensures that any cork fragments are in his glass.

If the host is a man, he may pour wine for the women first, then the mens' glasses, filling his own last. Or guests may pass their glasses for filling. A woman can do the same, or she can ask a guest to pour the wine while she serves the meal. Less formally, the wine can be passed for guests to help themselves. It is correct to leave the bottle on the table; traditionally, if the wine is not in a decanter or claret-jug the bottle stands in a wine coaster which can be slid along the table and which also catches drips. The trick to pouring without a drip is to give the bottle a tiny anti-clockwise twist as the filling ends. Guests should feel free to refill their glasses, but a good host watches their glasses.

A wine basket looks party-like but is really only useful when an old red wine with sediment is served. The angle of the basket cradles the bottle so the sediment stays at the bottom.

A Small Wine Cellar

2 Red Bordeaux type
2 Red Burgundy type
1 White Burgundy
1 White Bordeaux type
1 Red Côte du Rhône
1 Chianti
1 Rhine wine type
1 Sparkling Rosé

A Larger Wine Cellar

4 Red Bordeaux type
3 White Bordeaux type
4 Red Burgundy type
2 White Burgundy type
1 German Rhine or Moselle
1 Loire or Rhône Valley
2 Chianti
2 Sparkling Rosé

Beer

Beer and pretzels, of course. Beer and cheese, or with roast pork, with sausages, with almost anything in the way of spicy meats. Beer contains protein and carbohydrates which means you had better allow for it if you are calorie-counting. (In fact, if you are watching calories, keep tab on all the alcohol, as the calories run surprisingly high. You can treat yourself to a small glass of dry wine . . .) Any 12-ounce bottle of beer weighs in at 175 calories and up.

Almost anytime is the right time to serve beer: with scrambled eggs, sausages or bacon. On a hot afternoon it is a poolside quencher, and at dinner, it is good with hearty food, hamburgers, and other barbecued treats, spareribs, pot roast, corned beef.

Beer deteriorates rapidly in sunshine and heat so keep it stored in a cool dark place, and before drinking store on the bottom refrigerator shelf which is about 40°F., a good temperature for lager. Ales and imported beers require five to ten degrees warmer. Remove the bottles from the refrigerator twenty minutes before serving. Fast chilling in the freezer will cloud beer.

Any glass that holds eight or more ounces is suitable. Whether you like a head is up to you: it's in the pouring. To minimize the foam tilt the glass or mug and pour straight down the side; for a head, straighten the glass and pour the last two-thirds straight down.

For a warm-weather party count on twelve ounces of beer per person every forty-five minutes.

After-Dinner Drinks

Some gourmets insist that an after-dinner drink aids the digestion. In any event, a brandy or a liqueur is a pleasant way to end a meal and to finish the evening. While we tend to serve these drinks after dinner, they can be served at anytime, late afternoon, before dinner (although the sweet types will dull the palate), and late at night. They should be poured with a light hand and, for most liqueurs, into small glasses. However, don't use miniature dinkies from which it is impossible to drink. If you don't have a reasonably sized liqueur glass, use a sherry glass only don't fill it more than one-third full. These drinks, too, have an aroma and a large glass helps to develop it. Brandy should be served in a large glass for the same reason. And there is no need to go in for what connoisseurs will term nonsense—heating the glass with a candle warmer. Heated brandy loses its flavour. The glass is heated by holding it in the hand, which is sufficient to develop the aroma. And the super-sized so-called snifters are an affectation.

The Brandies

Brandy is the pure distilled spirits of grape wine. There are also other fruit wine brandies such as apple, cherry, plum, raspberry. As it comes from the still grape brandy is a colourless liquid but it is aged as much as twenty years in casks of new wood. In the cask it takes on colour, loses alcohol through evaporation and develops bouquet and body. The longer in the wood, the finer the brandy because aging stops once the liquid is bottled. Price is the best indicator of age and quality. Authentic brandies are marked: for example, V.S.O.P. means Very Superior Old Pale, V.S. is Very Special—superior but not especially old. There are three basic grape brandies: cognac, armagnac and marc. Napoleon brandy has nothing to do with the emperor, it is a trademark.

Cognac is the finest of brandies and is distilled from wines grown in the Cognac region of

France. Old cognac is expensive and should always be served undiluted. Younger cognacs can have a splash of soda water, or be used in coffee. All cognac is brandy, but not all brandy is cognac!

Armagnac is produced from wines grown in the designated French area in southern France. This brandy improves with age; a young armagnac is very raw.

Marc is French brandy made from the last pressing of the grapes. It's woody, dry and an acquired taste. There is an Italian counterpart: grappa.

Other brandies are made wherever grapes are grown, and wine is made in such places as Australia, California, and South Africa. In general, these do not have the smoothness of the French brandies and are best served in coffee, or diluted with soda, over ice.

FRUIT BRANDIES: Fruit wines are distilled into brandy: apple is calvados, cherry is kirsch (a sweet fiery liquid generally used to flavour fruit cups, desserts, cheese fondue), and plum, slivovitz. Or they may be labelled, Apricot Brandy, Pear Brandy, and so on. These are all fairly expensive and are served in small amounts after dinner, usually accompanied with black coffee in demi-tasse.

The true fruit brandy shouldn't be confused with fruit-flavoured brandy. The fruit-flavoured are made with a brandy base to which are added a sweet fruit flavouring, generally at least two and a half times as sweet as the real fruit brandy.

The Liqueurs

They are sweet drinks, served after dinner and are referred to as cordials, liqueurs and crèmes. Basically they are all cordials, subdivided into liqueurs and crèmes.

These drinks are nearly always sweet and usually strongly alcoholic, and are therefore served in small quantities. They are made of a syrup and brandy base (or some other spirit such as whisky) then flavoured with roots, leaves, petals, peels or herbs. A crème differs in that its sugar content is usually very much higher to the point of being creamy.

Each and every ingredient of these liqueurs is never known except to the manufacturer who guards the recipe jealously. Some have been made in exactly the same way for hundreds of years, others are relative newcomers. Like all food and drink, there are personal preferences. Since these are all expensive, buying one you don't like is a problem; although it need not be wasted (see p. 110). If possible try all these brandy-based drinks from small bottles, either the miniature, or the half bottle. If not available to you, then before you spend a great deal of money, have one the next time you dine out and taste-test it.

What Does it Taste Like?

ADVOCAAT: very thick, creamy; made of brandy and egg yolks, and resembling eggnog. It has a low alcoholic content (15 to 18 per cent) and is sometimes eaten with a spoon.

ANIS AND ANISETTE: respectively Spanish and French versions of the same drink. Clear aromatic, its licorice flavour derives from the seed of the star anise plant. It can be diluted with water, which clouds it with a pale greenish tinge.

APRICOT LIQUEUR: made from a very sweet brandy base and mashed apricots.

AQUAVIT: colourless, unsweetened Scandinavian drink made from rectified potato spirits and flavoured with caraway seeds.

BENEDICTINE D.O.M.("Deo Optimo Maximo," "To God the Best, the Greatest"): perhaps the oldest and certainly one of the most famous of liqueurs, dating back to 1510. No longer made by the Benedictine religious order which originated it, it's privately manufactured today. Greenish-yellow and flavoured with a variety of ingredients —exactly what they are only three people know at any given time. An official "B&B" is also marketed, a half-and-half mixture of Benedictine and brandy.

BLACKBERRY LIQUEUR: made from steeping blackberries in a blackberry brandy, sometimes with a touch of red wine.

CHARTREUSE: another grand old liqueur, 250 years younger than Benedictine; still manufactured by the original religious order (Carthusians). The base is brandy, but the numerous plant and herb flavourings (estimated at as many as 230) are still secret. There are two varieties: tangy green, and a sweeter yellow.

CHERRY HEERING: Danish, not oversweet, famous throughout the world. The brandy base is flavoured with cherry stones.

CURAÇAO: flavoured with the skins of oranges. Originally a Dutch liqueur, but now generic for all orange-flavoured cordials. Cointreau, Grand Marnier and Triple Sec are the best-known proprietory names.

DRAMBUIE: one of the most popular liqueurs in this country, it's a 200-year-old Scottish drink with a Scotch whisky base and heather honey and herb flavourings.

GALLIANO: Italian, gold-coloured, its dominant flavour is vanilla.

GOLDWASSER: flavoured with aniseed and caraway, it is distinguished by the flakes of 22 karat gold suspended in the clear liquid.

IRISH MIST: pure Irish whiskey and heather honey combination, a counterpart to Drambuie.

KÜMMEL: high alcoholic sweet, aromatic, white dates back to the sixteenth century. Distilled from pure grain alcohol and flavoured with caraway seeds.

MILLEFIORI: pale gold in colour, from Italy; purportedly made from the extracts of a thousand Alpine flowers. Look for a twig floating in each bottle.

PARFAIT AMOUR: very sweet, spiced, either red or violet.

PERNOD: very dry, bitter, of high alcoholic content, flavoured with aniseed. Like anis, it becomes cloudy when mixed with water.

SLOE GIN: heavy, aromatic, flavoured with sloeberries (fruit of the blackthorn bush) steeped in gin.

SOUTHERN COMFORT: American, peach-flavoured and 100 per cent proof.

STREGA: Italian, sweet, yellow in colour; similar to yellow chartreuse.

CRÈME DE CACAO: sweet, syrupy, cocoa-flavoured; dark chocolate colour or clear.

CRÈME DE CAFÉ: sweet, syrupy, coffee-flavoured. Tia Maria from Jamaica is the most popular label; Kahlua is the Mexican variety.

CRÈME DE CASIS: dark, moderately sweet; low proof and flavoured with black current.

CRÈME DE FRAISES: sweet, strawberry-flavoured.

CRÈME DE FRAMBOISE: sweet, raspberry-flavoured.

CRÈME DE MENTHE: pungent, aromatic; flavoured with various mints, primarily peppermint; available in white or green (artificially coloured), the former somewhat drier.

CRÈME DE NOYAUX: bitter, almond-flavoured, ruby-hued.

You Don't Like It or
You Want Another Use for the Liqueur

□ If it is one of the unusual flavoured liqueurs such as aniseed-flavoured, give it to a friend.

□ Most of the sweet liqueurs, Tia Maria, Cherry Heering, Crème de Cacao, pour over a vanilla ice-cream or a fruit sherbet. Or layer in tall glasses with a small amount of liqueur between layers of mousse, custard, ice-cream or sherbet.

□ Add a small amount of Pernod or Aniseed to any dish containing sauerkraut, or add to a rich dark sauce made from the gravy of roast duck, orange juice, peels, etcetera.

□ Add to food in small amounts so that there is sufficient to point up the flavour but not so much that the liqueur drowns the natural flavour of the food itself.

The Bar

A bar can be an elaborate piece of furniture, a serving cart or one or two sturdy bridge tables. A large occasional or small dining table will serve as a bar. Less practical but still useful is a hutch cupboard, a "dry sink" or a sideboard. If you are using a fine piece of furniture, cover it with a cloth over a double-folded sheet or pad to absorb all moisture and any spills.

For most parties the bar can be set up the night before. Put out one bottle of every kind of liquor you plan to offer so guests can see what's available at a glance. Keep the extras under the table in a box. Put out glasses, napkins, coasters, stirrers, dishes that will be filled later with olives, lemon wedges, etcetera. And don't forget such items as ice tongs, measures and toothpicks.

Glass Basics

For party use don't buy crystal or hand-blown glass. Save those for quiet get-togethers and small dinners. Use plastic around the pool and patio.

Buy good quality mass-produced glassware for large get-togethers and as a basic starter. Choose a simple style that can be replaced and select clear unpatterned glass. (Wine is distorted when served in coloured glass. And although some antique hock glasses are coloured, this was because early wines were off-colour. In some cases coloured glass with red wine can be nauseating.)

Buy at least a dozen of each shape and size. This is the minimum for eight people, allows for replacement for guests who just put glasses down, and for the inevitable breakages.

For a cocktail party you will need an assortment of highball or similar straight-sided tumblers and cocktail glasses if you are serving mixed drinks. Large receptions require a glass count of two per person equally divided among the glass types required for the drinks offered. This guarantees sufficient of any one type.

For a large party, and if you don't entertain on this scale more than twice a year, rent glasses.

Fine glasses need care. Don't put them in the dishwasher. Wash by hand and if there are greasy marks, a little household ammonia in the water will remove them. Rinse thoroughly in warm water and turn them upside down on paper towelling or lint-free cloth to drain. Dry as quickly as possible using a gentle action and a soft cloth. Wine glasses used less than gently will acquire nicked rims. These must be discarded. If the glass is valuable the edges can be reground; however, this is an expensive process.

Glassware should be checked well in advance of a party because they collect a greasy dusty film just standing on the shelf. If you are having a large party and don't want to use your fine crystal, rent inexpensive glasses. In any event, before a large party, check the number of glasses and arrange to rent. There's nothing as frustrating as running out of clean glasses, so a good rule of thumb is to have one-third more glasses than guests.

Bar Accessories

If you want to keep a home bar stocked with all the accessories you can run into a lot of equipment, some of it rarely needed: for example juicers, ice crushers, blenders. However, ice crushers and blenders can do double duty in the kitchen. But the basics include:

☐ A corkscrew: there are many to choose from. The simplest is the twist and pull type; choose one with a good heavy thread without sharp edges. There's the twist and pry, used by professional waiters. There's the Angel, a somewhat more elaborate mechanism but effective (the name comes from the two wings that are used in the lifting process), and the syringe type. The latter can build up air pressure and should be used with caution.

☐ A long-handled bar spoon used for stirring, and retrieving onions, olives, cherries, and so on.

☐ A bottle-opener: this should be strong, sturdy, with no sharp edges.

☐ Ice bucket: choose a big one with an easy to clean interior.

☐ Ice tongs.

☐ Liquor measures: there are a variety of types. You need only one size, the 1$\frac{1}{4}$ ounce, but you should have a few so you can use different ones for different spirits to avoid mixing flavours or else wash between mixing.

□ Pitcher with an ice guard for cold water. You may also need, depending on where and how you work, a sponge, a terry-cloth towel, and a tray. You can add to an elaborate bar set-up such equipment as a cutting board and a paring knife, a shaker, a strainer and a squeezer.

Stocking a Bar

Everyone has his own preferences, and this, plus the tastes of frequent guests, helps make the bar list for spirits. Table wines again follow personal taste and if possible keep on hand for table use, red, white and rosé wines in the standard sizes. For slightly larger parties there are some wines bottled in the 35-ounce size, and, of course, there are half bottles.

There are really no basics—all is based on the pocket book and taste, but here are a few suggestions.

Aperitifs

Sherry: there are many choices from sweet to
   very very dry
French and Italian Vermouth
St. Raphael, Campari, or similar aperatif

Spirits

Canadian Whisky (rye)
Scotch Whisky
Gin
Rum: again a wide variety; from dark to white,
   from heavy to light
Vodka
One thing about spirits, they aren't perishable and are always good for future hospitality.

The least expensive bar item is ice and it's one of the most important. A good guide is to have five pounds of ice for every fifteen guests.

You should allow three-quarts of mix for every quart of liquor. Soda water, tonic, ginger ale, bitter lemon, cola, and pitcher of ice water are basics. And a nice extra is bottled plain or mineral water.

Christmas Open House

Getting away from the traditional red and green, to a Scandinavian mood of red, white, and blue. The decoration is a grouping of bare branches sprayed with white paint and decorated with small birds. (see illustration opposite p. 33.)

The food is typical of many Scandinavian countries and is suitable for an open house that continues for a few hours. The menu includes a bowl of egg nog, rye breads, thin toast and a cheese spread, open-faced sandwiches made from horizontal slices of round rye loaf covered with cream cheese and garnished with sardines, hard-cooked eggs, tomatoes, and parsley and then cut in wedges. Dessert is fruit cake, sugar cookies, and crisp red apples.

The Pasta Party

A party for a crowd by hosts on a budget—only you wouldn't know it. The dark green candles and peppers give atmosphere. Pasta is easy to cook and both it and the sauce can come directly to the serving table from the stove. If you don't have a pasta boiler, use a preserving pan. Use plastic-coated plates, large paper napkins and keep the Italian theme going by serving espresso from a copper pot. The dessert is an inexpensive plain cake purchased from the bakery and iced at home.

The Bachelor's Party

Take-out foods can be dressed up to look different and to zip up the flavour. The food is set out on inexpensive plastic parsons' tables and guests can perch on chairs or sit on the floor. The chicken has a special sauce and the bread has been herbed. (See p. 157) A tip: the French fried potatoes usually sog, so serve crisp potato chips instead, and at the same time pick up some fresh home-made style country doughnuts for dessert.

Bar Sense

Should you buy the premium brands or the medium priced? For a very large cocktail party with many mixed drinks keep to the medium or lower-priced brands. Keep the premium for friends who drink the drinks, without mixes, savouring the true flavour of the drink—and for yourself.

There's no such thing as a "cooking" wine. Heat burns off the alcohol and leaves the basic flavour; if there isn't much to begin with, there will be none after cooking. Opt for a medium price range.

Estimating

If you are entertaining twenty-five to thirty-five guests, it will be busy around the bar, so eliminate the exotic drinks. Stick to the maximum of two standard cocktails such as martinis or Manhattans. If it's an informal evening, but with fewer guests (or your bar bill will go sky high), lead the guest to the bar for the first drink, then let the guest serve himself.

A 25-ounce bottle makes sixteen straight drinks. Here's a formula used by hosts to estimate volume requirements for liquor:

$$\frac{\text{number of guests} \times 1.5 \text{ drinks} \times \text{hours}}{15 \text{ drinks}}$$

=number of 25-oz. bottles needed.

Things get a little more complex when you try to break down this quantity estimate into specific types, such as gin, Scotch, rum and Canadian whisky. It helps if you know the tastes of your individual guests.

There are many books on bartending available, some free from distillers, others from bookstores and the following guide will help you understand bartender argot:

1 jigger	1½ oz.
1 pony	1 oz.
1 wineglass	4 oz.
1 bar spoon	1 level teaspoon
1 teaspoon	⅛ oz.
1 dash	3 or 4 drops

Mixing Drinks

The inexperienced should keep to straight drinks using a measure accurately. Never get careless after the first round. However, if you want to serve mixed drinks, follow implicitly a bartender's guide. The following tips are applicable to all mixed drinks.

□ There's a difference between shaking and stirring. Shaking means to put the liquid in a capped container and shake vigorously.

□ Serve drinks really cold. The mixing glass should be stored in the refrigerator for at least three hours.

□ A good cocktail is never watery and shouldn't be allowed to stand. Mix only enough for one round, or for the number ordered.

Before the second round, drain the container and never re-use ice.

Serving Tips

□ Clear cloudy ice cubes by sprinkling with lukewarm water.

□ Chill cocktail and long cold drinks (Collins, etcetera) before serving.

□ Don't keep drinks standing unless absolutely necessary.

□ Always replace the caps on bottles because liquor can pick up food, smoke, cooking, onion odours.

□ Have plenty of coasters on hand.

□ Prepare garnishes in advance. Slices and wedges of lemon, lime, orange, as well as saucers of olives, onions, and maraschino cherries give mixed drinks a professional touch, as do twists of lemon peel. Have cherries and olives ready speared on toothpicks.

□ Check on supplies of Angostura Bitters, Tobasco and Worcestershire sauce. And always use with a light hand!

Bar Recipes

GIN

Admiral Cocktail

Juice of 1/2 lime
1/2 oz. cherry cordial
2 oz. gin
Shake with ice and strain.

Yellow Bird Cocktail

3/4 oz. Yellow Chartreuse
2 oz. gin
Shake with ice and strain. Top with lemon peel.

Alexander Cocktail No. 1

1/2 oz. cream
3/4 oz. Crême de Cacao
1 1/2 oz. gin
Shake with ice and strain. Top with nutmeg.

Bijou Cocktail

1/2 oz. chartreuse
4 dashes sweet vermouth
2 oz. gin
Stir with ice and strain. Decorate with cherry. Twist of lemon peel over drink.

Blue Moon Cocktail

1/2 oz. Crême de Yvette
2 oz. gin
White of egg
Shake with ice and strain.

Bronx Cocktail

1/4 oz. orange juice
1/4 oz. sweet vermouth
1/4 oz. dry vermouth
2 oz. gin
Shake with ice and strain.

Clover Club Cocktail

Juice ½ lemon
White of egg
4 dashes grenadine
2 oz. gin
Shake with ice and strain. Serve in wine glass.

Flamingo Cocktail

Juice ½ lemon
3 dashes grenadine
½ oz. Apricot Brandy
2 oz. gin
Shake with ice and strain.

French "75"

Juice ½ lemon
1 tsp sugar
2 oz. gin
Serve in tall glass with cracked ice. Filled with
    chilled champagne. Stir.

Gimlet Cocktail

Juice ½ lime
¼ oz. Triple Sec
2 oz. gin
Shake with ice and strain.

Gibson Cocktail

¾ oz. dry vermouth
2 oz. gin
Stir with ice and strain.
Decorate with small pearl onion.

Gin Buck

Crush juice of ¼ lemon in highball glass.
1½ oz. gin
2 ice cubes
Fill with ginger ale. Stir.

Gin Cocktail

2½ oz. gin
4 dashes aromatic bitters.
Stir with ice and strain.

Gin and Tonic

2 ice cubes
1½ oz. gin
Slice of lime or lemon
Serve in highball glass.
Fill with tonic water. Stir.

Gin Cooler

Cracked ice in tall glass.
1 tsp sugar or 4 dashes grenadine
2 oz. gin
Peel rind of lemon in spiral form.
Fill with club soda. Stir.

Gin Daisy

Juice of ½ lemon
2 oz. gin
4 dashes raspberry or grenadine syrup
Serve in goblet with fine ice—fruit—stir.

Gin Fizz

Juice 1 lemon
1 tsp sugar
1½ oz. gin
Shake with ice and strain in highball glass
    with 1 ice cube.
Fill with club soda.

Gin Rickey

Insert juice of ½ lime and rind in highball
    glass with ice cube.
1½ oz. gin
Fill with club soda. Stir.

Gin Sling

1½ oz. gin
4 dashes aromatic bitters
Serve in tall glass with cracked ice.
Fill with club soda.
Twist of lemon peel. Stir.

Honolulu Cocktail

Juice $1/2$ lime
$1/2$ oz. pineapple juice
$1^1/2$ oz. gin
4 dashes curacao
Shake with ice and strain.

International Cocktail

$3/4$ oz. dry vermouth
2 dashes Absinthe
2 oz. gin
Stir with ice and strain.

Martini

$3/4$ oz. dry vermouth
2 oz. gin
Stir with ice and strain.

Napoleon Cocktail

2 dashes port wine
2 dashes curacao
2 dashes Fernet Branca
2 oz. gin
Shake with ice and strain.
Squeeze lemon peel on top.

Perfect Cocktail

$3/4$ oz. dry vermouth
$3/4$ oz. sweet vermouth
$1^1/4$ oz. gin
Stir with ice and strain.
Twist of orange peel.

RUM

Rum Cocktail

$1^1/2$ oz. white rum
$1/2$ oz. lemon juice
1 dash egg white
1 dash grenadine
1 maraschino cherry
Shake well and strain into cocktail glass.
Add cherry before serving.

Between the Sheets

$1^1/2$ oz. lemon juice
$1/4$ oz. brandy
$1/4$ oz. light rum
$1/4$ oz. Triple Sec
Ice
Shake with ice and strain into cocktail glass.

Cuba Libre

$1^1/2$ oz. dark rum
2 oz. cola
$1/2$ oz. lemon or lime juice
Ice
Pour into ice-filled highball glass and serve with lemon or lime slice.

Daiquiri

$1^1/2$ oz. white rum
1 oz. lemon or lime juice
Shake well and strain into chilled cocktail glass.

Banana Daiquiri

$1^1/2$ oz. white rum
$1/2$ fresh banana or 1 oz. banana liqueur
1 oz. lemon juice
2 tsp sugar
1 cup cracked ice
Place all ingredients, including ice, in blender and blend until creamy. Should be served in chilled champagne glass.

Hot Buttered Rum

$1^1/2$ oz. dark rum
Small piece butter
1 lump of sugar
Boiling water
Combine first three ingredients in mug, then fill with boiling water and stir. Serve with sprinkle of nutmeg.

Mai Tai

2 oz. white rum
1¹/₂ oz. light rum
¹/₂ oz. lime or lemon juice
¹/₂ oz. almond liqueur
1 tsp sugar
Crushed ice
Shake with ice and pour into double-size old
 fashioned glass half full of crushed ice.
Stir gently and garnish with cherry, pineapple
 spear and sprig of mint before serving.

Navy Grog

1 oz. white rum
2 oz. dark rum
1 oz. fresh lime juice
1 oz. orange juice
1 oz. pineapple juice
1 oz. passion fruit nectar
Ice cubes
Mix well and serve with ice cubes in highball
 glass.

Planter's Punch

1 oz. dark rum
1¹/₂ oz. orange juice
¹/₄ oz. grenadine
¹/₂ oz. lime or lemon juice
Ice
Shake all ingredients and pour into ice-filled
 highball glass.
Decorate with orange slice and cherry.

Robin's Nest

1 oz. light rum
³/₄ oz. sweet vermouth
³/₄ oz. orange juice
Ice
Stir all ingredients with ice in old fashioned
 glass and decorate with orange twist.

Zombie

³/₄ oz. light rum
³/₄ oz. dark rum
³/₄ oz. Jamaican rum
³/₄ oz. Demerara Rum
¹/₂ oz. grenadine
1 oz. lemon juice
1 oz. orange juice
Ice
Shake with ice and strain into 14 oz. Zombie
 glass. Add cherry and orange slice and serve
 with straws.

Beachcomber Cocktail

Juice of ¹/₂ lime
2 dashes marashico
¹/₂ oz. Triple Sec
2 oz. rum
Serve in champagne glass with shaved ice
 banked on one side.
Serve with short straws.

Bolero Cocktail

Juice of ¹/₂ lime
4 dashes orange juice
1 oz. brandy
1 oz. rum
Shake with ice and strain.

El Presidente Cocktail

³/₄ oz. sweet vermouth
Dash curaçao
2 oz. rum
Stir with ice and strain. Decorate with orange
 peel.

Everest Cocktail

Juice of ¹/₂ lime
³/₄ oz. Triple Sec
2 oz. rum
1 tsp of coconut powder
Mix in electric mixer with shaved ice. Serve in
 champagne glass.

Honeymoon Cocktail

Juice of ½ lime
1 white of egg
2 dashes absinthe
¼ oz. honey
2 oz. rum
Shake with ice.

MacArthur Cocktail

Juice of ½ lime
½ oz. Triple Sec
2 oz. rum
3 dashes of Jamaica rum
Dash of egg white
Shake with ice and strain.

Mary Pickford

¾ oz. pineapple juice
3 dashes grenadine
2 oz. rum
Shake with ice and strain.

National Cocktail

¾ oz. pineapple juice
3 dashes lime juice
3 dashes apricot brandy
2 oz. rum
Shake with ice and strain.

Snow White

½ oz. pineapple juice
Juice of ½ lemon
1 tsp of sugar
2 oz. rum
White of egg
Shake with ice and strain.

Grog

1½ oz. rum (light or dark)
1 tsp blackstrap molasses
1 tbsp lemon juice
Freshly brewed hot tea
Stir rum, molasses and lemon juice in mug, add hot tea to fill. Sprinkle with grated lemon rind.

Coureur des Bois

1½ oz. white rum
½ oz. maple syrup
½ oz. lemon juice
Dash of Angostura bitters
Shake well with cracked ice and strain into cocktail glass.

Kapinski

1 oz. white rum
1 oz. Triple Sec
1 oz. unsweetened grapefruit juice
Shake with ice until chilled.
Strain into cocktail glass.

Tia Rumba

3 parts white rum
1 part Tia Maria
Serve on the rocks in old fashioned glass.

RYE

Rye Cobler

Fill goblet half with cracked ice.
2 oz. rye
1 slice of lemon
4 dashes curacao
Stir.
Decorate with fruit, sprig of mint.

Rye Cooler

Cracked ice in tall glass
1 tsp sugar or 4 dashes grenadine
2 oz. rye
Peel rind of lemon in spiral form.
Fill with club soda.

Rye Collins

Cracked ice in tall glass
Juice of small lemon
1 tsp sugar
2 oz. rye
Fill with club soda. Stir well.

Rye Daisy

Juice 1/2 lemon
2 oz. rye
4 dashes grenadine
Serve in goblet with fine ice — fruit — stir.

Rye Egg Nog

1 egg
1/2 pt. milk
1 1/2 tsp sugar
2 oz. rye
Shake well with ice and strain.
Serve in tall glass. Nutmeg on top.

Rye Fizz

Juice of 1 lemon
1 tsp sugar
1 1/2 oz. rye
Shake with ice and strain in highball glass with
    1 ice cube. Fill with club soda.

Rye Flip

1 1/2 tsp sugar
1 egg
2 oz. rye
Shake well with ice and strain.
Serve in wine glass. Top with nutmeg.

Rye Highball

Cubes of ice in highball glass
1 1/2 oz. rye
Fill with water, club soda, or ginger ale.

Rye Rickey

Juice of 1/2 lime and rind in highball glass with
    ice cube
1 1/2 oz. rye
Fill with soda.

Rye Scaffas

1 1/2 oz. Benedictine
Dash of aromatic bitters
1 1/2 oz. rye
Serve unchilled.

Rye Sling

1 1/2 oz. rye
4 dashes aromatic bitters
Serve in tall glass with cracked ice.
Fill with club soda.
Twist of lemon peel — stir.

Rye Smash

Crush half lump of sugar with 3 sprigs of mint in
    old fashioned glass.
1 ice cube
Slice of orange and a cherry
1 1/2 oz. rye
Top with club soda. Stir.

Rye Sour

Juice of 1/2 lemon
1/2 tsp of sugar
2 oz. rye
Shake with ice and strain in delmonico glass.
Top with a few dashes of club soda.
Decorate with slice of orange and cherry.

Rye Swizzle

Juice of 1/2 lime
1 tsp sugar
4 dashes aromatic bitters
2 1/2 oz. rye
Pour ingredients into a glass pitcher.
Churn vigorously with swizzle stick until it
    foams.
Serve in highball glass. Top with club soda.

Rye Toddy

1 tsp sugar
3 cloves on slice of lemon with small pieces of
    cinnamon
1½ oz. rye
Add boiling water.
Stir. Use old fashioned glass.

Rye Zoom

¼ oz. honey
½ oz. cream
2 oz. rye
Shake with ice and strain into wine glass.

Manhattan

2 oz. rye
¾ oz. sweet vermouth
Aromatic bitters (optional)
Stir with ice and strain. Decorate with cherry.

Rye Bazooka

Juice and rind of 1 lime
4 dashes grenadine
3 dashes curaçao
2 oz. rye
Serve in tall glass with shaved ice.
Decorate with fruit.
Fill with Bubble-up.

Buckaroo Highball

Place ice cube in tall glass.
1½ oz. rye
Fill with cola.

Rye Fix

1 slice of lemon in tall glass
2 tsp sugar
6 dashes cherry brandy
Juice of ½ lemon
2 oz. rye
Fill with shaved ice.
Stir well and decorate with fruit.
Top with club soda. Serve with straws.

Mint Julep

2 oz. rye
½ tsp sugar
4 sprigs mint (mash with muddler)
Fill a silver mug or tall glass with shaved ice.
Stir until the outside of mug or glass is frosted.
Top with a dash of Jamaica rum.
Decorate with mint sprigs.
Serve with straws.

Old Fashioned Cocktail

Muddle ½ lump sugar saturated with 1 dash
    aromatic bitters.
2 dashes of club soda in old fashioned glass with
    ice cube
1½ oz. rye
Decorate with twist of lemon peel.
1 slice orange
1 slice pineapple
1 maraschino cherry
Stir.

Rye on the Rocks

Old fashioned glass with ice cubes
2 oz. rye.

Partridge Cocktail

4 dashes Triple Sec
½ oz. sweet vermouth
2 oz. rye
Stir with ice and strain.

Stone Fence

Ice cubes in highball glass
Dash of aromatic bitters
1½ oz. rye
Fill with cider. Stir.

SCOTCH

Barbary Coast Cocktail

1/2 oz. cream
1/2 oz. Tia Maria
1/2 oz. gin
1/2 oz. Scotch
1/2 oz. rum
Shake well with shaved ice and strain in
    delmonico glass.

Boiler Maker

1 1/2 oz. Scotch with beer chaser.

Mamie Taylor

2 cubes of ice in tall glass
2 oz. Scotch
1 slice lemon
Fill with ginger ale. Stir.

Morning Glory Fizz

1 1/2 oz. Scotch
White of one egg
1 tsp powdered sugar
Shake with ice and strain into highball glass
    with 1 cube of ice. Fill with club soda.

Rob Roy Cocktail

3/4 oz. sweet or dry vermouth
2 oz. Scotch
Stir with ice and strain. Decorate with cherry or
    lemon peel.

Whisky Daisy

Juice of 1/2 lemon
2 oz. Scotch
4 dashes raspberry or grenadine syrup
Serve in goblet with fine ice. Stir.

Scotch Egg Nog

1 egg
1/2 pt. of milk
1 1/2 tsp sugar
2 oz. Scotch
Shake well with ice. Strain. Serve in tall
    glass — nutmeg on top.

Scotch Fizz

Juice of 1 lemon
1 tsp sugar
1 1/2 oz. Scotch
Shake with ice and strain in highball glass with
    one ice cube. Fill with club soda.

Scotch Flip

1 1/2 tsp sugar
Whole egg
2 oz. Scotch
Shake well with ice. Strain. Serve in wine
    glass — nutmeg on top.

Scotch Highball

Cubes of ice in highball glass
1 1/2 oz. Scotch
Fill with club soda.

Scotch Milk Punch

1/2 pt. of milk
1 1/2 tsp sugar
2 oz. Scotch
Shake with ice and strain. Serve in tall
    glass — top with nutmeg.

Scotch Mist

1 1/2 oz. Scotch
Serve in old fashioned glass with shaved ice.
Garnish with twist of lemon peel and short
    straws.

Scotch Old Fashioned

Muddle ½ lump of sugar saturated with 1 dash aromatic bitters. Add 2 dashes club soda in old fashioned glass with ice cube. Add 1½ oz. Scotch. Decorate.

Mint Cooler

1 oz. Scotch
3 dashes Crême de Menthe
1 lump of ice
Fill up glass with soda.

Scotch Rickey

1 lump of ice
Juice of half lime
Juice of a quarter lemon
1 oz. Scotch
Fill up glass with club soda.

Earthquake Cocktail

One third gin
One third Scotch
One third absinthe

Flying Scotsman

2½ oz. Italian vermouth
3 oz. Scotch
1 tsp bitters
1 tsp sugar syrup

Whisper

2 oz. Scotch
2 oz. French vermouth
2 oz. Italian vermouth
Cracked ice

Scotch Special

3 oz. Scotch
2 oz. French vermouth
½ oz. orange juice
Top with nutmeg.

Scotch on the Rocks

2 oz. Scotch with ice

Scotch Puff

½ pt. of milk
2 oz. Scotch
Shake and strain. Serve in tall glass with one ice cube and fill with club soda.
Serve with straws.

Scotch Scoffa

1½ oz. Benedictine
Dash of aromatic bitters
1½ oz. Scotch
Serve unchilled.

Scotch Sling

1½ oz. Scotch
4 dashes aromatic bitters
Serve in tall glass with cracked ice. Fill with club soda. Twist of lemon peel. Stir.

Scotch Zoom

¼ oz. honey
½ oz. cream
2 oz. Scotch
Shake with ice and strain into wine glass.

Scotch Swizzle

Juice of ½ lime
1 tsp sugar
4 dashes aromatic bitters
2½ oz. Scotch
Pour ingredients into glass pitcher. Add 2 scoops of shaved ice. Churn vigorously with a swizzle stick until it foams. Serve in highball glass. Top with club soda.

TEQUILA

Margarita

1¹/₂ oz. Tequila Arandas
1 oz. Triple Sec
Juice of ¹/₂ lime or lemon
Mix in a blender with crushed ice and strain into
  a chilled glass which has had the rim moistened with fruit rind and dipped in salt.

Sunrise

1¹/₂ oz. Tequila Arandas
4 oz. orange juice
Juice of ¹/₂ lime
Dash of grenadine
In order, mix in a tall glass over ice.

Brave Bull

1¹/₂ oz. Tequila Arandas
1¹/₂ oz. Tia Maria
Pour in an old fashioned glass over ice with a
  lemon twist.

Freddy Fudpucker

1¹/₂ oz. Tequila Arandas
1¹/₂ tbsp sugar
³/₄ oz. fresh lime juice
Dash of Galliano
Mix in a blender over cracked ice until smooth.
Serve in champagne glass and top with a cherry.

Bloody Maria

1¹/₂ oz. Tequila Arandas
2 oz. ice cold tomato juice
1 tsp lemon juice
1 dash tabasco sauce
1 dash celery salt
Pour tequila, tomato juice, lemon juice, Tabasco
  and celery salt into pre-chilled old fashioned
  glass.
Add rocks or ice slices to fill glass. Stir very well.
  Add lemon slice.

Bunny Bonanza

1¹/₂ oz. Tequila Arandas
1 oz. apple brandy
¹/₂ oz. lemon juice
1 tsp sugar
¹/₂ tsp curaçao
Shake tequila, apple brandy, lemon juice, sugar
  and curaçao well with ice. Strain into pre-
  chilled old fashioned glass. Add ice to fill
  glass. Garnish with lemon slice.

Chapala

1¹/₂ oz. Tequila Arandas
¹/₂ oz. orange juice
¹/₂ oz. lemon juice
1 dash orange-flower water
2 tsp grenadine
Shake tequila, orange juice, lemon juice,
  orange-flower water and grenadine well with
  ice. Strain over rocks in pre-chilled old
  fashioned glass. Add orange slice.

Coconut Tequila

1¹/₂ oz. Tequila Arandas
¹/₂ oz. cream of coconut
¹/₂ oz. lemon juice
1 tsp maraschino liqueur
¹/₂ cup crushed ice
Put all ingredients into blender. Blend 20 seconds at low speed. Pour into pre-chilled
  deep-saucer champagne glass. Perfect before
  a Polynesian brunch.

Frozen Blackberry Tequila

1¹/₂ oz. Tequila Arandas
1 oz. blackberry liqueur
¹/₂ oz. lemon juice
¹/₃ cup crushed ice
Put tequila, blackberry liqueur, lemon juice and
  crushed ice into blender. Blend 10-15 seconds
  at low speed. Pour into pre-chilled old
  fashioned glass. Add rocks to fill glass. Add
  lemon slice.

Frozen Matador

1¹/₂ oz. Tequila Arandas
2 oz. pineapple juice
¹/₂ oz. lime juice
¹/₃ cup crushed ice

Put tequila, pineapple juice, lime juice and crushed ice into blender. Blend at low speed 10-15 seconds. Pour into pre-chilled deep-saucer champagne glass. Add pineapple stick. Or pour over rocks in pre-chilled old fashioned glass. Add ice cubes to fill glass. Garnish with pineapple stick.

Mexico Pacifico

1¹/₂ oz. Tequila Arandas
¹/₂ oz. lime juice
1 oz. passion fruit syrup
¹/₃ cup crushed ice

Put tequila, lime juice, passion fruit syrup and crushed ice into blender. Blend 10-15 seconds at low speed. Pour into pre-chilled deep-saucer champagne glass. Add lime slice.

Mint Tequila

1¹/₂ oz. Tequila Arandas
6 large mint leaves
¹/₂ oz. lemon juice
1 tsp sugar
¹/₂ cup crushed ice

Put all ingredients into blender. Blend at low speed 15-20 seconds. Pour into pre-chilled old fashioned glass. Add a rock or two to fill glass to rim.

Prado

1¹/₂ oz. Tequila Arandas
³/₄ oz. lime juice
¹/₂ egg white
¹/₂ oz. maraschino liqueur
1 tsp grenadine

Shake tequila, lime juice, egg white, maraschino liqueur and grenadine well with ice. Strain into pre-chilled whiskey-sour glass. Add lemon slice and cherry.

Sloe Tequila

1 oz. Tequila Arandas
¹/₂ oz. sloe gin
¹/₂ oz. lime juice
¹/₂ cup crushed ice

Put tequila, sloe gin, lime juice and ice into blender. Blend 10-15 seconds at low speed. Pour into pre-chilled old fashioned glass. Add cucumber peel and fill glass with cubed or cracked ice.

Sunset

1¹/₂ oz. Tequila Arandas
¹/₂ oz. lime juice
¹/₂ oz. grenadine
¹/₂ cup crushed ice

Put tequila, lime juice, grenadine and ice into blender. Blend at low speed 10-15 seconds. Pour into pre-chilled old fashioned glass. Add ice slices or cubes to fill glass. Garnish with lime slice.

Tequila St-Raphael

1 oz. Tequila Arandas
1 oz. red St-Raphael

Pour tequila and St-Raphael into pre-chilled old fashioned glass. Add cubed or cracked ice to fill glass. Stir. Garnish with lemon slice.

Tequila Fresa

1¹/₂ oz. Tequila Arandas
³/₄ oz. strawberry liqueur
¹/₂ oz. lime juice
¹/₄ tsp orange bitters

Shake tequila, strawberry liqueur, lime juice and bitters well with ice. Strain over rocks in old fashioned glass. Add lime slice and a fresh strawberry.

Tequila Frozen Screwdriver

1½ oz. Tequila Arandas
3 oz. iced orange juice
⅓ cup crushed ice
Put tequila, orange juice and crushed ice into
    blender. Blend at low speed 10-15 seconds.
    Pour into pre-chilled old fashioned glass. Add
    orange slice.

Tequila Guayaba

1½ oz. Tequila Arandas
½ oz. guava syrup
½ oz. orange juice
½ oz. lime juice
Shake tequila, guava syrup, orange juice and
    lime juice well with ice. Pour into pre-chilled
    old fashioned glass. Add a rock or two to fill
    glass. Twist orange peel above drink and drop
    into glass. Pass a guacamole dip.

Tequini

1½ oz. to 2 oz. Tequila Arandas
½ oz. dry vermouth
Lemon peel
Stir tequila and vermouth well with ice. Strain
    into a pre-chilled cocktail glass. Twist lemon
    peel above drink and drop into glass. A Mexi-
    can martini. Olive may be added for a salty
    accent.

Tequila Fizz

2 oz. Tequila Arandas
1½ oz. lemon juice
2 tsp sugar
2 dashes Angostura bitters
1 small egg
Iced club soda
Salt
Shake tequila, lemon juice, sugar, bitters and
    egg well with ice. Strain into tall 14 oz. glass
    half filled with ice. Fill glass with soda. Stir.
    Sprinkle very lightly with salt.

Tequila Rickey

1½ oz. Tequila Arandas
¼ large lime
Iced club soda
Salt
Put three ice cubes into 8 oz. glass. Add tequila.
    Squeeze lime above drink and drop into glass.
    Add soda. Stir. Sprinkle lightly with salt. Fas-
    ten orange slice to cocktail spear. Munch it
    before or after each swallow.

Acapulco Cocktail

Juice ½ lime
½ oz. Triple Sec
6 dashes pineapple juice
2 oz. Tequila Arandas
Shake with ice and strain.

Tequila Cocktail

Juice ½ lime
1 tsp sugar or 4 dashes grenadine
2 ozs. Tequila Arandas
Shake with ice and strain.

VODKA

Black Russian

1 oz. vodka
1 oz. Tia Maria
Pour over ice cubes in an old fashioned glass.
    Stir.

Moscow Mule

½ lime squeezed and dropped in 2 oz. vodka
1 split ginger beer or ginger ale
2 cubes of ice
Serve in a mug. Stir.

Bloody Mary

2¹/₂ oz. tomato juice
3 dashes lime juice
2 dashes tabasco sauce
2 dashes L. & P. sauce
1¹/₂ oz. vodka
Salt and pepper to taste
Shake with ice and strain in delmonico glass.

Red Sea

2 oz. vodka
³/₄ oz. cherry liqueur
Serve on the rocks.
Decorate with cherry. Stir.

Screwdriver

1¹/₂ oz. vodka
Ice cubes
Fill with orange juice. Stir.

Vodka Cocktail

Juice of ¹/₂ lime
¹/₂ oz. cherry brandy
2 oz. vodka
Shake with ice and strain.

Ballet Russe Cocktail

4 dashes lime juice
2 oz. vodka
¹/₂ oz. Crême de Cassis
Shake with ice and strain.

Bullshot Highball

1 highball glass with ice cubes
1¹/₂ oz. vodka
Fill glass with beef consommé.
Salt to taste.
Twist of lemon peel. Stir.

Cafe Rainbow Room

¹/₃ oz. vodka
¹/₂ oz. Crême de Cacao
¹/₂ oz. heavy cream
1 tsp sugar
2 oz. Cafe Expresso
Shake well and top with cinnamon powder.

Flying Grasshopper Cocktail

³/₄ oz. White Crême de Menthe
³/₄ oz. Southern Comfort
³/₄ oz. vodka
Shake with cracked ice and strain into cocktail
    glass.

Gypsy Queen Cocktail

2 oz. vodka
4 dashes Benedictine
1 dash orange bitters
Shake with ice and strain.

Hurricane Cocktail

1¹/₄ oz. brandy
³/₄ oz. absinthe
³/₄ oz. vodka
Shake with ice and strain.

Kangaroo Kicker

³/₄ oz. dry vermouth
2 oz. vodka
2 dashes white Crême de Menthe
Stir with ice and strain. Top with lemon peel
    twist.

Salty Dog

Cube ice in highball glass
1¹/₂ oz. vodka
Fill with Wink.
Dashes of salt to taste. Stir.

Tovarich Cocktail
Juice 1/2 lime
1 1/2 oz. vodka
1 oz. Kummel
Shake with ice and strain.

Bolshoi Ballet
1 1/2 oz. vodka
1/4 oz. grenadine
1 1/4 oz. apple juice
Stir with ice and strain into chilled sour glass.
    Serve with cherry.

Bull Shooter
1 1/2 oz. vodka
1/4 oz. lemon juice
2 oz. beef broth
2 oz. tomato juice
5 drops L. & P. sauce
3 drops tabasco sauce
Salt & pepper to taste
Sprig of celery
3 ice cubes
Pour into 8 oz. highball glass containing ice
    cubes and garnish with celery sprigs.

Bull Shot
1 1/4 oz. vodka
1/4 oz. lemon juice
3 oz. beef broth
4 drops L. & P. sauce
Salt & pepper to taste
2 ice cubes
Pour over ice cubes in old fashioned glass.

Harvey Wallbanger
1 oz. vodka
1/2 oz. Galliano
Orange juice
Ice cubes
Pour vodka into 10 oz. glass filled with ice cubes,
    then fill glass 3/4 full with orange juice. Float
    Galliano on top.
Serve with orange slice.

Red Square
1 1/2 oz. vodka
1/2 oz. Cherry Whisky
4 oz. orange juice
Crushed ice
Pour over crushed ice in 14 oz. highball glass
    and stir.
Garnish with orange slice and two cherries and
    serve with straws.

Russian Cocktail
1 oz. vodka
1 oz. Crême de Cacao white
1 oz. gin
Shake well and strain into cocktail glass.

Salty Laika
1 1/4 oz. vodka
3/4 oz. grapefruit juice
3/4 oz. lemon juice
Sprinkle of salt
Shake with ice and strain into chilled sour glass.
Serve with sprinkle of salt.

Stargazer
1 oz. vodka
1 oz. orange juice
1/2 oz. lemon juice
1/2 oz. apricot brandy
Ice
Shake well with ice and strain into chilled cock-
    tail glass.

Vodka Sour
1 1/2 oz. vodka
1 1/2 oz. lemon juice
Ice
Shake with ice and strain into chilled sour glass.
    Garnish with cherry.

Vodka Stinger

1¼ oz. vodka
¾ oz. green Crême de Menthe
Ice
Shake well with ice and strain into chilled cock-
    tail glass. Add lemon twist and serve.

WINES AND LIQUEURS

Alexander Cocktail

½ oz. cream
¾ oz. Crême de Cacao
1½ oz. cognac
Shake with ice and strain. Top with nutmeg.

B & C

½ oz. Benedictine
½ oz. cognac
Serve in cordial glass.

Biarritz

Juice ½ lime
½ oz. orange curacao
2 oz. cognac
Shake with ice and strain.

Bourguignon Cocktail

2 dashes Crême de Cassis
3 oz. chilled white wine
Serve in wine glass.

Champagne Cocktail

1 lump of sugar in champagne glass saturated
    with aromatic bitters
Twist of lemon peel
Fill with chilled champagne.

Flicker

Juice of ½ orange
2 dashes of maraschino
Fill with chilled champagne.
Serve in champagne glass with ice cube.

The Home Wedding Reception

Take a summer's day, lots of flowers, and food that is dainty, bite-sized, and appetizing. The colour scheme is yellow and white and the ideas are adaptable to different seasons as well as to an indoor reception or wedding anniversary. The plentiful use of silver and crystal adds a festive touch and creates highlights. The tablecloth is made from dress fabric with cotton eyelet trim. There is no cutlery—just finger food and napkins.

Champagne cup is served with shrimp salad in tiny patty shells, rolled sandwiches, petit fours, meringues, candied orange slices, and mints. The cake with its single perfect rose is the focal point. It has understated simplicity, continues the colour scheme, and can be home-decorated. Borrowing a European custom, there are net bags of sugared or Jordan almonds for guest souvenirs.

St-Raphael Cocktail

1⅓ oz. St-Raphael
1⅓ oz. gin
Stir with ice and strain. Twist of lemon peel to
    decorate.

French ''90''

Pour juice of ½ lemon and 2 oz. cognac and
    ½ tsp sugar in tall glass.
Add cracked ice.
Fill with chilled champagne.
Stir and serve.

Jamaican Wonder

½ jigger Tia Maria
1 jigger navy rum
1 jigger lime juice
Fill with club soda.
Serve in highball glass.

Cappucino

⅓ Tia Maria
⅓ vodka
⅓ fresh cream
Shake with cracked ice, strain and serve in
    cocktail glass.

Sun Trap

⅓ Tia Maria
⅓ gin
⅙ lime juice
⅙ French vermouth
Shake with cracked ice, strain and serve in
    cocktail glass.

Black Maria

2 oz. Tia Maria
4 oz. strong black coffee
1 oz. navy rum
1 oz. sugar syrup
Serve over shaved ice or cracked ice in brandy
    snifter.

Hot Drinks on a Cold Night

Hot rum drinks including hot buttered rum with a cinnamon stick muddler, hot rum added to coffee and topped with whipped cream, and non-alcoholic drinks such as hot chocolate or foaming cocoa are warming and welcoming after a long winter walk, a skating party, or a sleigh ride. When appetites are sharp serve hot drinks with sweet-and-sour meatballs eaten from toothpicks.

Jamaican Cow

1/3 Tia Maria
2/3 milk
Serve cold on rocks.

Misty Cream

1/2 oz. Irish Mist
1/2 oz. cream sherry
Serve in liqueur glass.

The Mistake

2 ice cubes
1 oz. Irish Mist
1 oz. vodka
Pour in old fashioned glass. Stir.

Pink Garter

1 oz. Irish Mist
1/2 oz. vodka
1 oz. red wine
Shake well. Serve over ice in old fashioned
    glass.

Black Russian

1 oz. Tia Maria
2 oz. vodka
Pour over ice cubes in old fashioned glass.

Jupiter Cocktail

1 oz. Tia Maria
1 oz. Scotch
3/4 oz. dry vermouth
3 dashes orange curaçao
Stir with ice and strain. Decorate with cherry.

Cardinal Cocktail

Fill champagne glass with chilled champagne.
Add 4 dashes Crême de Cassis.

Mister Murphy

1 oz. Irish Mist
1 oz. white rum
Juice of 1 orange
Dash of Angostura bitters
Shake well and serve over ice cubes in old
    fashioned glass.

Irish Mist Sour

1 1/2 oz. Irish Mist
Juice 1/2 lemon
Ice
Shake well and serve over rocks or straight.

Side Car

Juice 1/2 lemon
3/4 oz. Cointreau
1 3/4 oz. cognac
Shake with ice and strain.

Diamond Fizz

Juice 1 lemon
1 tsp sugar
Serve in highball glass with 1 ice cube.
Fill with chilled champagne.

THE PUNCH BOWL

Wine Punch (for 1 gallon)

Juice of 12 lemons
1 pint brandy
1/2 pint curacao
2 bottles wine
1 bottle club soda
Sugar to taste
Cucumber rinds
Dress with fruits.
Block of ice
Stir.
Serve in punch glass.

Champagne Punch

2 tbsp lemon juice
Juice of 1 orange
4 oz. cognac
1/2 cup pineapple juice
1 bottle white wine
1 bottle champagne
Pineapple slices
Mix first 5 ingredients in large bowl. Add lump of ice and champagne. Garnish with pineapple slices. Makes 15-4 oz. cups.

Clog —Hot Wine Drink (serves 15)

3/4 cup sugar
1 pint sherry wine
2 oz. aromatic bitters
1 pint claret wine
1/2 pint brandy
Use large flame-proof casserole. Place over fire until piping hot.
Serve in old fashioned glass or mug.

Dickens Punch

Peel of 3 lemons
1 cup sugar
2 cups rum
1 cup cognac
6 tbsp lemon juice
4 cups boiling water
Heat first 4 ingredients in large saucepan. Off heat stir in lemon juice and boiling water. Stir well, cover for 5 min. Simmer 15 min. more. Garnish with lemon slices. Makes 15-4 oz. cups.

Egg Nog Large

8 egg yolks
3/4 cup sugar
2 cups rye
1 1/2 cups table cream
3 1/2 cups milk
8 egg whites
Beat egg yolks with sugar. Add rye, cream and milk. Whisk egg whites very stiff and fold into mixture. Sprinkle with nutmeg. Makes 16-4 oz. cups

Grande Marquise de Richelieu

1 bottle white wine
2 cups cognac
6 tbsp juice
1/2 lb. sugar
Handful whole cloves
3 cinnamon sticks
Heat first 4 ingredients until wine starts to form. Off heat add cloves and cinnamon sticks.
Makes 12-4 oz. cups

Hot Tea Punch

1 cup white rum
1 cup cognac
3 tbsp lime juice
7 1/2 cups freshly brewed hot tea
Sugar
2 sliced oranges
Mix first four ingredients in large bowl.
Add sugar to taste. Garnish with orange slices.
Makes 12-6 oz. cups.

Limonada

6 lemons
1 cup extra-fine sugar
1 bottle red wine
1 bottle white wine

With a small sharp knife or a vegetable peeler, remove the yellow peel from three of the lemons, being careful not to cut into the white underskin. Cut the peel into strips about 2" long and ¹/₂" wide.

Set them aside. Squeeze the juice from one of the peeled lemons and then slice the remaining 3 unpeeled lemons crosswise into ¹/₄" thick rounds. Combine the strips of lemon peel, the lemon juice, lemon slices, and sugar into a 3 to 4 quart serving pitcher. Pour in the red and white wine and stir until well mixed. Refrigerate at least 8 hours. To serve, stir again, taste, and add more sugar if you prefer the drink sweeter. Serve in chilled glasses, filled with ice cubes if you like. Serves eight.

Merry Mulled Wine

3-4 tsp sugar
1 cup water
6 whole cloves
3 small cinnamon stick pieces
Rind of 1 lemon
1 bottle red wine
Cloves
Cinnamon sticks
Lemon rind

Boil sugar in water. Add cloves, cinnamon sticks and lemon rind. When mixture comes to a boil add wine. Garnish with cloves, cinnamon sticks and lemon rind.
Makes 8-4 oz. cups.

Party Punch

Into large pitcher add:
1 cup brown sugar
8 oz. orange juice
6 oz. lemon juice
25 oz. light rum
Stir to dissolve sugar.

Pour into punch bowl with lumps of ice. Add 25 oz. dry ginger ale, 25 oz. soda water, several slices of fresh oranges and pineapple. Stir gently. Serves eight.

Royal Purple

2 bottles red wine
2 quarts ginger ale
Lemon slices
Whole cloves

Pour wine and ginger ale over ice cubes. Stir well. Garnish with clove-studded lemon slices. Makes 28-4 oz. cups.

Note: put a silver spoon into crystal or glass and pour hot liquids very slowly down it to prevent breakage.

Sangrià

¹/₂ lemon cut into ¹/₄" rounds
¹/₂ orange, cut into ¹/₄" rounds
¹/₂ large apple, cut in half length-wise, core, and cut into thin wedges.
¹/₄ to ¹/₂ cup extra fine sugar
1 bottle red wine
2 oz. cognac
Club soda
Ice cubes (optional)

Combine lemon, orange, apple and the ¹/₄ cup sugar in large pitcher. Pour in wine and cognac, stir until well mixed. Taste. If you prefer the sangrià sweeter, add up to ¹/₄ cup more sugar. Refrigerate for at least 1 hour. Before serving, pour in chilled club soda to taste, adding up to 24 ounces. Stir gently, serve at once in chilled glasses. Serves 4 to 6.

Strawberry Cup

4 cups frozen unsweetened strawberries
1 cup sugar
1 cup cognac
3 bottles cold white wine
Whole strawberries
Cover frozen strawberries with sugar and cognac. Shake bowl slightly and freeze 8 hours. Add wine before serving. Garnish with whole strawberries.
Makes 30-4 oz. cups.

Village Bowle

1 cup boiling water
Peel of 2 oranges
1 cup sugar
Juice of 1/2 an orange
1 tsp lemon juice
2 bottles red wine
Add boiling water to orange peel and sugar in saucepan. Let stand for 15 min. Add orange juice, lemon juice and wine. Heat to boiling. Garnish with clove-studded orange slices.
Makes 15-4 oz. cups.

WITH TEA AND COFFEE

By the Fire

1 1/2 oz. rye
1 tsp sugar
Freshly brewed hot tea
Cinnamon sticks
Mix whisky and sugar in mug. Add tea and 1 cinnamon stick. Stir well and top with sliced lemon.

Cafe Royale

Hold spoon with a lump of sugar over a mug of hot coffee.
Pour 1 oz. liquor on sugar.
Ignite and stir into coffee.

Canadian Coffee

8 oz. hot black coffee
2 tbsp maple syrup
1 oz. rye
Whipped cream slightly sweetened.
Pour coffee into two mugs and add syrup and whisky. Top with whipped cream.

Grog

1 1/2 oz. rum
1 tsp blackstrap molasses
1 tbsp lemon juice
Freshly brewed hot tea
Stir rum, molasses and lemon juice in mug.
Add hot tea to fill. Sprinkle with grated lemon rind.

Hot Milk With a Punch

1 tsp powdered sugar
1/2 oz. rum
1/2 oz. cognac
Hot milk
Mix sugar, rum, and cognac in mug. Fill with milk. Sprinkle with nutmeg.

Hunter's Mug

8 cups strong coffee
1 cup rum
2 cups whipped cream
Sugar
Mix coffee with rum in samovar or coffee server to keep warm. Place whipped cream, beaten stiff with sugar beside coffee so friends can pour coffee and spoon cream on top.
Makes 15-6 oz. cups.

Irish Mist Coffee

In a heated Irish Coffee glass pour 1 1/2 oz. Irish Mist.
Add hot black coffee to half inch of rim.
Top with heavy or whipped cream over back of spoon so that cream floats on top. Do not stir.

NON-ALCOHOLIC COCKTAILS

All Season Cocktail

¹/₂ tsp sugar
2 dashes bitters
Long twist of lemon peel
Add ice cubes and fill with soda water.
Stir gently.

Lemon 'n' Ginger

Ice cubes
¹/₂ tsp. sugar
Juice of ¹/₂ lemon
Fill with ginger beer.
Stir gently.

Holiday

Ice cubes
Juice ¹/₂ lemon
1 tablespoon grenadine
Fill with soda water.
Stir gently.

Fizz'n Ginger

Ice cubes
2 dashes bitters
¹/₂ tsp sugar
Juice of ¹/₂ lemon
Fill with ginger ale.
Stir gently.

NON-ALCOHOLIC PUNCHES

Grape Punch

Into punch bowl add:
Block of ice
Juice of 6 lemons
25 oz. grape juice
25 oz. cola
Stir gently.
Decorate with fruit.
Serves 8

Apple Special

Into punch bowl add:
Block of ice
16 oz. apple juice
2 oz. sugar syrup
8 slices of lime
Muddle and add:
25 oz. ginger ale
Stir gently.
Serves 6

7
Recipes

Kitchen and Cupboard Hints.

Recipes and Cookery Books

There are recipes in this book, but it is not a cookbook! I have used recipes from books, from friends, from magazines and made my own adaptations. They work for me, and the recipes are offered as a guide. Everybody has his own favourites. Everybody cooks one thing better than another—you will find few cookie or pie recipes here. Cookies take me too much time, and pastry is not my strong suite.

For additional recipes browse through cookbooks, libraries and book stores have hundreds of them, some are devoted to one subject, some are general purpose, others for the dedicated. Cookbook buying is very personal and it can also become a mania. However, for practical purposes, a selection of half a dozen books is usually sufficient.

My personal choices for everyday use are varied and range from a 1749, *English Housewifery* by Eliza Moxon* to
Robert Carrier *Great Dishes of The World*
Elaine Collett *The Chatelaine Cook Book*
Louis Diat *Gourmet's Basic French Cook Book*,
   Better Homes and Gardens Cook Book
   The Good Housekeeping Cook Book
   The Laura Secord Canadian Cook Book
Fannie Merritt Farmer *The Boston Cooking School Cook Book*
Duncan Hines *Dessert Book*
The Alice B. Toklas Cook Book
E. Aresty *The Delectable Past*

E. David *French Provincial Cooking*
   and so on.

---

*Eliza's Lemon Posset is cool, refreshing and easy to make. Serve it on a summery night with sliced Poundcake and tea or coffee, plus a bowl of unhulled strawberries.
1 pint whipping cream
grated rind and juice of two lemons
1/4 to 1/2 cup dry white wine
1/2 cup sugar
3 egg whites

Add the lemon rind to the cream and whip until stiff. Add the juice and stir in the wine and sugar to taste. In a separate bowl beat the whites until stiff enough to form peaks and gently fold into the cream. Serve in custard cups, small wine glasses or in Champagne flutes. Refrigerate until required.

Serves 6.

A Word About Quantities

(Quantity cooking p. 78.)
□ If a soup, casserole, or appetizer recipe says it will serve eight and you have never proven it, increase the quantities. It is always better to have too much than too little.
□ If you have a large party, you can double quantities for some foods such as chili, spaghetti sauce, and potato salad. But you can't successfully double cake recipes or those for many desserts. It is better to make two layer cakes and two

cold souffles. If a main course recipe is doubled, don't double the seasonings. Taste and add as needed. If the quantity is increased, the cooking time may have to be increased.

□ Chilling and refrigeration is important at all times, especially for creamy mixtures such as meat in sour cream sauce, eclairs, trifles, cream soups, etc. Large quantities should be cooled in shallow pans.

Dinner for Two

How Much to Buy Guide

The following is a suggested list of amounts for some basic food items. Much depends on your taste and what you consider reasonable-sized servings. To save time, cook two or more meals at once—just increase amounts given.

Amounts to buy for two servings:

Vegetables

Asparagus	1 pound
Beans, green or yellow	1/2 pound
Broccoli	3/4 pound
Cabbage (cooked)	3/4 pound
(salad)	1/2 pound
Carrots	1/2 pound
Cauliflower	1 small head
Mushrooms	1/2 pound
Peas	1 pound
Spinach	3/4 pound

Main Course

Minute steak	2
Club steaks	2
T-bone steak	1 (inch thick)
Chops	2 large or small
Ham slice	1 (1/2 to 1 inch thick)
Sausages	1/2 pound
Liver	1/2 pound
Hamburger	1/2 pound
Stewing meat	3/4 pound
Spareribs	1 1/2 to 2 pounds
Tenderloin (pork)	3/4 pound
Chicken	1 1/2-2 pound broiler split
Fish fillets	3/4 pound
Fish steaks	3/4 to 1 pound

Ways to Cook

Proper cooking utensils make cooking for two easy. Get the smaller sizes, exploit an electric frying pan and fuel-saving oven meals that can be cooked right in the serving dishes to save cleanup time. Ordinary stove-top cooking has its short-cuts, too — very important when a two-plate burner is the only means of cooking. Vegetables can be cooking in the lower section of the double boiler, while a pudding or sauce is simmering away on top. Warm up rolls in a covered dish set on simmering soup. Two vegetables can be cooked in one saucepan, or steamed together.

Desserts will not pose much of a problem —many of them come in individual portions: fruits, cheeses, ice cream sundaes, cupcakes, tarts, cup custards, waffles, and so on. Half a package of prepared pudding or half a cake mix baked as cup cakes may be enough at one time.

Tricks and Treats With Electric Frypans

BAKED APPLES: Set a pan of apples prepared for baking in the frying pan and cover. Turn control to 350°F. and bake 30 minutes. Baste, turn, and continue baking until tender, about 15 minutes. Apples may be cored, stuffed with sugar, cinnamon, and butter, wrapped loosely in foil, then set on a trivet or rack. Bake, covered, 45 minutes.

BAKE A CAKE: Prepare half the recipe of any butter-type cake batter, including mixes, and bake in a round or small square pan. Set on a trivet in the frying pan. Cover and bake 45 minutes at 300°F. Allow one hour for a two-layer cake batter. (Cake batter may be baked directly in the frying pan, but it's not easily turned out to cool. However, I have had success with a Teflon-coated pan.)

HOT GARLIC BREAD: Slit half a French stick into 1/2-inch slices through to the bottom crust. Spread with savory butter such as garlic, anchovy, parsley, herb or cheese and stand on a rack in the frying pan. Cover and bake 8 to 10 minutes.

GLAZED NEW CARROTS: Melt about 3 tablespoons butter in the frying pan at 200°F. then add 3 bunches whole little new carrots that have been trimmed and scraped. Sprinkle with salt and cover. Cook 10 minutes. Stir and sprinkle with 2 or 3 tablespoons brown sugar, then cover again and cook 5 minutes longer.

FROZEN MEAT PIES: Line the frying pan with heavy-duty foil and preheat pan to 400°F. Place the pie or pies directly in the pan and cover. Bake 40 minutes for one pie, 50 minutes for two.

Cooking With Wine

□ When alcohol is added to a cooking pan the heat causes the alcohol to evaporate almost immediately leaving only the basic flavour of the wine, spirit, or liqueur. For this reason there is no such thing as "cooking sherry". If it isn't worth drinking, it isn't worth using in cooking! These flavours are also somewhat volatile, so add as one of the last ingredients, or follow the recipe closely.

□ Use liquor, of any kind, with a light hand. You want to add flavour, not overpower the food.

□ Too much liquor in frozen foods such as mousse, ice cream, or parfaits will interfere with the freezing process and the mixture will remain soft and syrupy.

□ If you want to have a flaming main dish or dessert, don't try this technique for the first time at a party.

□ For success there must be sufficient alcohol in the liquor to flame. Therefore, table wines won't flame but fortified wines such as Madeira will, as will spirits such as brandy, rum, or vodka.

□ Cold liquor poured from the bottle onto the dish will not flame. The spirit chosen must be warmed in a ladle over a candle before it can be lit. Avoid overheating or it will burst into flames before you are ready.

□ You can either light the warmed liquor in a warm ladle and pour it over the food, or pour the hot liquid over hot food, then flame. The former method is easier and guarantees success!

□ Heated liquor will not flame if poured over a dish containing a lot of liquid.

□ Ignite liquor with a long wooden match, Don't lean over the candle or chafing dish flame to light the ladle. You may singe your hair or eyebrows.

□ Allow the flames to die down on their own.

Some Quick Tricks

A salad can be prepared ahead of the meal quite successfully if the greens are washed and torn into bite-size pieces. Store them in a paper-lined bowl and top with another paper towel. Refrigerate. Don't add sliced tomatoes, but celery, onions and other crisp ingredients can be added. Leave the dressing until the last minute—unless you want a wilted salad. Of course, you remove the paper, lift the greens with your hands into another bowl, dress, and add croutons if wanted.

A quick-to-make and easy-to-store vegetable dressing is made from soft butter beaten with a small amount of lemon juice and some chopped herbs. Refrigerate and spoon a firm lump of herbed butter over hot vegetables—good over broiled fish, breaded veal cutlets, and lamb chops.

Molded salads won't slide around the plate or collapse into a soft heap if the liquid is reduced. For every two cups of liquid called for, remove a quarter cup, don't take more out or the salad will become rubbery.

Toast or sautée almonds and coconut ahead of time. Never leave them while you are sautéeing them. Drain well on paper towels and leave uncovered until wanted.

Hard-cooked eggs passed through a sieve make a delicate garnish for pâté, spinach, green and potato salads, and hot or cold asparagus. The French call this Mimosa dressing.

Frozen Poultry Guide

Allow approximately ½ to 1 pound per serving

depending on parts being cooked. Breasts and legs yield more meat than wings and necks.

Turkey size (pounds)	Servings
4 to 8	4 to 10
8 to 12	10 to 20
12 to 16	20 to 30
16 to 20	30 to 40
20 to 24	40 to 50

Having guests galore? Then buy a big bird or two small ones. The bigger bird gives you a better buy—less bone and more meat. But it can cause a problem in today's small ovens. No matter what, choose a turkey large enough so you will have enough for seconds, and maybe even a return engagement—in hash, creamed turkey, or sandwiches.

Thawing the Unstuffed Frozen Bird

Should you thaw? Follow recipe suggestions. When braising, stewing, or cooking completely wrapped in foil, thawing is unnecessary as the meat surface will not dry out before the turkey pieces are cooked.

If you do thaw: Thaw frozen unstuffed poultry in original wrapping shortly before time to cook. To speed up thawing you can place wrapped turkey under cold running water. See the label directions that come with large birds such as turkeys.

Thawing timetable for frozen Turkeys (unstuffed)

Ready-to-cook weight (in pounds)	Days in refrigerator
4 to 12	1 to 2 days
12 to 20	2 to 3 days
20 to 24	3 to 4 days

Frozen Turkeys (stuffed)

These birds, weighing 5 to 17 pounds, are on the market already stuffed for your convenience. Most come with herbed bread stuffing. Ready-to-cook giblets are packaged with the bird. All you do is unwrap and roast the turkey (and stew the giblets, of course). Keep turkey frozen until you are ready to cook it. However, you may

transfer turkey from freezer to refrigerator the night before cooking; this cuts roasting time by about 1 hour. Follow exactly the directions that come with the bird.

Roasting the Bird

Roasting a turkey is easy, in fact it is one of the easiest cooking procedures. Put it in the oven. Don't do too much peeking—opening the door lowers the temperature. Since it is so easy, why have I included turkey recipes? Because every year more new-to-entertaining hosts are puzzled by this large bird.

Wash turkey, inside and out. Rub cavity lightly with salt. Stuff, using one cup of dressing per pound of poultry, and fasten opening.

Tie legs snugly against the tail and place wing tips on back.

To cook: Cover top and sides of bird with fat-moistened, clean cheesecloth, or greased brown paper, or foil (capons and turkey only).

Place breast side down on a rack in a shallow roasting pan, with no lid, and no water, and roast according to the chart.

Turn breast up during last hour of cooking.

What Is the Recommended Roasting Temperature and Time?

Ready to cook Weight	Oven Temperature	Internal Temperature	(Approximate) time
6 to 8 lbs	325°F.	165°F. (stuffed)	3 to 4 hours
8 to 12 lbs	325°F.	190-195° (unstuffed)	4 to 4½ hours
12 to 16 lbs	325°F.	190-195°	4½ to 5½ hours
16 to 20 lbs	325°F.	190-195°	5½ to 6½ hours
20 to 24 lbs	325°F.	190-195°	6½ to 7 hours

For unstuffed turkeys shorten time ½ to 1½ hours. The shorter time is for birds up to 12 pounds and the longer time for birds over 12 pounds.

Preheat oven to 325°F. Times are for unstuffed chilled turkey and are approximate only. For stuffed turkey, add 30 to 45 minutes to the total roasting time.

After a 12 lb. and over turkey has lightly browned, cover it with a loose tent of foil and continue cooking.

The Pantry Shelf

NIBBLES: canned anchovies, smoked oysters, baby shrimp, herring tidbits, cocktail sausages, olives, crackers in variety, canned nuts, and toothpicks.

MAIN DISHES: canned chicken, fish, sea food, ham, luncheon meat. These make quick casseroles when combined with cream soups and poured over rice or noodles. Eggs are a great standby for scrambling, turning into omelets, or adding hard-cooked to casseroles as extenders.

DESSERTS: fruits—fresh, canned, or frozen. Mix, add a dash of wine or liqueur, or add a creamy instant pudding as a sauce. (Add approximately half a cup extra milk. Or make as directed and fold in one cup whipped cream to make a rich but light topping.) Stretch canned fruits and perk them up with fresh orange slices or banana slices and coconut. Use fruits either whole or pureed in a blender as sauce for ice cream. Keep a variety of frozen breads, rolls, coffee cakes, buns, and cakes on hand. Make an extra batch of Christmas cake; it freezes well, thaws quickly, and is welcome with a drink at any time.

Grocery stores are filled with interesting party items from sauces to pudding mixes, as well as quick cooking rice and pasta, a variety of sweet cookies, cheeses, and they become part of party fare in minutes.

After the party remember to store pretzels, cookies, and chips in airtight containers; however, once opened and unless you plan another party within a week or so, you may as well enjoy them while they are fresh.

Party Quick

The simplest party fare is a selection of drinks, hot and cold, plus a cheese tray with crackers, fruit, and olives. Or tea, coffee, or a drink with pound cake, fruit, or a rich cookie.

□ Add finely chopped anchovies and pitted olives to commercial sour cream and use as a dip for raw vegetables.

□ Melt semi-sweet chocolate or chocolate chips in a chafing dish and use as a dip for fresh sliced fruits.

□ Mix drained crabmeat with mushroom soup, heat and serve over poached eggs on split toasted English muffins.

□ Pour the creamed seafood mixture over hot buttered noodles.

□ Toss freshly cooked noodles with a mixture of sour cream and chopped parsley and chives. Sprinkle with grated Parmesan.

□ Serve old-fashioned hot cocoa, but put a spoonful of brandy in the adults' mugs and top with whipped cream.

Quick Drinks

IRISH COFFEE: fill mugs with hot strong black coffee, add sugar to taste and one jigger of Irish whiskey. Top with whipped cream. Do not stir because the coffee should be sipped through the cream.

TRINIDAD COFFEE: add 1½ ounces of light rum to hot coffee and top with whipped cream.

COFFEE-CACAO: pour iced coffee into tall glasses and add 2 ounces Crême de Cacao per serving. Top with cream if liked.

ICED TEA VARIANT: pour iced tea, sweetened to taste, over ice cubes. Add a twist of lemon and 1½ ounces Bourbon.

Impromptu Party Basics

Apart from food and drink, keep in a closet some of the following party basics and you'll keep fuss and dishwashing to a minimum.

—a supply of paper plates, napkins, guest towels, tablecloths

—a set of 8-ounce glasses and some coffee mugs candles and candlesticks

—baskets for crackers and warm breads

—a salad bowl that doubles for nuts, chips, pretzels

More Store Cupboard Ideas

Instant puddings are a godsend when you are organizing an impromptu party or thinking of what dessert to set before the unexpected guest. These puddings come in many flavors and set in minutes, but chocolate, vanilla, and butterscotch are among the most versatile. Make them as directed and pour into tall glasses alternating a dollop with a spoonful of whipped cream until the glass is filled, then top with whipped cream and add shredded chocolate or chopped nuts.

Ice cream is among the most versatile of foods. If you have a true freezer (not one incorporated within a refrigerator) the ice cream stays sufficiently hard so that you can surprise your guests with Baked Alaska. Cover a wooden board with foil. Using a white cake layer as a base (the kind sold for fruit shortcake is ideal), put a generous layer of ice cream (never use sherbet) over the cake and within an inch of the edge. Make a stiff meringue by beating three egg whites until almost stiff, adding flavouring such as vanilla and six tablespoons of fine sugar beaten in. The meringue should be stiff but not dry. Spread it over the ice cream and onto the cake, sealing the edges well. Put the board under the broiler and watch, as soon as the meringue turns golden remove and serve immediately.

Ice cream and sherbet make instant mock parfaits. It's nice to own tall parfait glasses but not necessary—use any tall glass. Pour a spoonful of liqueur into the bottom of the glass—Crème de Menthe, Crème de Cacao, or the orange-flavoured types are delicious. Add a layer of ice cream and/or sherbet, then another spoonful of liqueur. End with liqueur and whipped cream. Freeze until ready to serve.

Cheeses help add interest as well as bulk to the salad course, and add richness when stirred into the sauce for a noodle- or rice-based casserole. Cheeses are useful snacks to be enjoyed while you prepare the main course, and versatile enough to turn up as dessert accompanied by fruit such as apples, grapes and pears. If a glass of port is served, the impromptu meal becomes a party. Cheeses keep well but when they become dry and hard, grate and use as toppings on salads, casseroles, and soups.

Keep herbs and spices fresh (throw out when you can no longer smell their aroma). Store them away from light and in as cool a place as possible. Their uses and combinations are endless. A touch of dry mustard to the cheese sauce perks up homely macaroni and cheese. Curry powder is a zippy touch for creamed chicken, mushroom, and shrimp soups. But use sparingly and taste.

Dried parsley flakes give colour and flavor to a multitude of main course dishes, vegetables, soups, and salads. Onion flakes store well, leave no smell on the hands and are great to have on hand when cooking in a hurry.

Canned brown bread, date breads, and similar puddings steam well and can be served with an instant pudding sauce. Make the sauce with an extra 1/2 cup of milk and add a dash of vanilla, rum, or brandy.

Canned milk is a great cooking standby and takes the place of rich milk or cream in appetizers and desserts. It is especially good in Quiche or Crème Brulée.

Garnishes

Garnishing conjures up radish roses and hotel buffets built around ice carvings, or worse still, ducks or pigs made from lard. The problem with garnishes is that they can become time-consuming. They can also get out of hand and have been used, too often, to disguise a poorly cooked dish. However, garnishing can also increase the appetite, add subtle flavours to a dish and, today, should never be elaborate. When the host is the chef, there's no reason to try to copy hotels. The first rule of garnishing is that it should be appropriate; chives or watercress on a creamy vegetable soup, sliced oranges around a duckling. Avoid great sprigs of parsley. We all know that parsley (and paprika) does marvels for the appearance of soups, salads, and main courses but it is overdone especially when everything is sprinkled with green or red!

The most effective garnishes are the simplest; a bunch of watercress or mint tucked beside a roast, a few pieces of mushroom tossed on top of a salad. And when it comes to cocktail bites, avoid the garnish trap or you will have garnishes all over the rug.

Fried Bread or Melba Toast Triangles

Fried bread should be cooked slowly and evenly in butter, then drained throughly. In this calorie counting age, Melba toast or homemade oven-dried rusks are a useful garnish and accompaniment for soups. And these almost crisp breads are delicious when served with stew or coq au vin.

Lemon

Quarters of lemon are easier to use (and a garnish should be usable if not always completely edible) than the usual dinky slices. Mashing a slice to get the juice is rarely successful, but squeezing a quarter lemon is, and is permissible. Of course, if you feel very fancy you should remove the seeds. You can be very four-star and wrap the quarters in little pieces of cheesecloth to prevent the juice from hitting other guests in the eye. However, if you trim the stringy centre of the lemon segment away the juice won't deflect. Lemon is particularly good with fish but it is also delicious with fresh asparagus, broccoli, or over fried chicken. It is always a temptation to use lemon slices because they look so pretty. Use them as pure garnish across poached salmon, but also serve a wedge.

Olives

When used as a garnish particularly for Mediterranean type foods they should be pitted. They look good among raw vegetables, and they give a lift when sliced into salads. The trouble with them is two-fold. Some people never acquire a taste for them. Those that do have a tendency to use them on, over, and in everything. It's like owning a can of red paint.

Radishes

Radishes are ubiquitous. They can be sliced into petals by peeling back the skin with a sharp knife. If plunged into heavily iced water the flowers will open up. If you have the time, the fancy, sharp knife, and the patience, flowers, other than "roses", can be made. However, they are just as effective and possibly more digestible if thinly sliced.

Paper Frills

These are the ultimate and were once de rigeur. Now they are a little affected but can be fun to use since they disguise the fact that the drumstick is charred! However, they serve a purpose in that they are traditionally used to cover bone ends, chicken or other poultry drumsticks, the ham bone, or, and this is the ultimate, to decorate a crown roast. Today, they are hard to come by and when they are discovered (usually through catering supplies) they are sold in enormous quantities at very high cost.

If you feel the urge, they can be made at home. In fact its a task you can set children doing or bored guests. For poultry you need a length of foil, wax or parchment paper about a foot long. For larger bones such as ham frills, you'll need about two feet long. The paper should be about six inches wide. Fold the paper in half lengthwise. Take a sharp pair of scissors and snip the folded side in one inch straight cuts parallel with the end of the paper. Fold it lengthwise again but the opposite side from the first fold. Do not press down. You will find you can vary the cuts; the large one- or two-inch cuts are good for large birds and roasts. The smaller half-inch cuts look better on smaller bone ends. Secure one end with a straight pin and wrap the frill around the bone . Secure with another pin. It looks glamourous, sounds complicated, but actually takes a few minutes.

Almonds

Almonds seem to be very popular and unfortunately they turn up in the most inappropriate dishes, usually slightly charred and often rather greasy. The blanched almonds (either buy them split and blanched, or blanch them by pouring boiling water over them. In a few seconds the skins will slip. Drain and remove skins. Don't let them soak or the result will be bitter.) Almonds can be used as is, lightly sautéed. When browning almonds, don't leave them because they char easily. After they are browned, drain onto paper towelling. These can be made ahead and stored in well-stoppered refrigerator jars. They are now a cliché with green beans—but still taste good and crunchy. Excellent with broiled or sautéed fish, brussel sprouts, broiled or fried chicken pieces. Pecans lightly toasted in the oven are good sprinkled over salads, squash, or ice cream desserts as well as with pumpkin pie. Walnuts in the shell served with cheese and Port or Madeira is a traditional dessert, good tasting and very satisfying.

Flowers

Flowers are used successfully by the Japanese who tuck them into plates and shred them over bowls of steaming broth. Europeans often use nosegays to garnish plates of meat, or add nasturtiums, both flowers and leaves, to salads. For most of us, flowers are best kept in vases unless we are very adventurous. However, the leaf of a geranium and a couple of petals makes a dash in a finger bowl. Finger bowls sound very Victorian-snobby but they make a great deal of sense when finger food such as spareribs are served. And as mentioned elsewhere, you don't need to collect antique crystal bowls; the fruit nappies will do. Or if you eat outdoors and the fingers are likely to be greasy, go oriental, and pass small guest or face towels that have been sprinkled with cologne before pouring boiling water over them. Roll them before heating and

drain before serving. Simpler but not as much fun are the small packages of scented towelettes. Use them not only for adult parties but insist on them when entertaining children who have tucked into hot dogs followed by chocolate cake.

Appetizers

Food To Go With Drinks

Groceries and delicatessens offer an abundance of delicacies and nibbles. If all else fails there's the salted peanut and the potato chip! A few substantial appetizers look better than a trayful of tired over-decorated doodads, which require far too much preparation time, anyway.

Nuts and Crunchies

Canned salted nuts keep fresh for a long time and are excellent standbys. Salted almonds, filberts, et cetera, are expensive and it doesn't take much time to prepare your own.

Salted Nuts

Spread shelled nuts on a large flat cookie sheet, sprinkle with salt and dot lightly with butter. Bake at 350°F. for 25-35 minutes or until the nuts are lightly toasted. Watch them, or the toasting turns to charring. Remove nuts and let them cool and drain on paper towelling.
Variations: sprinkle with garlic powder, or add curry to taste to the butter before putting on the nuts. Chili powder and a mixture of herbs such as green onion, dill, garlic can be substituted too.

Crunch

Combine various unsweetened breakfast cereals, bite-size shredded wheat, rings of oatmeal, crispies, crunchies, nuts, small pretzels. To 2 quarts of cereal add 1 pound peanuts, a sprinkling of garlic powder (optional), salt to taste, dot with butter, and bake at 300°F. for about 45 minutes, shaking and stirring often. Store in an airtight container.

Patés and Spreads

Quick Pâté

Combine a pound of liverwurst, 1/2 pound of cream cheese, garlic to taste, and 1/4 cup brandy. Beat well together and pile into a bowl. Serve with thin toast.

Liver Pâté

Sauté and cook:
1lb. chicken livers
1 crushed clove of garlic
2 large sliced onions
1/4 cup butter and
1 tbsp oil
1/2 tsp. gelatine
1 can consommé
1 hard-cooked egg
Dissolve and heat 1/2 teaspoon plain gelatine in 1/4 can undiluted canned consommé. Sauté livers and garlic in the melted butter and oil in a covered pan over low heat. When the livers have lost redness, remove them from heat and add remaining consommé to pan juices, stirring to loosen any small pieces from the pan.

In a blender, put small batches of liver, onions, and some of the juices. Scoop batches into mixing bowl. When all is blended add gelatine mixture, stir and adjust seasoning with salt, pepper, and a dash of brandy.

Refrigerate several hours. Top with Mimosa garnish: a hard-cooked egg riced through a strainer. Cover the top with foil or plastic wrap. Can be made the night before. Cover any leftovers; refrigerate and use within two days.

Pâté D'Auverne

2 tbsp. butter
1/2 lb. chicken livers
2 hard-cooked eggs
1-8 oz. pkg. cream cheese
1/2 tsp. salt
1/2 tsp. Tabasco
1/2 tsp. Angostura

3 tbsp. Cognac
Parsley
Jellied consommé

Sauté chicken livers in butter until tender, about 5 min. Put livers and eggs through fine blade of food grinder. Cream cheese until light and fluffy. Add salt, Tabasco, and bitters to cheese. Gradually blend in livers and eggs. Add cognac last. Chill 24 hours. Garnish with parsley and jellied consommé broken into pieces with a fork.

Makes 2 1/2 cups.

Spreads

Fill small bowls with spreads and surround with assorted breads and crackers plus plenty of small spreader-knives.

Avocado Spread

Mash three or four very ripe peeled avocados and add 1/4 cup chopped green onions, add 1 teaspoon chili powder and sufficient chili sauce, about 3 tablespoons to mix. Beat well, season with salt, chopped garlic to taste.

Salmon Spread

1-7 3/4 oz. can Sockeye salmon
1/3 cup minced celery
1 tbsp. minced pimento
Dash of Tabasco
2 tbsp. mayonnaise
Toss together.

Seafood Spread

1-2 1/2 oz. salmon and shrimp spread
1/4 tsp. curry powder

Blend spread with curry powder and chill 1 hour.

Makes 1/4 cup.

Canapé Alternatives

Antipasto Tray

Thin slices of salami, tongue, ham, devilled eggs, ripe and pimento stuffed olives, sliced Swiss and Cheddar cheese. Arrange foods in spoke-fashion around the tray. Fill the centre with a grapefruit speared with olives, smoked oysters, and cauliflowerettes on toothpicks.

Crab Pastries

1 (8-ounce) can refrigerated butterflake biscuits
2 egg yolks, well beaten
1 cup (1/4 pound) shredded Cheddar Cheese
1 (6 1/2-ounce) can crabmeat, drained and flaked
1/2 teaspoon onion salt
1/4 cup snipped parsley
2 egg whites, well beaten

Split biscuits into 24 pieces. Using fingers to flatten each piece, push outwards to form a small rim (diameter 1 1/2 inches). Brush with beaten yolks. Combine cheese, crabmeat, onion salt, and parsley. Fold in egg whites. Place a heaping tablespoon of mixture on each biscuit. Place on ungreased cookie sheet. Bake in a 450° oven for 10-12 minutes.

Yields 2 dozen.

Crudités

Crisp finger food salad with unlimited combinations: cauliflowerettes, celery, olives, radishes, cucumber spears, cherry tomatoes, zucchini. Have a bowl of thick, highly-seasoned mayonnaise for dipping. Suggested flavours: garlic, blue cheese, or anchovy.

Mayonnaise

You don't have to make mayonnaise at home. In fact, it is trickly unless you have a blender. If you are using commercial mayonnaise, buy quality and dress it up yourself.
1. Stir in a dash of anchovy paste to taste.

The Bar

A permanently installed bar is glamourous and decorative, and allows the host to place everything within reach. However, you don't have to go to such lengths; a card table, kitchen counter, or a tea wagon are good locations to set out glasses, beverages, and accessories. No matter where the location, it is the placing of the equipment that is important. A neat arrangement with openers, corkscrews, jiggers, and tongs makes for easy serving. Where you place them depends on the types of drinks you are mixing and whether you work left- or right-handed.

A heavy woven placemat or towel at the mixing area sops up spills. The ice should be kept in a closed insulated bucket and only enough for one round placed on the counter. A good tip for any gathering.

2. Stir in chopped parsley, green onions, and a touch of tarragon.

3. Add the juice of a lemon and stir well.

4. Add a ½ cup of commercial sour cream, a dash of garlic powder, and swirl paprika through it.

However, if you own a blender there's nothing like the rich, home-made sauce. If there's any left, it will keep in the refrigerator for about a week (if tightly capped). Stir before using.

1 egg
½ tsp. dry mustard
½ tsp. salt
Dash of chopped garlic
2 tbsp. white vinegar
1 cup salad oil or half lemon juice, half oil

Break the egg into the blender and add the seasonings and about ½ cup oil. Cover and blend at low speed. Uncover and pour the remaining oil in a steady stream. Stop blender once the mixture thickens. Adjust seasoning.

For a sumptuous dressing for cold poached salmon, seafood cocktail, hard-cooked eggs used as an hors d'oeuvre, try Green Mayonnaise.

The same ingredients as above, but add 1 tbsp. chopped chives or green onions and a pinch of tarragon to the dry ingredients.

Seafood Mushrooms

Large fresh mushrooms
Lemon juice
Smoked salmon spread
Dash Worcestershire sauce.

Snap off stems and wipe mushrooms with damp cloth. Rub caps with lemon juice. Mix spread with Worcestershire and fill mushrooms. Chill 1 hour.

Dunks

These dips are good for raw vegetables, boiled shrimp, and other cooked shellfish.

The Tea Trolley Bar

An excellent way to assemble drinks, mixes, and fixings for a small party. Put the mixes on the bottom shelf. Put the bottles and glasses on the top, and wheel the wagon into the living room. When finished collect the empties and wheel it all back to the kitchen. If your trolley has a pullout or a leaf that can be raised, you will have additional room to set out nibbles. A cloth sops up any spills, adds colour, and makes service quieter. Pick up colour with bowls of cherries, onions, slices of fruit and match them to your coasters and napkins.

Herb Dunk
Combine 1 pint commercial sour cream with ³/₄ teaspoon salt, ¹/₂ cup each chopped parsley, chives, and green onions. Blend, adjust seasoning to taste.

Lemon Dip
2 cups mayonnaise, juice of one lemon, ¹/₂ cup chopped green onions, ¹/₄ cup chopped parsley. Stir, adjust seasoning.

Basic Dip
1 pint commercial sour cream
1 envelope onion soup mix
Combine and refrigerate one hour.

After you've made one basic dip you can vary it with the addition of canned or fresh shredded crabmeat or lobster, lobster paste, or anchovy, and ring the changes by serving potato chips, raw vegetables, melba toast, or bread sticks.

Yogurt Dip
1 cup plain yogurt
¹/₂ tsp. dill weed
¹/₂ tsp. onion salt
¹/₂ tsp. dried parsley flakes
¹/₂ tsp. garlic
1 cucumber peeled and cut in sticks
1 zucchini peeled and cut in sticks

Combine yogurt, dill weed, onion salt, and parsley flakes: chill. To serve stand vegetable sticks up around edge of deep bowl. Spoon yogurt mixture into bowl.

Italian Appetizer
(Travels well to picnics and makes a hearty meal-salad, good for an appetizer, stores well in refrigerator and takes minutes to make.)
1 - 7 oz. can solid pack tuna, drained
1 can pitted ripe olives, drained
1 lb. mushrooms sliced
1 - 15 oz. can of artichokes, drained, or frozen thawed artichokes

1 cup sweet mixed pickles
1 - 4 oz. jar of cocktail onions drained
¹/₂ cup sliced celery
1 cup pitted green olives
1 - 8 oz. can tomato sauce
¹/₄ cup wine vinegar
2 tbsp. salad oil
Salt and pepper to taste.

Break up the tuna into large chunks. Add remaining ingredients. Toss gently. Chill. Store in lidded refrigerator jars.

Makes about 6 cups.

Soups

Quick Cold Borscht

Cold soups are delicious any time and Borscht has a tasty sweet-sour tang. For a hot soup — mix the beets, consommé, lemon juice, and onion. Serve and pass the sour cream.
1 large can beets
1 can condensed consommé
3 tsp. lemon juice
1 small onion
1 cucumber
1 cup commercial sour cream
Dill—if available

Put beets in blender with onion and soup, a small amount at a time. Add half a cup iced water to mixture and chill. Peel cucumber, remove seeds, and cut into small strips. Add to soup, season to taste. Serve topped with a dollop of cream sprinkled with dill.

Serves 6.

Quick Crab Bisque

This elegant, luxurious soup points up the delicate crab flavour. For additional luxury, add ¹/₂ cup of thinly sliced and sautéed mushrooms.
1 can cream of mushroom soup
1 can milk

6 oz. canned crabmeat
1/2 cup cream

Combine and heat but don't boil. Before serving add 1/4 cup sherry.

Serves 4.

Consommé Royale

This is one of the classic soups that show off culinary know-how. Quick and delicious, it shouldn't frighten calorie-counters.
Beat two eggs thoroughly. Add salt, pepper, and a tablespoon of finely chopped parsely. Heat a 10-inch frying pan or omelette pan and add one tablespoon of butter. When the butter is hot, but before it browns, pour in the egg mixture. Cook gently, lifting the edges to let the uncooked liquid slip beneath. As soon as set, flip the egg mixture onto a piece of wax paper. With sharp scissors cut into strips, or with tiny cookie cutters cut out shapes.
    Heat canned consommé to near boiling. Just before serving add 1/4 cup dry sherry or Madeira and the egg garnish. Serve immediately.

Crème Sénégale

The curry should be sufficient to be discerned but should not overpower the delicate, creamy chicken.
Mix one can cream of chicken soup as directed, stir in 1 to 2 teaspoons of curry powder, or to taste. Heat to extract flavour from the curry powder; do not boil. Serve reheated later or icy cold. Garnish the bowls with a slice of hard-cooked egg.

Serves 4.

Gazpacho

This soup-salad is Spanish in origin but frankly much tastier than the genuine mixture!
1/2 clove garlic
2 tsp. salt
1/4 tsp. pepper
1/2 cup slivered mushrooms
1/2 cup chopped onion
2 cups chopped peeled tomatoes
1 cup chopped red and green peppers
1 cup chopped cucumber
3 cups tomato juice
1 can condensed consommé

FIRST METHOD: crush garlic and combine all the ingredients in a glass bowl and chill for several hours. Serve with plain or garlic croutons.
SECOND METHOD: put juice, consommé, garlic, and seasoning in a bowl. Blend the vegetables leaving out a 1/4 cup of each for garnish. Add to liquid and chill. Serve with the garnish.
THIRD METHOD: blend liquids and add a dash of Tabasco. Serve the vegetables in separate bowls for guests to add as desired.

Serves 8-10.

Pea Soup

A rib-sticking meal in a soup bowl that conjures up memories of snowy days and wood-burning fires.
1 cup split peas
3 cups cold water
1 ham bone
1 onion finely chopped
1 cup finely chopped celery
3 quarts boiling water
2 bouillon cups
salt, pepper

Soak peas overnight in cold water or follow package directions. Combine remaining ingredients, apart from salt and pepper, cover. Bring to a boil, reduce heat and simmer three hours. During the last half hour of cooking taste for seasoning, and if liked, one large shredded carrot can be added.

Serves 10-12.

Tomato Bisque

This Bisque has no connection with tomato soup. It is simple to make, compliments the seafood, and the dash of vodka is the secret ingredient!

1 can condensed tomato soup
1 cup milk
1/2 cup table cream
Pinch of tarragon
1 tsp. chopped onion
1 tbsp. chopped chives or green onion
1 cup cooked shrimp, coarsely chopped
1/4 cup vodka

Stir together the first five ingredients and heat well but do not boil. Just before serving add the remaining ingredients. Soup bowls can be garnished with a slice of lemon.

Salads

How to Make a Super Salad

The best salads are the simple ones and some gourmets go so far as to say that only greens are permissible and that there is no place for a tomato or a radish in a salad. It's a matter of taste.

First buy the very best of ingredients: salad oil (corn or olive), wine vinegar, peppercorns, salt, herbs, and above all the freshest of greens. These can include spinach, escarole, chicory (in small amounts), and the many varieties of lettuce, the least of which is the familiar iceberg that is almost tasteless.

Don't wash lettuce, cucumber, celery or any ingredient until just before making the salad —which can be made early in the day provided it is cooled and no dressing is applied. Wash ingredients carefully, and dry even more carefully by patting with paper or linen towels or using one of the swing-around baskets sold at kitchen shops. Then tear the greens into bite-size pieces, slice everything thinly or cut into small pieces. There is nothing more ungainly than trying to get a too large piece of lettuce into the mouth while conversation is taking place.

After cutting and slivering, the mixture should be put into a wooden bowl, which may be lightly rubbed with garlic—a matter of taste. If garlic is enjoyed first throw some coarse salt into the bowl, then spear a peeled garlic clove with a specially reserved fork and rub it around the salt which will pick up the flavour, yet keep the garlic flavour from being overwhelming. Remove the salad bowl from the refrigerator at least a half hour before serving so that flavor develops—it can't if the ingredients are too cold. Just before serving add the dressing and toss. Taste for seasoning. Serve immediately.

Pick and Choose Salad Bar

One of the drawing cards at restaurants from coast to coast, and very adaptable to the home host who asks fellow workers in for a surprise supper, when the cocktail party guests stay on and on, when the weekend guests hug the pool.

Salad Bar

Romaine and Bibb lettuce
Spinach
Cherry tomatoes
1/2 lb. fresh mushrooms sliced
1 zucchini sliced
1 small cauliflower broken into flowerets
1 English-style cucumber—about 1 1/2 cups
1 cup sliced celery
1 cup chopped green onions
1/2 lb. slivered Swiss cheese
1 lb. thinly shredded meat, ham, tongue, etc.
1 - 8 oz. can salmon, drained and broken into chunks
1 - 8 oz. can of tuna, drained and chunked
1 - 8 oz. package frozen cooked shrimp

Place lettuce in salad bowl. Arrange remaining ingredients in individual bowls or on a large platter. Guests help themselves to the food. Supply a variety of dressings: Blue Cheese, French, Italian Style, Creamy Green Onion, et cetera.

Menu

A meal built around a Salad Bar and purchased foods.

Hot Onion Soup
Cheese Straws
Salad Bar
Croissants
Fresh Fruit   Cheese
Cookies

All the food is adaptable in quantity, the choice is enormous and just about everything can be purchased at a quick one stop shop.

For a Salad Bar party before arranging the salad, put the soup on to heat, pop the croissants into a warm oven. If from the baker, about 6 minutes at 350°F. If frozen, follow instructions. By the time wine is poured, salad arranged, the soup will be ready to be served in mugs, and the rolls will be warm and flaky.

SUMMER VARIATION: serve cold potato soup (Vichysoisse). A nice trick is to stir in sour cream and fresh chives before serving, and put one ounce of vodka in every soup bowl.

Bean Salad

This is a variation in salads and a great way to use left-over cooked beans, peas, or cauliflower.

1-9 oz. package of thawed frozen French-style green beans or use garden-fresh Frenched beans cooked until lightly tender
1 onion thinly sliced
1/2 lb. mushrooms thinly sliced
Italian style dressing

Pour boiling water over beans, drain immediately. Combine with other vegetables. Add about 1/3 cup salad dressing and toss. Pour into screwtopped jar. Place in cooler chest. Before serving spoon into a bowl and surround with hard cooked eggs and tomato wedges.

Spinach and Mushroom Salad

Another salad that seems to belong only to restaurants. It shouldn't because it is quick to assemble and the flavour is delicious. It is equally at home with cold poached fish as it is with Cornish hen.

1 package (10 oz.) spinach
1 cup fresh sliced mushrooms
1/3 cup oil
3 tbsp. lemon juice
1/2 tsp. salt
1/4 tsp. pepper
Garlic salt

Trim and tear spinach leaves into large pieces, discard the stems. Toss in mushrooms. Combine oil, lemon, salt and pepper to make dressing. Season to taste.

Serves 4 to 6.

Meat

Beef Bourguignon

Really a beef stew—but with a difference and, like all stews, it tastes better the next day.

3/4 lb. small fresh mushrooms
3 tbsp. butter
12-18 very small onions
3 tbsp. shortening
3 lbs. lean boneless beef chuck, cut in 2-inch cubes
3 tbsp. flour
1 can (10 oz.) beef broth or stock
2 cups dry red wine
1 tbsp. tomato paste
1-4 cloves of garlic, finely minced
1 tbsp. thyme
1 tsp. salt
Freshly-ground black pepper
4 sprigs parsley
1 bay leaf
Chopped fresh parsley for garnish

In large skillet, sauté mushrooms lightly in butter. Remove and set aside. Add shortening to pan, and brown the onions well over moderate heat. Remove and set aside with mushrooms. Add beef chunks to pan a few at a time, browning them well on all sides (add extra fat if needed). Remove beef to a heavy 4 or 5-quart casserole. To fat remaining in skillet, stir in flour, then beef stock, wine, tomato paste. Bring to boil, whisking constantly as sauce thickens. Add garlic, thyme, salt, a little pepper, parsley and bay leaf. Pour sauce over beef in casserole. It should almost cover the meat; add more wine or stock if necessary. Cover casserole tightly and bake in 350°F. oven for 2-3 hours or until meat is tender. Gently stir in onions and mushrooms. Bake 20-30 minutes longer. Remove bay leaf; skim off any fat. Taste sauce and adjust seasoning if necessary. Sprinkle beef with chopped parsley and serve directly from casserole, with French bread and red wine.

Serves 6-8.

Beef Courvoisier

Can a steak dish be different? This one is and once the method is mastered it is a great standby. A tasty variation for cooking steaks. The chief difference is in the method, which is to dust the steaks with garlic and pepper, sear them quickly on both sides at high heat, then put them on a serving platter in a 250°F. oven for 15 minutes. They will be pink through. Add 1/4 cup of red wine (per person) and 1 tablespoon butter to the pan juices, stir and simmer for a couple of minutes to blend perfectly, pour over the steaks, and flame them at the table with one oz. Cognac per steak. The resulting sauce is highly esteemed by bread and gravy devotees.

Ground Beef Stroganoff

Originally "Bif Stroganof", this Russian favourite was made from beef strips, sour cream, and mushroom sauce and served on rice. The Russians have long enjoyed the appeal of the sour taste and they use sour cream lavishly. By using ground beef length of preparation, cooking time, and cost drop significantly. For variety, Stroganoff can be served on noodles.

Stroganoff, made with ground beef, is a dish with subtle, creamy yet spicy sauce. It is easy to prepare, attractive, and lends itself to self-service. It is perfect for a chafing dish or electric skillet, but is served equally well from the kitchen in a casserole or serving dish.

Every good buffet combines hot and cold food temperatures. Guests will appreciate a hearty green salad of cauliflower, celery, tomato, cucumber, and green onion with crisp lettuce leaves.

1 1/2 cup chopped onion
2 tbsp. fat
1 lb. ground beef
2 tbsp. flour
1 tsp. salt
1 garlic clove, minced
1/4 tsp. pepper
1 - 10 oz. can mushrooms, drained
1 - 10 oz. can condensed cream of chicken soup
1/2 pint (1 1/4 cups) dairy sour cream
3 cups cooked noodles (6 ozs. uncooked)

Sauté onion in fat until transparent. Add ground beef and brown. Drain off excess fat. Stir in flour, salt, garlic, pepper, then mushrooms and soup. Bring to boil, then reduce heat and simmer uncovered 10 minutes. Stir in sour cream and heat thoroughly but do not boil. Serve over noodles.

6 Servings.

This is a recipe that can be doubled or tripled without a problem.

Broccoli Ham Bake

This recipe is a little time-consuming but the results are worth it. Not only is it deliciously flavoured but there is a texture contrast and the colour combination is most appetizing.
1-1/2 lb. broccoli
Boiling water
3/4 tsp. salt
12 slices cooked ham (3/4 pound)
5 tbsp. butter
5 tbsp. flour
1/2 tsp. salt
1/8 tsp. pepper

1/2 tsp. dry mustard
1 1/2 cups milk
3/4 cup grated cheddar cheese

Trim broccoli. Stand upright (stem ends down) in 1-inch boiling water. Sprinkle with salt. Cover and cook gently until almost tender (about 10 minutes). Drain and divide in 12 portions. Roll a ham slice around each portion. Arrange in a greased baking dish. Melt butter. Blend in flour and seasonings. Gradually add milk. Stir and cook until smooth and thick. Add cheese and stir until melted. Pour over ham rolls. Bake at 350°F. until broccoli is tender (20-25 minutes).

6 servings.

Chili Con Carne

There are as many chili recipes as there are curry recipes. Just add herbs, spices and vegetables to suit yourself. Some like it very hot, others add diced potatoes and Texans like more vinegar.
1/2 cup sliced onions
2 tbs. oil
1/2 lb. ground beef
1 cup canned tomatoes
1 1/2 tsp. chili powder
1 tbsp. vinegar
1 tsp. sugar
Dash of garlic
2 cups canned red kidney beans

Cook onion until tender, add ground beef until it loses redness. Add remaining ingredients and adjust seasoning. Simmer uncovered for at least an hour, stirring occasionally. If the mixture becomes too thick, add some tomato juice. Serve with hot crusty French bread and a green salad.

This serves four but just keep adding for a crowd.

Ham

A ham sounds extravagant but it gives value —from a beautiful party meat to slices cut off to be broiled for brunch and finally the necessary ingredient for split pea or dried bean soups.

Place ham, fat side up, on a rack in an open pan. Use no water and no lid. Bake in a 325°F. oven. To bake a ready-to-eat ham:

Heating Schedule

16 to 20 lbs	8 mins/lb	2 1/2 hours
12 to 15 lbs	10 mins/lb	2 hours
8 to 11 lbs	10 mins/lb	1 1/4 hours

When meat thermometer is used, heat to an internal temperature of 130°F.

To Glaze Ham

After ham is baked, remove rind. Score fat in squares or diamonds. Cover ham with one of the following glazes and return to a 400°F. oven for about 15 minutes or until glaze is shiny. Stud with cloves and garnish with fruit—pineapple rings or chunks, sautéed banana strips, sliced peaches or apricot halves.

Ham Glazes

Red Wine—mix 2 cups brown sugar with 1/2 cup red wine.

Orange-mustard—mix 1 can (6 ounces) thawed frozen concentrated orange juice with 2 tablespoons dry mustard and 1 tablespoon Worcestershire sauce.

Currant jelly—soften 1 cup currant jelly with 2 tablespoons hot water; stir in 2 tablespoons prepared mustard and 1/4 teaspoon ground cloves.

Lazy daisy—glaze unscored top with 1/2 cup honey until it is shiny. Remove from oven, decorate with daisies of halved seedless grapes and maraschino cherries.

Peach—1 1/2 cups brown sugar, 1/3 cup juice from canned peaches, 3 tablespoons vinegar, 3/4 teaspoon cloves. Trim ham with peach halves.

Honey-Garlic Glazed Ribs

The ultimate in barbecued foods but just as popular at a finger-licking indoor party. And if you feel expansive serve them as appetizers at a crowd get-together.

5-6 lb. pork or lamb ribs
1 cup liquid honey
$^1/_2$ cup lime juice
4 cloves of garlic, crushed
2 tsp. salt
$^1/_4$ cup chopped fresh mint
1 green pepper, cut in strips
Lime slices and mint for garnish

Cut ribs in serving-size pieces. Simmer ribs in salted water until tender, about 1$^1/_2$ hours. Drain and arrange in large shallow pan. Combine honey, lime juice, garlic, and salt. Sprinkle mint and green pepper strips over ribs; pour honey mixture over. Allow to marinate at least 2 hours; drain and reserve marinade. Grill ribs over hot coals (or in oven broiler) until crisp, well browned and glazed, turning and brushing often with reserved marinade. To serve, sprinkle lime slices, mint, and green pepper strips over ribs for garnish.

8-12 servings.

Javanese Curry

Curry is delicious! Have it mild, medium, or hot. And look through your local delicatessen for Oriental-type breads. Usually they are canned, come with directions, and really do compliment the curry.

1 medium onion, cut in chunks
1 medium green pepper, cut in chunks
2 tbsp. fat
1 lb. ground beef
1 tsp. salt
1 to 2 tbsp. curry powder
1 cup raisins
$^1/_2$ cup water
1 cup canned or frozen peas

Sauté onion and green pepper in fat until tender. Add beef and brown. Drain off excess fat. Add remaining ingredients except peas, and simmer 20 minutes. Add peas and simmer 10 minutes more. Serve over rice with selection of condiments*.

6 servings.

---

*Curries are usually served with condiments to act as a moderation for this fiery spice. Suggested condiments are chutney sauce, mandarin orange sections, walnuts, banana slices, tomatoes, coconut, cucumber, peaches. A basic curry has many variations depending on the condiments you choose. Remember curry is only as hot as you make it.

Lasagna

One of the most glamorous of casseroles. It isn't frightening or complicated to make and the following recipe serves 10 people. A great party dish when served with a spinach, lettuce, and mushroom salad, bread and followed by Spumoni ice cream and bar cookies.

Lasagna can be made in advance and reheated. An added advantage is that it freezes well. In fact, the following recipe can be divided between two medium-sized casseroles and frozen. Freeze unbaked.

Sauce:
2 tbsp. oil
1$^1/_2$ lbs. ground round or chuck beef
1 medium onion chopped
$^1/_4$ tsp. garlic salt
1 tsp. salt
$^1/_2$ tsp. pepper
1 tsp. rosemary
14-oz. can tomato sauce
10-oz. can mushrooms *or* stems and pieces
1 chopped green pepper
2 cups hot water
Other Ingredients:
8 lasagna noodles
2 tsp. salt
1 cup cottage cheese
8 large slices Mozzarella cheese (2 packages)

In a large pot or very large frying pan sauté the meat and onion in the oil and brown lightly, stirring all of the time to break up the meat. Add the garlic salt, salt, pepper, rosemary, tomato sauce, green pepper, mushrooms, and hot water and simmer uncovered for 30 minutes.

Meanwhile cook the 8 lasagna noodles in a large pot in 2 or 3 quarts of boiling water with the 2 teaspoons salt for 20 minutes. Drain in colander and rinse in cold water to prevent clinging together.

Into a very large pan or small roaster (or foil pan) measure 2 cups of the sauce. Arrange layers as follows: 4 lasagna noodles, cottage cheese, 4 slices Mozzarella, *half* of remaining sauce, 4 lasagna noodles, *all* of remaining sauce and finally 4 slices Mozzarella. Cover snugly with buttered doubled foil. Bake at 350°F. for 30 to 40 minutes. Let rest 15 minutes before serving for cutting into squares.

Manicotti Stuffed with Meat

There is no better hot dish for a buffet. And the recipe can be doubled or tripled. The savory stuffed pasta looks as good as it tastes.

Filling:

1/2 lb. ground beef
1/4 lb. ground pork
1/4 lb. ground veal
1 egg
1/2 cup bread crumbs
1/3 cup grated Parmesan cheese
2 tbsp. chopped parsley
1 tbsp. lemon juice
1 tbsp. cheese spread
1/4 tsp. garlic powder
1/4 tsp. oregano
1/2 tsp. salt
1/8 tsp. pepper

8 oz. Manicotti
14 oz. can spaghetti sauce with meat
1/2 cup grated Parmesan cheese

Combine filling ingredients. Chill.

Prepare Manicotti in large amount of boiling salted water as package directs.
Drain.
Grease 9″ x 13″ baking dish. Stuff Manicotti with prepared filling. Arrange in single layer. Pour spaghetti sauce over and sprinkle with grated Parmesan cheese.

Bake, covered, in moderately hot 375°F. oven 30-35 minutes.

4-6 servings.

Orange Glazed Pork Chops with Baked Squash

The flavour of orange seems to increase the meaty taste of the pork in this update of a very old recipe that is ideal for family or party dinners during the fall and winter.

6-8 thick pork chops
1/4 cup brown sugar
1 tsp. cornstarch
1 cup orange juice
2 tsp. grated orange rind
1 tsp. salt
1/4 cup finely chopped onion

In large skillet, brown pork chops on both sides; sprinkle with salt and pepper. Drain off excess fat. Combine remaining ingredients and pour over chops. Cover and simmer until chops are tender, stirring occasionally and adding a little water if necessary. Remove lid and continue to cook while spooning sauce over chops to glaze. Arrange on platter with wedges of baked squash. Brush squash with some of the orange glaze if desired.

6-8 servings.

South Seas Meatballs

Meatballs are easy to make and this recipe can be used as a main course or as an appetizer. For a main course pass a large bowl of rice—plain or tossed with raisins and nutmeats.

1½ lb. ground beef
Mushroom caps, about 4 oz.
2 tbsp. sugar
1 tbsp. cornstarch
2 tbsp. vinegar
2 tsp. soy sauce
1 can (14 oz.) pineapple tidbits
1-2 tbsp. light rum
1 small green pepper, cut in small pieces

Season ground beef with salt and pepper and shape into small balls. Brown evenly on all sides in a little hot oil. Remove from pan. Sauté mushroom caps lightly; remove from pan and drain off excess fat. Combine sugar, cornstarch, vinegar, soy sauce, and liquid drained from pineapple. Pour into pan; cook and stir over moderate heat until smooth and thickened; stir in rum. Return meatballs and mushrooms to sauce in pan. Add pineapple tidbits and green pepper. Heat thoroughly, spooning sauce over meatballs to glaze. Keep hot in chafing dish.

Spaghetti Caruso

A main course dish that can be expanded, and expanded.

Sauce
1 large can tomatoes
1 large can tomato paste
1 clove minced garlic
¼ cup chopped parsley
1 tsp. sugar
2 tsp. Basil
1 tsp. Marjoram
Black pepper and salt to taste
1 cup chopped onions
1 cup green pepper in strips (half for garnish)
2 tsp. oil
1 lb. chicken livers
½ lb. mushrooms

Sauté onions and green peppers until limp. Add remaining ingredients and simmer for two hours. Sauté the chicken livers and mushrooms until the livers lose their pinkness. Add to sauce and simmer 5 minutes. Just before serving add remaining green pepper slivers. Serve over hot spaghetti.

Spaghetti with Meatballs

Spaghetti and noodles make tasty family and party dishes, all of them can be frozen, or made ahead, refrigerated, and reheated. And the charm of them is the fact that they require few accompaniments, are adaptable to large scale entertaining and require only a green salad. Above all, they can be eaten with a fork when seating is at a premium. However, supply the largest size table napkins you own!

Meatballs:
½ lb. ground beef
¼ lb. ground pork
¼ lb. ground veal
2 eggs
½ cup dry bread crumbs
⅓ cup grated Parmesan cheese
¼ tsp. garlic powder
½ tsp. oregano
1½ tbsp. chopped parsley
1 tsp. salt
¼ tsp. pepper
Dry bread crumbs
½ cup vegetable oil
14 oz. can spaghetti sauce with meat
16 oz. spaghetti
⅓ cup grated Parmesan cheese

Mix together meatball ingredients. Shape into small balls. Roll balls in additional dry bread crumbs.

Brown meatballs in the oil. Add spaghetti sauce; simmer 20 minutes.

Prepare spaghetti in large amount of boiling salted water as package directs. Drain.

Pour sauce over cooked spaghetti arranged on serving platter. Sprinkle with grated Parmesan cheese.

6-8 servings.

Tourtière

The traditional winter dish of Quebec that's a must for Christmas Eve parties. Tradition aside, it is a good meat pie for cold evenings. Tourtière and mulled cider are great after a day in the snow. Or, serve it with hearty wine or cold beer after a TV game party.

1 lb. lean pork shoulder
1 lb. lean veal shoulder
1 cup water
1 onion chopped
1 clove garlic, chopped
1 tsp. salt
1/4 tsp. pepper
1/2 tsp. nutmeg
Dash mace
Dash cayenne
1/4 tsp. celery salt
Pastry

Remove meat from bones and chop meat finely but do not grind. Place in a saucepan with meat bones and next nine ingredients. Cover and simmer over medium heat until meat is tender, 45-60 minutes, adding water if necessary as the meat cooks. When cooked, the mixture should be thick. Remove bones and cool. Line two 8" pie plates with pastry. Fill with the meat mixture, add top crust, cut to let steam escape. Bake in a 425°F. oven 40 minutes.

Serves 4 to 6.

Poultry

Chicken Casserole

A smooth rich chicken dish with an unusual twist—artichokes.

2-2 1/2 lb. frying chickens, cut in serving pieces
4 tbsp. butter or margarine
1/2 cup chopped onion
1/3 cup flour
1 1/2 tsp. dried rosemary
1 1/2 tsp. salt
1/4 tsp. pepper
1 cup chicken broth
1 cup dry white wine
1 lb. mushrooms
1 package frozen artichokes thawed (optional)*

Brown chicken pieces in butter. Transfer to 13 x 9-inch baking dish or shallow 3-quart casserole. Arrange artichoke hearts among chicken pieces. Add onions to skillet and cook just till tender. Blend in flour and seasonings; add chicken broth and wine. Cook, stirring constantly, until mixture is thickened. Add mushrooms. Spoon evenly over chicken, (casserole may be made in advance, covered, and refrigerated). Bake, covered in 375°F. oven 55 to 60 minutes or until chicken is tender. If chilled allow 20 to 25 minutes more.

Makes 8 servings.
Serve with buttered noodles.

---

*If you substitute canned artichokes, drain and add ten minutes before serving.

Chicken Curry

A curry dinner or buffet is fun. Everyone enjoys sampling the condiments. Just be sure to have plenty of them and a generous rice bowl.

3-4 lb. chicken
4 tbsp. oil
1 medium onion, finely chopped
3 cloves of garlic, finely minced
2 tbsp. imported curry powder
Salt, pepper, thyme
Chicken stock or water

Cut chicken in small pieces. In large skillet or Dutch oven, fry onion and garlic with curry powder in hot oil. Add chicken pieces a few at a time and brown lightly, sprinkling with a little salt, pepper and thyme (or add a stalk of dried thyme with the liquid). Add a little stock or water, cover tightly and simmer until chicken is tender, adding more liquid if necessary. Adjust seasoning as desired. Makes about 6 servings.

Serve with hot rice and 3 or 4 side dish condiments: grated coconut, chopped cucumber, chopped tomatoes, chutney, sliced bananas.

Chicken and Mushrooms

This is a simple adaptation of one of the great French recipes. The only reminder—go easy on the tarragon. It must not overwhelm the dish.

In a large pan brown chicken pieces in a mixture of 1/4 cup butter and 2 tablespoons oil until golden brown on both sides. Season with salt and pepper. Lower heat and cook covered for 35 minutes or until tender. Baste occasionally with pan juices. In another pan sauté 1 pound slivered mushrooms and 2 tablespoons chopped onion. When chicken is tender remove to a warm platter. Skim off any excess fat from pan juices, and add any mushroom juices. Simmer, adding 1/2 cup whipping cream and cook until slightly reduced. Add a sprig of fresh tarragon or a 1/4 teaspoon dried tarragon. Pour sauce over chicken and arrange mushroom slices over all. (The chicken can be browned and simmering while you wait for guests).

Chicken Livers with Madeira

Even those who don't care for liver seem to like the delicate flavour of chicken livers. The dash of Madeira adds richness. The addition of mushrooms makes this dish even more heavenly.

1 pound chicken livers
3 tbsp. oil
3 tbsp. chopped onion
salt and pepper
1/4 cup Madeira

Trim the livers. Heat the oil until hot, quickly stir in livers, turning constantly. Cook approximately six minutes. (The livers should be brown outside and rosy inside.) Add onion and stir, salt and pepper to taste. Lower heat, scrape and loosen any pan scraps; add Madeira and heat until the mixture bubbles. Serve over rice, noodles or crisp dry toast.

Serves 4.

Chicken Paprika

It is smooth, creamy, and tangy and the sauce is so good you should serve this with noodles, rice, or French bread for soppings. Traditionally it is served with noodles sprinkled with poppyseeds—but that's not everybody's taste. However, try it—it tastes nutty and crunchy.

1 - 3 1/2 pound chicken, cut up
1/2 cup chopped onion
1/4 cup vegetable oil
1-2 tsp. paprika
Salt to taste
1/4 cup hot water
1 cup commercial sour cream
1 tbsp. flour
1 1/2 tbsp. water
1 tsp. lemon juice
Chopped parsley

Sauté the onion in the oil, remove, and brown the chicken. Then sprinkle with the cooked onion, paprika, salt, and hot water. Cover and simmer over low heat for 45 minutes or until tender. Remove chicken to a hot platter and keep warm. To the skillet add the flour stirred into the water and cook over gentle heat removing all the scrapings into the sauce. Add the sour cream; heat but do not boil. When hot, add the lemon juice and stir in the parsley. Pour over the chicken.

Serves 4 generously.

Hunter's Chicken

Batter-coated finger-licking fried chicken, cole-slaw, and the bonus bread can be very good straight from the box when you are pressed for time. When you want a change and still don't have much time, try this recipe.

2 chopped tomatoes
1/4 lb. chopped mushrooms or one can drained
2 tbsp. dried onion flakes
Salt, pepper, dash of tarragon or oregano
2/3 cup white wine and juice of a lemon
1/2 can bouillon
2 tsp. cornstarch
Carry-home fried chicken

Mix cornstarch to a paste with the wine. Using a large skillet (10-12 inch) add all ingredients except wine paste. Bring to a boil, simmer for 2 minutes, slowly add wine paste. Cook stirring until mixture thickens, add fried carry-home chicken pieces and simmer until hot and blended.
BREAD: slice, spread with soft butter, sprinkle with dried garlic, parsley, and herbs to taste. Wrap in foil and put in a 400°F. oven while chicken heats.
COLESLAW: Add one chopped apple to a 2-4 serving of carry-home coleslaw.

Roast Duckling with Orange Glaze

A great classic dish and, like all famous recipes, it isn't very time-consuming or complicated.

2 (4-5 lb.) ducklings
1/2 tsp. salt
Freshly ground black pepper
1/2 cup honey
1/4 cup orange juice
4 cups brandy

Rub cavity of ducklings with salt and pepper. Prick with a fork all over. Place ducklings on a rack in a roasting pan. Roast in a 350°F. oven for 1 1/2-2 hours or until the meat is tender.

Meanwhile, prepare the glaze. Combine honey and orange juice. Place on simmer until heated. Add the brandy. Baste ducklings with glaze twice, 15 minutes before serving. Heat and serve the remainder at the table after carving the duck.

Spaghetti Tetrazzini

A classic Italian main course dish. It is elegant enough for a buffet party or a superb way of using up leftover chicken or turkey.

4 chicken breasts
2 tbsp. butter or margarine
1/4 cup dry white wine or chicken broth
1 1/2 cups sliced fresh mushrooms
1/2 tsp. salt
1/4 tsp. pepper
Sauce:
1/3 cup butter or margarine
1/3 cup flour
1 1/2 cups chicken broth
1 cup milk
1/4 tsp. salt
Dash pepper
1/4 tsp. paprika
1/2 cup grated Parmesan cheese, divided
12 oz. spaghetti

Remove chicken from bone and cut in strips. In frypan, brown strips of chicken in butter. Add wine, sliced mushrooms, salt, and pepper. Simmer until chicken is tender.

In a small saucepan, prepare cream sauce. Blend together butter and flour. Gradually add chicken broth and milk, salt, pepper, and paprika. Cook and stir until thickened and smooth. Add chicken mixture and 1/4 cup of grated Parmesan cheese. Simmer 2-3 minutes.

Prepare spaghetti in large amount of boiling salted water as package directs.
Drain.

Pour prepared sauce over cooked spaghetti. Sprinkle with remaining grated Parmesan cheese.

4-6 servings.

Spanish Chicken

Once again you can begin with carry-home chicken and with a little of this and that you have a different and delicious supper.

1 package Spanish Rice
1 cup frozen peas
2 tablespoons dried onion
Sliced ripe olives

6-8 pieces ready fried carry-home chicken. Prepare rice mix as directed, stir in remaining ingredients and put in a baking dish, keeping chicken to the top. Bake uncovered at 350°F. for about ½ hour.

Turkey Tetrazzini

If after-holiday parties are a headache and leftovers another pain, toss together this great Italian casserole. Makes a marvelous crowd dish.

1-8 oz. package of spaghetti or noodles
1-8 oz. can tomatoes
1 can beef consommé or bouillon or one bouillon cube and 10 oz. water
½ to one cup chopped onion
4-5 cups cut-up cooked chicken or turkey
2 tbsp. each flour and butter
1 cup evaporated milk
½ pound grated cheddar cheese (about 2 cups)

Cook pasta and drain. Simmer tomatoes and bouillon ten minutes, then add onion. Season to taste: salt, pepper, dash of cayenne, Worcestershire Sauce. Add meat.

Additional but optional: add one can mushrooms drained or a cup of sliced fresh mushrooms as well as ¼ cup chopped parsley.

Mix together and set on one side.

Blend the butter and the flour and melt in a small saucepan over low heat, stir in the milk and half the cheese. Cook, stirring constantly, until thick and smooth. Gradually add to tomato-bouillon mixture. Mix in pasta and turn into a lightly greased 2½ quart casserole. Sprinkle with remaining cheese and bake at 350°F. for 30-40 minutes. Serves 8 generously. If you plan to freeze the casserole, do not top with cheese, do not bake. Before cooking, thaw overnight in the refrigerator.

Serves 6-8.

Seafood

Baked Red Snapper
(or other whole fish suitable for baking)
One 3-4 pound fish will give 4-6 servings. Remove backbone if desired. Whole fish may be stuffed, or the inside spread with finely chopped onion and sprinkled liberally with seasoned salt and black pepper. Place fish in well-oiled baking pan, cover loosely with buttered paper or foil. Bake in 400°F. oven about 30 minutes (10-15 minutes per inch of thickness), basting occasionally with butter if desired. Serve whole on large platter garnished with lemon.

Paella

Named for the large open pan used in Spain to cook and serve. However, you can use any pan that's large enough because Paella seems to keep on growing.

½ lb. uncooked shrimp
2 frozen rock lobster tails
1 can clams (or one dozen fresh)
1 can mussels (or one and a half dozen fresh)
1 frying chicken cut into pieces
¼ lb. piece of salami or other cured sausage
1 clove garlic
1 onion, chopped
3 fresh tomatoes or one small can of tomatoes
1 small package frozen peas

2 cups rice
Saffron*, salt, pepper, water
1/4 cup oil

Cook seafood and set aside. In a heavy skillet or a paella heat the oil and add the chicken pieces. Cook until well browned. Add the chopped garlic and onion and cook until the onion is limp. Add salt, pepper to taste, and either chopped fresh or canned tomatoes. Cook for 10 minutes.

Add rice and four cups of water and stir to combine. Then heat over low heat for 15 minutes. Add the frozen peas and continue to cook for another 10 minutes. Dissolve the saffron in a spoonful of water and pour over mixture. With a large spoon turn the rice and the mixture over from top to bottom so that it is all mixed and the rice is a pale gold. Continue cooking for another 10 minutes, then add the shelled shrimp and the lobster tails which can be cut into portions. Test the mixture for doneness.

If cooked in a paella dish it can go directly to the table, if cooked in a skillet transfer to a shallow casserole. Before serving add the cooked clams and mussels and gently heat.

Serves 6-8.

The charm of paella is that any mixture of chicken, fish, and vegetables can be cooked and served together. And the dish can be extended by using more rice. It can be garnished with slivered almonds, pimiento strips, sautéed mushrooms, or sliced stuffed olives.

---

* Saffron: this is the most expensive spice in the world. If you use saffron let it soak for a few minutes in warm water to draw out the yellow colour. As a substitute for colour but not flavour, use a 1/2 teaspoonful of mace. After mixing check colour. Use a little more if desired but watch the additions carefully. Too much mace gives a rank flavour.

Seafood Casserole

Friends descending for lunch or dinner and nothing prepared? With a collection of canned seafood and five minutes preparation, this is a dish for the gods. Serve it with noodles or rice and end the meal with fruit and cheese.

1 can shrimp
1 can lobster
1 can crab
3 tbsp. flour
3 tbsp. butter
1 1/2 cups light cream
salt and pepper to taste
1 cup grated mild cheese
1 tsp. commercial French mustard
1/4 cup sherry
1/2 cup buttered crumbs

Heat oven to 350°F. Grease a casserole. Mix seafood in a large bowl. Mix flour and butter together to make a paste and heat in saucepan over low heat. Gradually add the cream and stir until the sauce thickens. Add seasoning and cheese. Remove from heat and stir in mustard and sherry. Pour over the seafood and mix well, then scrape into the casserole. Sprinkle with buttered crumbs. Bake about 30 minutes until lightly brown and bubbley.

Vegetables

Seaside Avocados

1 – 7 oz. tin solid white tuna, drained
1 medium tomato, peeled and chopped
2 tsp. lemon juice
1 tsp. Worcestershire sauce
1/2 tsp. salt
1/4 tsp. Tabasco
3 avocados
Black olives

Combine first 6 ingredients. Peel avocados, cut in

half and remove pits. Fill hollows with tuna mixture and garnish with olives.

Serves 6.

Serve as a main course salad or quarter the avocados and turn into a salad appetizer.

Jamaican Rice and Peas

A great tropical dish for poolside parties, and a perfect extender and accompaniment to ribs or chicken.

1 cup small red peas
2 cups rice
1 small onion, finely chopped (or 2-3 scallions)
1 tbsp. butter
Small piece of hot pepper, optional
Salt to taste

Boil peas until tender in 3 cups salted water. Drain and measure the cooking liquid; add water to make 4 cups. Return liquid to peas in saucepan; add rice, onion, butter, hot pepper if desired, and salt to taste if needed. Simmer covered until liquid is absorbed and rice is tender. Makes about 12 servings.

Note: If possible, 1 cup coconut milk made from grated coconut should be used as part of cooking liquid for the rice. To make coconut milk, cut or break coconut meat into small pieces (it is not necessary to remove the brown skin); grate coconut into a bowl; add an equal quantity of warm water. (Coconut may be grated in some electric blenders with an equal quantity of water). Squeeze the coconut meat with its liquid through a bag of muslin or double cheesecloth, into a bowl. Wring the cloth firmly to extract all the milk; discard the pulp.

Cinnamon Sweet Potatoes

1/4 cup finely chopped onion
1 tbsp. Worcestershire sauce
2 tbsp. brown sugar

Summer Drinks

Long, icy cold drinks with a fruit base are refreshing and welcome as the temperature rises. No one would attempt to make all the varieties shown at one party—these are just an indication of the changes that can be rung with glasses and garnishes. For recipes see the chapter on drinks.

½ cup water
¼ cup lemon juice
2 tbsp. chili sauce
½ tsp. cinnamon
4 sweet potatoes, boiled in their jackets.

Mix first 7 ingredients together and simmer for 5 mins. Peel cooked potatoes and slice into shallow buttered baking dish. Pour sauce over top and bake at 400°F. for 15 minutes.

Serves 6.

Yams

¼ cup light brown sugar, firmly packed
½ tsp. salt
¾ tsp. cinnamon
2 cans (19 ounces) yams, drained
⅓ cup melted butter or margarine

Combine brown sugar, salt, and cinnamon. Slice yams ¼-inch thick lengthwise and place a layer in a greased 8″ round shallow baking dish. Sprinkle lightly with some sugar mixture and spoon on some melted butter. Arrange another layer starting at edges of dish, overlapping slightly. Sprinkle with some sugar mixture and butter. Bake in a 350°F. oven for 25 minutes or until yams are hot and sugar is bubbly.

Serves 4 to 6.

Eggs and Cheese

Fondu

Swiss and French fondu are made with old cheese and new wine. Old cheese doesn't glob and new wine is acidic which helps break down the cheese. To approximate these conditions, the cheese should be grated the night before, and the lemon juice added to the wine. You'll never taste it.
¾ lb. grated Gruyère cheese
Dash of Cayenne
2 tbsp. flour
1½ cups dry white wine

Beef Bourguignon
A hearty, spicy dressed-up beef stew.

Salad Bar
A large platter of vegetables, seafood, hard-cooked eggs, and other good things together with oil and vinegar for a help-yourself salad.

Glazed Fruit Tart
A rich thin shell holds a splendid array of colourful fruits under a light and not-too-sweet glaze.

Irish Coffee
Fresh, hot, strong coffee poured over Irish Whiskey liqueur and topped with a layer of thick whipped cream.

2-3 tbsp. lemon juice
1 to 2 cloves garlic
¼ cup whipping cream
3 tbsp. brandy or 2 tbsp. kirsch

Toss cheese with cayenne and flour. Heat wine, lemon juice, and garlic until simmering. Keep the heat low and gradually stir in handfuls of the cheese mixture using a fork. Keep the action steady and wait for each addition to dissolve. When thick and creamy, lower heat and add sufficient cream to make the fondu thick enough to coat a spoon. Season with salt, freshly ground pepper, and remove garlic cloves.

Add brandy or kirsch to taste (kirsch makes the dish slightly sweeter).

Place chafing dish container over hot water, put heater in place. Serve immediately with pieces of crusty French bread speared with long fondu sticks.

This can be made an hour before guests arrive and set over warm water, if it thickens, add a little more cream.

The Elegant Pot-Luck-Omelets

Buy a good quality omelet pan from a kitchen supply shop—and keep it only for omelets. Omelets should be light and tender, and can be a main course or an unusual dessert. Practice makes an omelet, and should you fail, think nothing of it, serve the mixture as scrambled eggs and try another time.

Serve omelets with crisp bread, butter, and a salad; dessert omelets with fruit sauces and hot coffee.
Omelet mixture (one serving)
2 eggs
1 tbsp. water
Dash of salt and pepper
1 tbsp. butter
Beat all ingredients except the butter

(Tip: mix a party size batch by multiplying the ingredients, then pour a ½ cup mixture per serving.)

Heat an 8-inch omelet pan, add butter and heat until it sizzles. Tilt pan to butter sides. Pour in mixture. Keep heat at medium. Tilt and lift the edge of the cooked mixture so that the egg runs underneath. Cook 2-3 minutes. Spoon filling on to cooked egg. Roll up omelet and slide on a plate.

Hollandaise

Hollandaise is one of the glamour sauces. Made with a blender it won't curdle and it is all done in minutes. Excellent over poached eggs. The celebrated Eggs Benedict are simply poached eggs on cooked ham on a split, toasted English muffin. Hollandaise gives cauliflower sparkle and is the classic sauce with poached salmon, sole, or other delicate fish. Try it with fresh asparagus too.

In a small saucepan heat to bubbling, but don't brown, ½ cup of butter. (The unsalted is best.) Into the blender put 3 egg yolks or 2 whole eggs, 2 tbsp. lemon juice, ½ tsp. salt, a dash of cayenne (if liked).

Cover blender and turn to low speed. Remove cover and pour in the hot butter. The butter-and-egg mixture should thicken in the blender. If not, pour the sauce into the small saucepan and gently stir over a very low heat. Don't rush this or you'll have scrambled, buttery eggs.

Serves 4.

Hard-Cooked Egg Casserole

This can be thrifty or party. Either way it is simple, delicious, and serves 4 generously.

8 eggs
2 cups wide noodles (packed)
2 qts. water
1 tsp. salt (first amount)
3 tbsp. margarine
2 tbsp. chopped green pepper

2 tbsp. chopped onion
1 tsp. salt (second amount)
2 tbsp. flour
1½ cup milk
1 cup shredded cheese
1 cup fresh breadcrumbs (preferably whole wheat)

Now be careful hard-cooking the eggs. The approved and successful method is to put them in a pot, cover with cold water, bring quickly to boil. Reduce heat at once to simmer, cover, and cook over lowest possible heat for 15 minutes. At once flood with cold water to chill. (This method prevents discolouring of surface of the yolk.)

Roll the eggs between your palms to crack the shells and carefully peel.

Meanwhile cook the noodles in salted water (1 tsp.) at least 15 minutes until tender. Drain through colander and tip into large shallow casserole. (I used an oval stainless steel casserole 12 x 7 inches.)

Cut eggs in halves crosswise and stand them, cut side up, in noodles, pressing them down a little to make them steady in the "nest" of noodles.

In a frying pan melt the margarine and gently sauté the green pepper and onion until soaked but not brown. Stir in flour and salt (second) amount) and when mixed stir in milk until thick. Stir in cheese. Pour hot sauce all over eggs and sprinkle crumbs on top.

Bake at 350°F. for 20 minutes until bubbly and brown. For a party add drained shrimp, tuna, or salmon.

Noodles Alfredo

So quick to make, and yet it is not only delicious but famous as one of the classics of Italian cooking. In fact one restauranteur made his name by serving Noodles Alfredo with gold serving spoons.

12 oz. pkg. wide noodles
1 cup dairy sour cream
2 tbsp. soft butter or margarine
¼ cup chopped fresh chives
¼ cup grated Parmesan or Romano cheese
Dash pepper
Dash paprika

Prepare noodles in large amount of boiling salted water as package directs. Drain. Return to saucepan.

Blend together remaining ingredients. Add to noodles.

4 - 6 servings.

Serve with a green salad and crusty bread.

This recipe can be doubled or tripled.

Quick Quiche

3 eggs
1 cup evaporated milk
½ cup milk
½ tsp. salt
Pepper to taste
1 tbsp. flour
1 cup grated cheese

Beat all ingredients except cheese. Pour into a 9-inch unbaked pie shell. Bake 10 minutes at 450°F., reduce heat to 350°F. and bake 20 minutes more or until mixture is set and knife blade comes out clean.

Variation: Cheese and onion pie.

Slice three onions thinly and sauté in 2 tablespoons oil until lightly golden. Cover the pan and steam over low heat until tender, about 5 minutes, remove lid, and evaporate any liquid. Arrange over a 9-inch unbaked pie shell and pour the Quiche mixture over. Bake as before.

Served in small slices as an appetizer, or accompanied by a salad and crisp French bread this makes a main course.

Breads and Cakes

Batter Bread

There's nothing quite like a house that smells of warm baked bread. Start the bread in the morning and have it ready for tea, or supper.

2 envelopes active dry yeast
2¹/₂ cups warm water
2 tsp. sugar
¹/₄ cup shortening
¹/₄ cup sugar
1 tbsp. salt
5 cups all-purpose flour

Dissolve 2 teaspoons sugar in warm water; sprinkle yeast into water and let stand 10 minutes. In large mixer bowl, combine shortening, ¹/₄ cup sugar, salt, and dissolved yeast. Add 3 cups flour; blend well, then beat 2 minutes at medium speed, scraping bowl occasionally. (By hand, beat vigorously.) Stir in remaining flour until smooth. Cover and let rise in warm place until doubled, about 1 hour. Stir down batter and beat about 20 strokes. Spread batter evenly in two well-greased 9 x 5-inch loaf pans or 3-quart casserole or cast iron pan. Smooth top of batter by patting with floured hand. Cover and let rise again until doubled, 1 to 1¹/₂ hours. Bake in 375°F. oven about 45 minutes for small pans, 60 for large; bread should sound hollow when tapped. Brush top with soft butter. Remove from pans and cool on rack. Makes 2 small or 1 large loaf.

Cheese Cake

Guests ooh and aah at homemade cheese cake. And there are hundreds of recipes. This one must be made with a blender. It is rich, yet very light because of the blender and because it uses cottage cheese.

1³/₄ cups graham crackers finely crushed
¹/₂ cup butter melted
¹/₂ cup sugar

Combine. Press into the bottom and up the sides of a 9-inch spring form pan.

24 oz. cottage cheese
4 eggs
1 cup sugar
Pinch of salt
1¹/₂ tsp. vanilla

Blend the ingredients in small amounts at high speed until the consistency of whipped cream. Scoop into the mixing bowl and stir together. Pour into prepared pan of graham cracker base and bake at 350°F. for approximately 30 minutes. Insert a skewer to test for doneness—it should be slightly moist but set and the top uncoloured.

Mix together by stirring gently with a spoon ¹/₂ pint commercial sour cream, ¹/₄ cup sugar and 1 teaspoon vanilla. Spread over cooked cheese cake and return to oven to set for 10 minutes. Topping does not brown. Remove and chill. Don't remove from pan until cooled for several hours. Refrigerate until serving time. Serve as-is, or, with a sauce made from sliced strawberries lightly sugared and sprinkled with Cointreau; or blend slightly thawed raspberries until of a sauce consistency. Serve very cold.

Serves 10—can be doubled to serve 18-20.

Chocolate Log

A traditional European Christmas treat. But why save it for once a year? Once you've mastered the jellyroll technique the variations are endless.

6 squares sweet baking chocolate
4 tbsp. water
5 eggs, separated (large)
³/₄ cup sugar
1 cup whipping cream, whipped
3 tbsp. rum
Chocolate butter icing or confectioners' chocolate
  icing
Preheat oven to 350°F.

Melt the chocolate over warm water with the water. Beat the yolks with the sugar until light and creamy. Beat the whites until stiff. Let the chocolate cool slightly and add to the yolk mixture. Fold in the whites.

Oil a jelly roll pan and line it with a sheet of wax paper extending about 5 inches either end. Lightly oil the paper. Pour batter onto the paper. Bake for 12-15 minutes until just set. Remove from oven and cover with a damp towel and let cool for several hours. Cover the counter with a large sheet of waxed paper and turn cake onto the wax paper, peeling off the pan liner carefully. Stir the rum into the whipped cream and spread over cake. Roll-up lengthwise and roll onto a board or platter. Cover with a chocolate icing using the tines of a fork to simulate tree bark. Chill.

Christmas or White Wedding Cake

This white fruit cake can be baked in a 10-inch tube pan plus a small pan or in the small, medium, and large square Christmas Cake pans.
1 lb. blanched slivered almonds
1 lb. red and green cherries
1 lb. candied citron peel, diced
1 lb. white raisins
1/2 lb. candied pineapple cut into slivers

Mix the fruit, cut the cherries if desired, and put into a large bowl sprinkling with 1/2 cup all-purpose flour. Line and grease pans with brown paper and corn oil.
Assemble remaining ingredients:
3 1/2 cups all-purpose flour
3/4 cup butter
3/4 cup shortening
1 tbsp. almond extract
2 cups granulated sugar
6 eggs, separated
1 tsp. cream of tartar
1 cup brandy

Set oven at 275°F. Cream butter and shortening, add extract, work in sugar until the mixture is light and fluffy. Beat egg yolks until thick and add to the butter mixture. Add brandy and flour to the mixture alternately. Beat egg whites until foamy and add cream of tartar. Continue beating until whites hold their shape but are not dry.

Add butter-brandy batter to fruit and nuts (you will need a large container). Fold in egg whites and put in prepared tins.

Bake with a container of water on the lowest shelf. The medium sized cake should take about 2 hours. Allow to become cold before taking from pans and before wrapping. Place on large pieces of heavy-duty foil. Sprinkle cold cake with brandy, wrap securely and store in a cool dry place.

Cornbread (Johnnycake)

A pioneer recipe that has been updated. Serve it at a coffee party, for a Sunday snack, or as an accompaniment to roast pork or chicken.

1 cup cornmeal
3/4 cup buttermilk
1/2 cup shortening
1/2 cup granulated sugar
1 egg
1 1/4 cups sifted all-purpose flour
1 tsp. baking powder
1 tsp. baking soda
1/2 tsp. salt
1 cup buttermilk

Combine with 3/4 cup buttermilk; set aside. Cream shortening with sugar; beat in egg. Combine flour, baking powder, soda and salt; mix thoroughly. Add dry ingredients to creamed mixture alternately with 1 cup buttermilk. Stir in cornmeal mixture. Pour into greased 8-inch square pan (or 10 x 6-inch cast iron pan). Bake in 350°F. oven for 40-45 minutes or until toothpick inserted in center comes out clean. Serve with butter, honey, or maple syrup.

Magic Fruit Cake

This is an old favourite and one of the easiest fruitcakes to assemble.

2½ cups all-purpose flour
½ tsp. salt
1 tsp. baking soda
2 eggs
3 cups mince meat
1 can milk
2 tbsp. sherry (optional)
1 cup walnuts, coarsely chopped
2 cups mixed candied fruit

Preheat oven to 300°F. Grease 9-inch tube pan. Line with brown paper; grease again. Sift flour, salt and baking soda. Set aside. In large sized bowl, slightly beat eggs, add mince meat, sweetened condensed milk, sherry, nuts, and fruit; mix well. Stir in sifted dry ingredients. Turn into prepared pan.

Bake in slow 300°F. oven for 2 hours. Cool in pan for 5 minutes. Turn out of pan; remove paper. Cool. Decorate. Wrap in plastic and store in refrigerator.

Munchies

What happens when you mix chocolate, butterscotch, peanuts, and chow mein noodles? "Munchies", that's what. "Munchies" are drop cookies with a heavenly blend of flavours and texture. They get crunchy crispness from the chow mein noodles which absorb the nut-like sweetness of the other ingredients. This is a no-bake and I promise you a sure-fire success.

6-oz. package (1 cup) chocolate chips
6-oz. package (1 cup) butterscotch chips
1 cup chow mein noodles
1 cup peanuts

Melt 6-oz. package (1 cup) chocolate chips and 6-oz. package (1 cup) butterscotch chips in a 1½-quart bowl over hot water. Stir in 1 cup chow mein noodles and 1 cup peanuts. Drop with two teaspoons onto wax paper. Chill until firm. Makes 2 dozen.

Orange Pecan Bread

A very delicious quickbread that is especially yummy served with sweet butter into which the rind of an orange has been grated.

2¼ cups sifted all-purpose flour
1 cup granulated sugar
3½ tsp. baking powder
½ tsp. salt
¾ cup finely chopped pecans (or walnuts)
2 tbsp. grated orange rind
1 egg
½ cup frozen orange juice concentrate, undiluted
¼ cup vegetable oil
¾ cup milk

Combine flour, sugar, baking powder, salt, pecans and orange rind; mix thoroughly. Beat egg and add orange juice concentrate, oil, and milk; beat to blend thoroughly. Add liquid to dry ingredients all at once, stirring only until completely moistened. Pour into greased 9 x 5-inch loaf pan. Bake in 350°F. oven for 1 hour or until toothpick inserted in centre comes out clean.

Super Health Bread

Baking bread is uplifting to the soul—never mind what it does to appetites!

1 cup raisins
½ cup boiling water
1 egg
1 cup lightly-packed brown sugar
1 cup whole wheat flour
1 cup rolled oats
1 cup all bran cereal
¼ cup wheat germ
1½ tsp. baking soda
½ tsp. salt
1 cup buttermilk

Pour boiling water over raisins: let stand until cool. Beat egg and blend in brown sugar. Add dry ingredients (mixed together), buttermilk, raisins, and their liquid. Stir until thoroughly combined. Pour into greased 9 x 5-inch loaf pan. Bake in 350°F. oven for 45 minutes or until toothpick inserted in centre comes out clean.

Desserts

Apples Courvoisier

Baked apples sound like baby food—but not Apples Courvoisier. They are definitely for adults with a flair for food.

For two, select a matched pair of large, well shaped, red Delicious apples, slice off the tops carefully, remove the core without puncturing the bottom, while leaving a firm enough shell of the apple to retain its shape, scoop out and dice the pulp (use diluted lemon juice to prevent discoloration of pulp and shell.)

In advance, soak in sufficient hot St. Raphael (Red or Golden) to absorb ¼ cup raisins and two diced pieces of dried apricots. Drain the diced apple and simmer for 10 minutes in one tablespoon each of honey and St. Raphael and a pinch each of cinnamon and nutmeg. Add raisin-apricot mixture and one piece diced preserved ginger, drain and put in apple shells. Carefully pour in one ounce of cognac per apple, sprinkle with bread crumbs and grated Parmesan cheese, dot with butter, heat in a 350°F. oven for 10 minutes then put under the broiler to brown the cheese.

Serve hot.

Baked Pears

Too often pears are neglected. They are excellent cooked and have an affinity with liqueurs.

6 ripe pears
Butter
Sugar
1 liqueur glass of Irish Mist
1 glass gin

Peel and core pears, leaving them whole (core them carefully from the bottom). Place whole pears upright in well-buttered and heated saucepan. Heat over medium heat for about 5 minutes basting with the butter. Place upright in buttered muffin pans or baking dish sprinkling remaining butter over pears. Sprinkle liberally with sugar. Bake at 500°F. for 5 minutes or until soft, but not brown. Remove to warm serving plates immediately. Combine Irish Mist and gin and heat until hot. Ignite, and while flaming, serve at once over pears.

Makes 6 servings.

Black Bottom Pie

This pie has been a favourite of the southern United States for generations. But this recipe uses Tia Maria to enhance the rich chocolate flavour.

1 envelope unflavoured gelatine
1 cup sugar, divided
1¼ tbsp. cornstarch
4 eggs, separated
2 cups scalded milk
2 squares unsweetened chocolate, melted
1 tsp. vanilla
1-9-inch baked pie shell
½ cup Tia Maria
Grated semi-sweet chocolate

Mix gelatine, ½ cup of the sugar, and cornstarch in the top of a double boiler. Beat egg yolks and milk: add to gelatine mixture and cook over boiling water, stirring constantly until mixture coats spoon. Divide custard in half. To one part add melted chocolate and vanilla; mix well and turn into pie shell. Chill until it starts to thicken. Beat egg whites until frothy. Gradually add remaining sugar and continue beating until egg whites hold their shape. Fold in chilled custard and turn onto chocolate layer. Top with grated chocolate; chill.

Brandy Alexander Pie

I have never been able to resist this sumptuous dessert. It is rich, beautiful to look at, and not really a complicated recipe.

1 envelope unflavoured gelatine
1/3 cup sugar
1/8 tsp. salt
1/2 cup cold water
3 beaten egg yolks
1/3 cup Crême de Cacao
3 egg whites
3 tbsp. brandy
1/2 cup sugar
1 cup whipping cream
9-inch graham cracker crust
Chocolate curls

In small saucepan, combine gelatine, 1/3 cup sugar, and salt. Stir in water and egg yolks. Cook over low heat, stirring constantly, until gelatine dissolves and mixture thickens slightly. Remove from heat; stir in Crême de Cacao and brandy. Chill till partially thickened. Beat egg whites to soft peaks. Gradually beat in 1/3 cup sugar till stiff; fold in thickened gelatine mixture. Whip cream; fold in. Chill again till mixture mounds slightly. Pile in crust and chill several hours or overnight. Top with chocolate curls. (To make chocolate curls, have a 4-ounce bar of sweet baking chocolate or large milk chocolate bar at room temperature. Place chocolate flat on firm surface. Hold bar firmly; press a floating blade potato peeler against chocolate and draw from one end of bar to the other.) Or top with grated chocolate.

Makes 8 servings.

Graham Cracker Crust

1 1/4 cups fine graham-cracker crumbs
1/4 cup sugar
6 tbsp. butter or margarine melted
Mix together all ingredients. Press firmly into 9-inch pie plate. Bake in 375° oven 6 to 8 minutes till edges are browned; cool.

Chocolate Cups

A little fiddley to make, but with patience there's a dessert you just can't buy.

1 cup chocolate chips
2 tablespoons butter
Melt the chocolate and butter in a double boiler over low heat. Stir until very smooth. Using a teaspoon line small paper baking cups. Tip the cups to spread the mixture evenly. Set the chocolate lined baking cup in a muffin pan and refrigerate, at least six hours. Peel off the paper cup and refrigerate each cup as finished. Before serving fill, gently, with soft ice cream, or, pour a spoonful of liqueur in the cup and top with whipped cream. Serve immediately.

Cointreau Soufflé

4 tbsp. each butter and flour
1 cup light cream
pinch of salt
6 eggs, separated
3/4 cup sugar
grated peel of one orange
1/4 cup Cointreau
Whipped cream
Cointreau

Melt butter in a saucepan and add flour. Stir in cream and salt. Cook until thickened. Remove from the heat. Beat the yolks with half the sugar, add the peel and the liqueur.

Whip the whites until they hold peaks, then beat in remaining sugar. Beat egg yolks into the sauce. Fold the whites into the mixture very gently.

Pour into a butter and sugar-dusted 2-quart soufflé dish. If necessary fit a lightly buttered foil collar around the dish. It should extend above the dish about 1 inch. Bake at 375°F. for 15 minutes, remove collar but do not jar the soufflé or remove from the oven. Continue baking for 25 minutes. Serve immediately. Over each serving spoon whipped cream and a little slightly warmed liqueur.

Serves 6.

Cold Chocolate Soufflé

So simple to make, the flavour belies the simplicity!

4 eggs
1/2 cup sugar
3 tbsp. instant coffee
2 oz. semi-sweet baking chocolate
3 tbsp. water
1/4 cup dark rum
1 pint whipping cream

Separate eggs and beat yolks with sugar until thick, add coffee and beat until mixed. Melt chocolate slowly over warm water, adding the water and rum. When smooth stir into the eggs. Whip cream and fold into the egg/chocolate mixture. Whisk egg whites stiff and fold in gently. Pour into individual soufflé dishes or parfait glasses and refrigerate covered with plastic or wax paper. Before serving top the dishes with a rosette of whipped cream and grated chocolate or with a chocolate "coffee bean"

Serves 6-8.

Coeur à la Crème

One of the great desserts from France. Again simple to make but you'll find guests asking for more so you might as well make two hearts.

Purchase a traditional porcelain heart-shaped mould (with holes in the bottom) from a gourmet utensil shop. Line the mould with cheesecloth that has been wrung out in cold water (makes it easier to unmould), and set mould on a dish that will catch any drips.
1/2 lb. creamed cottage cheese
11/2 cups commercial sour cream
1/2 pint whipping cream, whipped

1/4 cup fine white sugar
Pinch of salt

Blend the cottage cheese or push through a sieve until very smooth and mix lightly with all other ingredients. The mixture should be very thick and smooth. Pour the mixture into the mould and set in refrigerator overnight, or at least six hours. Unmould onto a serving plate. The heart can be decorated with whirls of whipped cream and crystallized fruit. Serve with sponge lady fingers, and sweetened strawberries, raspberries, or other sliced fruits.

Serves 6-8.

Crème Brulée

It is creamy, cold, and very smooth with the contrast of the rich taffy topping.

4 egg yolks slightly beaten
2-4 tbsp. granulated sugar
Pinch of salt
2 cups canned evaporated milk, scalded
4 tbsp. brandy
Brown sugar

Combine the eggs, sugar, salt, and milk and cook over boiling water until the mixture coats a wooden spoon, stirring constantly. (If it starts to lump, put the mixture in the blender immediately and whorl.) Pour into a round, shallow, oven-proof dish and cool, then chill. Pour brandy over the top and chill thoroughly; overnight is best. Before serving, preheat broiler. Cover the custard surface with a thick layer of brown sugar. Place dish on a tray of ice, place under broiler and wait until the top melts to a brown glaze. Be careful, it browns quickly and can catch fire so don't leave it. Remove from broiler and from ice tray. Serve by scooping into sherbet glasses. If you like, spoon over slightly sugared strawberries and/or raspberries. Good with sugared blueberries, too.

Glazed Fruit Tart

Making this tart is like painting a picture—the variations of fruit, texture, and colour are infinite.

Baked 9 or 10-inch pastry shell in flan ring or
  quiche pan
Filling: About 2 cups French Pastry Cream (recipe
  below) OR vanilla instant pudding
Topping: Sliced fresh or canned fruit, well
  drained (strawberries, peaches, pineapple,
  green grapes)
Glaze: About $1/2$ cup apple jelly or red currant
  jelly
  1 tablespoon Cointreau or kirsch

Spread cooled filling in baked pastry shell. Drain fruit very well on paper towelling; arrange fruit attractively over filling. For glaze, use apple jelly with Cointreau for light coloured or mixed fruit; red currant jelly with kirsch for strawberries alone. Melt jelly thoroughly in small saucepan, add liqueur, allow to cool slightly, then brush liberally over fruit. Refrigerate at least 2 hours. Serve with whipped cream if desired.

French Pastry Cream

In small heavy saucepan, beat 3 egg yolks with $1/4$ cup sugar until thickened and pale in colour. Beat in $1/4$ cup all-purpose flour, then add $1 1/4$ cups hot milk gradually, beating with a wire whisk. Cook over moderate heat, stirring constantly with whisk until mixture thickens; beat vigorously to keep it smooth as it gets very thick. Lower heat and continue to cook and stir 2-3 minutes longer. Beat in 2 teaspoons butter and 1 teaspoon vanilla. Pour into bowl, cover surface with waxed paper and chill thoroughly.

Hot Spiced Brandied Fruit

This is an old but still popular dessert and one that moves fast!

One large can each of canned red sour cherries, apricot halves, peach halves or slices, Bartlett pears.

Drain the fruit and reduce the syrup over a low heat for about 1 hour. Add to the boiling syrup the shredded rind of one orange and one lemon, a clove if liked. Remove from the heat and add $1/4$ cup brandy, juice of a lemon, and a scraping of fresh nutmeg.

Meanwhile, arrange the fruit in a large oven-proof dish and sprinkle with more shredded lemon rind. Strain the syrup and pour over the fruit (not more than a cup to prevent overflow). Put dish in a 400°F. oven on an oven tray to catch the drips. After 20 minutes cover with foil and lower oven heat. This dish can be left for at least an hour. Continue to add syrup as the liquid lowers. Serve very hot, adding a dash more brandy if required. Excellent with a cold custard sauce or with vanilla ice cream.

Pot de Crème

This is very rich and the ultimate in chocolate desserts. Portions should be very small.

9 oz. semi-sweet chocolate
4 oz. unsweetened chocolate
$1/2$ cup strong cold coffee
$1/4$ cup rum
6 eggs separated

Put the chocolate, coffee, and rum into a double boiler and melt gently over simmering water. (Too high heat makes the chocolate oil.) Remove from heat and stir smooth and cool slightly. Beat egg yolks until very thick and gradually add to chocolate. Return to low heat and cook for a few minutes until smooth and thick. Add a pinch of salt to the whites and beat until stiff. Gently fold into slightly cooled chocolate mixture. Spoon immediately into chocolate pots, demitasse, or custard glasses. Refrigerate several hours. Before serving top with a spoonful of whipped cream. Pass ladyfingers or sugar cookies.

Syllabub

Once upon a time, fashionable ladies made syllabub by milking a cow into a teapot or punch bowl. Cows were scrubbed and brought to the drawing room! This updated version keeps all the flavour but dispenses with the "back-to-nature" requirement.

1 pint whipping cream
Grated rind and juice of two lemons
1/4 cup white wine
2 tbsp. brandy
Sugar to taste—about 1/2 cup
3 egg whites

Add the rind and juice to the whipping cream and whip until thick and stiff. Add sugar to taste. Beat egg whites until very stiff and fold into cream mixture. Gradually add the liquid. Pour into custard, parfait, or champagne glasses.

Trifle

A genuine trifle is an elegant dessert and is not a catch-all for leftovers. This is so good that you will find yourself snitching the leftovers—if there are any!

1 package frozen raspberries or strawberries
1 baked baker's sponge cake
1/2 cup brandy
Homemade custard made with three eggs, one can of milk, 1/4 cup sugar, cooked until thick over simmering water
1/2 pint whipping cream
Sugar
Crystallized violets, angelica, and/or chopped nuts, chocolate curls, etc.

Blend slightly thawed fruit (add sugar if necessary) and pour into deep serving bowl. Cover with pieces of cake and pour over the liquor. When custard is cooked pour over the cake. Refrigerate covered for several hours. Garnish by topping with whipped cream whipped until smooth and thick and sweetened to taste. Garnish as desired. Refrigerate until serving time.

Vanilla Mousse Maria

Its light, its delicate, and it looks like a magazine picture.

1 1/2 cups sugar
1 cup water
8 egg yolks
1/2 cup Tia Maria
1 quart whipping cream
2 tsp. vanilla extract

Dissolve sugar in water and cook syrup rapidly for 5 minutes. Cool. Beat egg yolks in top of a double boiler and whip in the syrup gradually. Add Tia Maria. Cook over hot, not boiling, water, stirring constantly, until custard becomes thick and creamy. Strain through a fine sieve, and stir custard over cracked ice until it cools. Whip cream until stiff, flavouring it with vanilla extract. Fold whipped cream into the cooled custard. Fill a mold with mixture. Cover mousse with buttered wax paper, adjust cover of mold, and bury mold in ice or freeze it in the refrigerator for 2 or 3 hours. Unmold mousse and garnish it lavishly with whole fresh raspberries or other fresh lightly-sugared fruits.

Zabaglione

The French call this Sabayon but with any name it is delicious. However, like a hot soufflé, you must make your guests wait while you make it.

3 to 6 egg yolks (allow one plus per person)
1/4 cup granulated sugar
1/4 cup Marsala, Sherry, Madeira, or Tia Maria
1 tbsp. brandy

Beat egg yolks and add sugar and put into the top part of a double boiler. Keep the water beneath simmering. Whisk the mixture until it triples in bulk and is very light and frothy. Add liquor, and whisk keeping the sides of the pan scraped down. Serve immediately in small glasses, demitasse, or over sliced berries.

Speedy Finales for Dinner Parties

With a few items from your cupboard and freezer you can make spectacular desserts that take minutes to prepare and can be served at once or baked or chilled while you eat the main course.

Black Forest Cheese Cake

16 thin slices chocolate-flavoured Swiss roll
1/2 lb soft cream cheese
1/2 cup milk
1 tsp. vanilla
1 envelope whip-and-chill-type dessert mix
  (vanilla or chocolate)
1/2 (19 oz.) can cherry-pie filling

Grease a deep 9-inch pie pan and stand slices of Swiss roll around the inside edge and over the bottom close together. Beat cheese, milk, and vanilla together until fluffy, scraping the bowl occasionally. Add the dessert mix and beat until thick and smooth. Taste and add sugar if you like a sweeter filling. Spread in the prepared pie shell and chill in the freezer for 5 minutes. Cover with cherry filling and chill in the refrigerator until serving time. Cuts into 8 wedges.

Pineapple Ambrosia

A fold-together trifle that is ready to serve in less than 10 minutes.
1 envelope of dessert-topping mix OR
  1 cup whipping cream, whipped
1 (12 oz.) can crushed pineapple, well drained
1 tbsp. lemon juice
3/4 cup miniature marshmallows
1/2 cup flake-type coconut
1 cup sponge-cake cubes or
8 broken lady fingers

Prepare dessert topping according to directions or whip the cream. Combine the remaining ingredients. Fold mixture into the dessert topping

and spoon into 8 to 10 compotes. Garnish with maraschino cherries, if you wish. Chill until serving time.

Raspberry Torte

A no-cook cake-type dessert.

1 (15 oz.) pkg. frozen sweetened raspberries
1/2 pint whipping cream, whipped
1 large baker's angel or chiffon cake
1 envelope vanilla instant pudding mix
Flake-type coconut

Partially defrost raspberries or break up the solid container with a fork and defrost in a bowl over warm water. Whip the cream and refrigerate. Split the cake into 4 layers. Spoon-spread 3 bottom layers with raspberries letting the juice soak in thoroughly. Cover raspberries with vanilla pudding prepared according to directions, spreading almost to the edge of each layer. Reassemble the cake. Cover with the whipped cream and sprinkle with the coconut. Chill at least 30 minutes.

Cuts into 10 generous wedges.

Strawberries Romanoff

1 quart strawberries
1/2-1 cup fruit, brown, or granulated sugar
1-2 cups commercial sour cream

Wash the strawberries. Do not hull. Place in a bowl. Put sugar, sour cream in separate bowls. Pass fruit and accompaniments and let guests spoon sugar over the berries and dip in cream.

If you don't like fingerfoods, wash, hull, and dry the berries. Just before serving slice and put into glasses. Add brown sugar lightly to the sour cream and pour over fruit.

Serves 4-6.

Index

Food, Menu, and Recipe Index